also by america's test kitchen

The Complete Plant-Based Cookbook

Vegetables Illustrated

Bowls

The Ultimate Meal-Prep Cookbook

The Chicken Bible

Meat Illustrated

The Complete One Pot

Foolproof Fish

Cooking for One

How Can It Be Gluten-Free Cookbook Collection

The Complete Summer Cookbook

The Side Dish Bible

100 Techniques

Easy Everyday Keto

Everything Chocolate

The Perfect Pie

How to Cocktail

Spiced

The Ultimate Burger

The New Essentials Cookbook

Dinner Illustrated

America's Test Kitchen Menu Cookbook

Cook's Illustrated Revolutionary Recipes

Tasting Italy: A Culinary Journey

Cooking at Home with Bridget and Julia

The Complete Diabetes Cookbook

The Complete Slow Cooker

The Complete Make-Ahead Cookbook

The Complete Mediterranean Cookbook

The Complete Vegetarian Cookbook

The Complete Cooking for Two Cookbook

Just Add Sauce

How to Braise Everything

How to Roast Everything

Nutritious Delicious

What Good Cooks Know

Cook's Science

The Science of Good Cooking

The Perfect Cake

The Perfect Cookie

Bread Illustrated

Master of the Grill

Kitchen Smarts

Kitchen Hacks

100 Recipes: The Absolute Best Ways to Make the True Essentials

The New Family Cookbook

The America's Test Kitchen Cooking School Cookbook

The Cook's Illustrated Baking Book

The Cook's Illustrated Cookbook

The America's Test Kitchen Family Baking Book

America's Test Kitchen Twentieth Anniversary TV Show Cookbook

The Best of America's Test Kitchen (2007–2021 Editions)

The Complete America's Test Kitchen TV Show Cookbook 2001–2021

Toaster Oven Perfection

Mediterranean Instant Pot

Cook It in Your Dutch Oven

Vegan for Everybody

Sous Vide for Everybody

Air Fryer Perfection

Multicooker Perfection

Food Processor Perfection

Pressure Cooker Perfection

Instant Pot Ace Blender Cookbook

Naturally Sweet

Foolproof Preserving

Paleo Perfected

The Best Mexican Recipes

Slow Cooker Revolution Volume 2: The Easy-Prep Edition

Slow Cooker Revolution

The America's Test Kitchen D.I.Y. Cookbook

the cook's illustrated all-time best series

All-Time Best Brunch

All-Time Best Dinners for Two

All-Time Best Sunday Suppers

All-Time Best Holiday Entertaining

All-Time Best Soups

cook's country titles

Big Flavors from Italian America

One-Pan Wonders

Cook It in Cast Iron

Cook's Country Eats Local

The Complete Cook's Country TV Show Cookbook

for a full listing of all our books

CooksIllustrated.com

AmericasTestKitchen.com

praise for america's test kitchen titles

"Here are the words just about any vegan would be happy to read: 'Why This Recipe Works.' Fans of America's Test Kitchen are used to seeing the phrase, and now it applies to the growing collection of plant-based creations in *Vegan for Everybody*."

THE WASHINGTON POST ON *VEGAN FOR EVERYBODY*

"True to its name, this smart and endlessly enlightening cookbook is about as definitive as it's possible to get in the modern vegetarian realm."

MEN'S JOURNAL ON *THE COMPLETE VEGETARIAN COOKBOOK*

"This is a wonderful, useful guide to healthy eating."

PUBLISHERS WEEKLY ON *NUTRITIOUS DELICIOUS*

"Another flawless entry in the America's Test Kitchen canon, *Bowls* guides readers of all culinary skill levels in composing one-bowl meals from a variety of cuisines."

BUZZFEED BOOKS ON *BOWLS*

Selected as the Cookbook Award Winner of 2019 in the Health and Special Diet Category

INTERNATIONAL ASSOCIATION OF CULINARY PROFESSIONALS (IACP) ON *THE COMPLETE DIABETES COOKBOOK*

"Diabetics and all health-conscious home cooks will find great information on almost every page."

BOOKLIST (STARRED REVIEW) ON *THE COMPLETE DIABETES COOKBOOK*

"*The Perfect Cookie* . . . Is, in a word, perfect. This is an important and substantial cookbook. . . . If you love cookies, but have been a tad shy to bake on your own, all your fears will be dissipated. This is one book you can use for years with magnificently happy results."

THE HUFFINGTON POST ON *THE PERFECT COOKIE*

"The sum total of exhaustive experimentation . . . anyone interested in gluten-free cookery simply shouldn't be without it."

NIGELLA LAWSON ON *THE HOW CAN IT BE GLUTEN-FREE COOKBOOK*

"The book's depth, breadth, and practicality makes it a must-have for seafood lovers."

PUBLISHERS WEEKLY (STARRED REVIEW) ON *FOOLPROOF FISH*

"Offers a real option for a cook who just wants to learn some new ways to encourage family and friends to explore today's sometimes-daunting vegetable universe. This is one of the most valuable vegetable cooking resources for the home chef since Marian Morash's beloved classic *The Victory Garden Cookbook* (1982)."

BOOKLIST (STARRED REVIEW) ON *VEGETABLES ILLUSTRATED*

"If you're a home cook who loves long introductions that tell you why a dish works followed by lots of step-by-step hand holding, then you'll love *Vegetables Illustrated*."

THE WALL STREET JOURNAL ON *VEGETABLES ILLUSTRATED*

"A one-volume kitchen seminar, addressing in one smart chapter after another the sometimes surprising whys behind a cook's best practices. . . . You get the myth, the theory, the science, and the proof, all rigorously interrogated as only America's Test Kitchen can do."

NPR ON *THE SCIENCE OF GOOD COOKING*

"The 21st-century *Fannie Farmer Cookbook* or *The Joy of Cooking*. If you had to have one cookbook and that's all you could have, this one would do it."

CBS SAN FRANCISCO ON *THE NEW FAMILY COOKBOOK*

"Some 2,500 photos walk readers through 600 painstakingly tested recipes, leaving little room for error."

ASSOCIATED PRESS ON *THE AMERICA'S TEST KITCHEN COOKING SCHOOL COOKBOOK*

"The go-to gift book for newlyweds, small families, or empty nesters."

ORLANDO SENTINEL ON *THE COMPLETE COOKING FOR TWO COOKBOOK*

"Some books impress by the sheer audacity of their ambition. Backed by the magazine's famed mission to test every recipe relentlessly until it is the best it can be, this nearly 900-page volume lands with an authoritative wallop."

CHICAGO TRIBUNE ON *THE COOK'S ILLUSTRATED COOKBOOK*

"It might become your 'cooking school,' the only book you'll need to make you a proficient cook, recipes included. . . . You can master the 100 techniques with the easy-to-understand instructions, then apply the skill with the recipes that follow."

THE LITCHFIELD COUNTY TIMES ON *100 TECHNIQUES*

the complete SALAD cookbook

A Fresh Guide to 200+ Vibrant Dishes Using Greens, Vegetables, Grains, Proteins, and More

AMERICA'S TEST KITCHEN

Library of Congress Cataloging-in-Publication Data

Names: America's Test Kitchen (Firm), author.
Title: The complete salad cookbook : a fresh guide to 200+ vibrant dishes using greens, vegetables, grains, proteins, and more / America's Test Kitchen.
Description: Boston, MA : America's Test Kitchen, [2021] | Includes index.
Identifiers: LCCN 2020049539 (print) | LCCN 2020049540 (ebook) | ISBN 9781948703567 | ISBN 9781948703574 (epub)
Subjects: LCSH: Salads. | LCGFT: Cookbooks.
Classification: LCC TX740 .A658 2021 (print) | LCC TX740 (ebook) | DDC 641.83--dc23
LC record available at https://lccn.loc.gov/2020049539
LC ebook record available at https://lccn.loc.gov/2020049540

AMERICA'S TEST KITCHEN
21 Drydock Avenue, Boston, MA 02210

Manufactured in Canada
10 9 8 7 6 5 4 3 2 1

Distributed by Penguin Random House Publisher Services
Tel: 800.733.3000

pictured on front cover Tomato Salad with Steak Tips (page 241)

pictured on back cover Quinoa Lettuce Wraps with Feta and Olives (page 301), Summer Dinner Salad with Scallops (page 104), Sesame Lo Mein Salad (page 378), and Roasted Grape and Cauliflower Salad with Chermoula (page 173)

editorial director, books Adam Kowit

executive food editor Dan Zuccarello

deputy food editor Stephanie Pixley

senior editors Leah Colins, Joseph Gitter, Kaumudi Marathé, Sara Mayer, and Russell Selander

associate editor Camila Chaparro

test cooks Samantha Block and Sarah Ewald

executive managing editor Debra Hudak

editorial assistant Emily Rahravan

design director Lindsey Timko Chandler

deputy art director Katie Barranger

photography director Julie Bozzo Cote

photography producer Meredith Mulcahy

senior staff photographers Steve Klise and Daniel J. van Ackere

staff photographer Kevin White

additional photography Joseph Keller and Carl Tremblay

food styling Joy Howard, Catrine Kelty, Chantal Lambeth, Kendra McKnight, Ashley Moore, Christie Morrison, Marie Piraino, Elle Simone Scott, Kendra Smith, and Sally Staub

PHOTOSHOOT KITCHEN TEAM

  photo team and special events manager Alli Berkey

  lead test cook Eric Haessler

  test cooks Hannah Fenton and Jacqueline Gochenouer

  assistant test cooks Gina McCreadie and Christa West

senior manager, publishing operations Taylor Argenzio

imaging manager Lauren Robbins

production and imaging specialists Tricia Neumyer, Dennis Noble, and Amanda Yong

copy editors Christine Campbell, April Poole, and Rachel Schowalter

proofreaders Tess Berger and Sara Zatopek

indexer Elizabeth Parson

chief creative officer Jack Bishop

executive editorial directors Julia Collin Davison and Bridget Lancaster

contents

welcome to america's test kitchen

This book has been tested, written, and edited by the folks at America's Test Kitchen, where curious cooks become confident cooks. Located in Boston's Seaport District in the historic Innovation and Design Building, it features 15,000 square feet of kitchen space including multiple photography and video studios. It is the home of *Cook's Illustrated* magazine and *Cook's Country* magazine and is the workday destination for more than 60 test cooks, editors, and cookware specialists. Our mission is to empower and inspire confidence, community, and creativity in the kitchen.

We start the process of testing a recipe with a complete lack of preconceptions, which means that we accept no claim, no technique, and no recipe at face value. We simply assemble as many variations as possible, test a half-dozen of the most promising, and taste the results blind. We then construct our own recipe and continue to test it, varying ingredients, techniques, and cooking times until we reach a consensus. As we like to say in the test kitchen, "We make the mistakes so you don't have to." The result, we hope, is the best version of a particular recipe, but we realize that only you can be the final judge of our success (or failure). We use the same rigorous approach when we test equipment and taste ingredients.

All of this would not be possible without a belief that good cooking, much like good music, is based on a foundation of objective technique. Some people like spicy foods and others don't, but there is a right way to sauté, there is a best way to cook a pot roast, and there are measurable scientific principles involved in producing perfectly beaten, stable egg whites. Our ultimate goal is to investigate the fundamental principles of cooking to give you the techniques, tools, and ingredients you need to become a better cook. It is as simple as that.

To see what goes on behind the scenes at America's Test Kitchen, check out our social media channels for kitchen snapshots, exclusive content, video tips, and much more. You can watch us work (in our actual test kitchen) by tuning in to *America's Test Kitchen* or *Cook's Country* on public television or on our websites. Download our award-winning podcast *Proof*, which goes beyond recipes to solve food mysteries (AmericasTestKitchen.com/proof), or listen to test kitchen experts on public radio (SplendidTable.org) to hear insights that illuminate the truth about real home cooking. Want to hone your cooking skills or finally learn how to bake—with an America's Test Kitchen test cook? Enroll in one of our online cooking classes. And you can engage the next generation of home cooks with kid-tested recipes from America's Test Kitchen Kids.

Our community of home recipe testers provides valuable feedback on recipes under development by ensuring that they are foolproof. You can help us investigate the how and why behind successful recipes from your home kitchen. (Sign up at AmericasTestKitchen.com/recipe_testing.)

However you choose to visit us, we welcome you into our kitchen, where you can stand by our side as we test our way to the best recipes in America.

facebook.com/AmericasTestKitchen
twitter.com/TestKitchen
youtube.com/AmericasTestKitchen
instagram.com/TestKitchen
pinterest.com/TestKitchen

AmericasTestKitchen.com
CooksIllustrated.com
CooksCountry.com
OnlineCookingSchool.com
AmericasTestKitchen.com/kids

list of recipes

list of recipes continued

getting started

salad days

A salad has the potential to be the star of the table: a complete meal that's unique, refreshing, colorful, and full of flavor. It's fun to bring together, easy on the eye, and fabulously satisfying to the palate.

This book contains more than 200 imaginative, tried-and-tested recipes that will make you curious, make you hungry, and inspire you to embrace salad making like you never have before.

Salad and lettuce are often thought of in the same breath. And while there are lots of lettuce and other green salads here, that's just the start. We also present recipes where ingredients such as sweet potatoes, celery root, grapefruit, edamame, or farro are the star.

Try our Roasted Pattypan Squash and Corn Salad, which showcases ingredients native to the Americas (page 210), and our Crispy Lentil and Herb Salad (page 255), for which we fried green lentils, arranged them on a bed of yogurt, and drizzled pomegranate molasses over top. This salad is just begging to be scooped up with pita and devoured. And then there is our tangy, hearty Pinto Bean, Ancho, and Beef Salad with Pickled Poblanos (page 277), which gets added oomph from a chopped dark chocolate garnish.

As for the classics? They're here. We just gave them new life in recipes such as Grilled Chicken Cobb Salad (page 112) and Fiddlehead Panzanella (page 192). Naturally, we couldn't resist turning favorites like fajitas or soba noodles into salads, too.

When it comes to serving, salads are totally flexible. Fill up your bowl as many of these are substantial enough to be a meal, or serve smaller portions alongside other foods.

We paired greens and vegetables with proteins ranging from chicken and steak to duck, crab, scallops, and tofu to make eye-catching mains. But many of the purely vegetable combinations make salads that are plenty hearty, too, as do the salads built around beans, grains, pasta, and noodles.

We have salads you can assemble just before serving and salads that are great make-ahead options. There are dishes you must eat immediately and others that taste wonderful even after a day or two.

In true test kitchen fashion, we explored techniques to elevate the flavors and textures of our salads, from shaving, spiralizing, and grating ingredients so that they could more effectively hold dressing to wilting them ever so slightly in a warm dressing. We paired foods in intriguing ways to contrast textures and flavors and sought to prevent waste by using every part of a vegetable.

People sometimes say, "I don't need a recipe to make a salad. I like to wing it." In The Architecture of a Salad and Wing It, with a Flight Plan, we give you techniques and tips to help your spontaneous experiments succeed by suggesting ways to prep and combine ingredients creatively and layer varied tastes, textures, aromas, and colors.

Whether you choose one of our recipes or follow your own path, using our tips, the result will be a gorgeous, satisfying salad that you are happy to put before your family or a table full of dinner guests.

how salad got its name

In the spring, the ancient Romans and Greeks ate greens dipped in salt. After a long winter without fresh vegetables, eating fresh lettuces must have felt revitalizing. The salt that people dipped their greens in ("sal" is "salt" in Latin) led to that salad being called herba salata ("salted greens"). Romans quickly figured out that they were not limited to just using salt. They started making dressing by adding olive oil and vinegar to the salt. And voilà, you have the dish that gave rise to the Old French word "salade."

what kind of salad are you?

Salads can be differentiated by their cutting techniques, cooking methods, assembly, and serving styles to create a variety of looks, textures, and flavor profiles.

torn or crumbled

The easiest way to prepare greens is to tear them into bite-size pieces, which creates jagged edges that pick up and hold on to dressing, as in Bitter Greens and Chickpea Salad with Warm Vinaigrette (page 65). We also tear other ingredients such as tofu so that they can soak up marinades. As for crumbling, that's the easiest way to treat soft cheeses such as feta and goat cheese.

chopped or sliced

Greens and other ingredients can be chopped into bite-size pieces of different widths, thicknesses, and shapes. In Chopped Winter Salad with Butternut Squash (page 69), chopping allows us to play up colors—orange squash, red and white radicchio, and white feta—and helps us taste every component in each bite by making ingredients easier to eat.

shaved

Shaving vegetables thin gives them a pretty translucent look and creates more surface area to be coated with dressing. It also allows vegetables to be softened by acid, as in Shaved Zucchini Salad with Pepitas (page 249).

spiralized

Spiralizing "pasta" from vegetables has the same effect as shaving them. The noodles look different from their shaved counterparts but gain surface area to coat with dressing, as in Zucchini Noodle Salad with Tahini-Ginger Dressing (page 248).

grated or shredded

Grating or shredding vegetables also creates more surface area for dressings to adhere to, as in our Brussels Sprout, Red Cabbage, and Pomegranate Slaw (page 155). We grate other ingredients, such as hard-cooked egg yolks and whites too for our Spinach Salad with Egg and Red Onion (page 127).

boiled

Naturally we boil vegetables such as potatoes and beans for Salade Niçoise (page 216) and cook pasta and some noodles in lots of boiling salted water, too. We also use the method to prepare grains and rice. Boiling in plentiful liquid and spreading the cooked grains on a baking sheet to cool helps them stay distinct rather than clumpy, which is essential for a salad.

grilled

To make the most of the summertime, we grill vegetables for smoky char and then dress them, as we do for radicchio for our Grilled Radicchio Salad with Corn, Cherry Tomatoes, and Pecorino Romano (page 114). For Grilled Panzanella (page 148), we grill bread and an assortment of vegetables, and fruit gets the same treatment for some salads.

roasted

Wintertime is for turning on the oven to cook meats and vegetables so that they suffuse your home with warmth and aroma. But you might still feel like eating a salad, so our roasted vegetable salads give you the best of both worlds. The tender browned vegetables pair with the tang of a dressing that gives them lightness, as in our Roasted Pattypan Squash and Corn Salad (page 210), or with pickles, as in our Carrot and Smoked Salmon Salad (page 169).

warmed and wilted

A warm dressing is flavorful and allows vegetables and greens to get slightly cooked and gently wilted, making them more tender and taming their bitterness. For Wilted Spinach Salad with Strawberries, Goat Cheese, and Almonds (page 129), we make the dressing in a Dutch oven, turn off the heat, and toss the spinach and dressing together in the still-warm pot. For Pea Green Salad with Warm Apricot-Pistachio Vinaigrette (page 61), pea greens, whole peas, and endive are tossed in the skillet with the warm, nutty dressing.

tossed
For these salads, ingredients are prepped and then tossed with a vinaigrette or dressing. Tossing works well when different colorful and textural elements are combined, as in Purslane and Watermelon Salad (page 58).

composed
Let your creativity run free; arrange ingredients artfully on a platter. Composed salads are presented ready to eat, so elements are dressed before being arranged, like our Grilled Peach and Tomato Salad with Burrata and Basil (page 214).

wrapped
For some salads, lettuce is neither part of the tossing nor the composition. It may be the vessel, as in Quinoa Lettuce Wraps with Feta and Olives (page 301).

bound
These salads are held together by a thick mayonnaise-based or other creamy dressing and can be presented composed, tossed, or as wraps. Our bound salads, such as Tuna Salad with Hard-Cooked Eggs, Radishes, and Capers (page 76) and Curried Chicken Salad with Dried Apricots (page 73) are great served on greens, with toast, or in sandwiches.

layered
A layered salad looks attractive and is easy to transport, keeping ingredients distinct till they are ready to be tossed with creamy dressing or spooned up to serve. Our Layered Tex-Mex Salad (page 262) does a one-two on classic seven-layer salad, leaving out eggs and bacon and using salsa, black beans, corn, and tortilla chips instead.

the architecture of a salad

Build a tossed or composed salad in four parts. Lay the foundation of a hearty base, build the structure with flavorful add-ins, add a glistening facade of dressing, and embellish with detail: croutons, cheese, dried fruit, and nuts.

foundation

This base layer will be the bulk of your salad—greens, sweet potatoes, or any ingredients you choose. Each chapter of the book offers a different base.

detail

Decorate your tossed or composed salad with garnishes. Cheese, croutons, and nuts are classic, but get creative (see pages 44–51 for ideas).

structure

Meats, vegetables, and fruits allow you to layer flavors, textures, colors, and shapes (see page 11 for some suggested combinations). To prevent heavier ingredients from crushing delicate ones, add them just before tossing. Save meats and vegetables to arrange on composed salads just before serving.

facade

A dressing brings salad ingredients together and gives them a glossy face. For a tossed salad, build the dressing in the bowl, add other ingredients, and toss gently. For composed salads, dress components separately before placing them on the base.

wing it, with a flight plan

A salad is the perfect opportunity to improvise in the kitchen and try new ingredient combinations. Think about where you'd like to go with your salad. Do you want it to be filling or light? Is it going to be the whole meal or just the starter? Once you've decided, you can play with ingredients.

SALAD IMPROV GAME PLAN

1 use top-notch ingredients

We use top-quality ingredients in our salads. When the ingredients are uncooked, quality is especially critical because you don't have the transformative power of cooking to help disguise wilted greens, substandard oil, or overripe fruit.

2 experiment

We experiment with ingredients for every recipe we develop. You can do the same. Never thought capers would pair well with peaches? Give them a shot. No sour cream at home? Try using plain yogurt for your dressing instead.

3 got leftovers?

Open the fridge and look in. Leftovers make great salad fixings. Are there leftovers you don't want to warm up for lunch? Transform them into a salad with lettuce, fruit, and Make-Ahead Vinaigrette, a dressing you quickly shake up (page 29).

4 magic pantry

Turn to your pantry for inspiration. What can work in a salad or dressing? Anchovies? Jam? Crackers? Here's an idea: Try crushed-up crackers instead of croutons. But be sure to add them just before serving so that they stay crisp.

5 jot down your ideas

Think about what ingredient combos worked for you. Then write down your successes (and failures) so that you don't forget.

EASY WAYS TO MARRY FLAVORS

combine two contrasting greens

Create nuance and variety by pairing differently flavored or textured greens: bitter and mild (dandelion greens and red leaf lettuce), tender and crunchy (Bibb and frisée), or grilled and raw (charred radicchio and raw romaine).

treat one vegetable different ways

Use ingredients in multiple ways in a single salad. We use rhubarb in a dressing as well as a tart, crunchy salad base in Rhubarb, Celery, and Radish Salad (page 224).

balance richness with fruit or pickles

A dressing brings acidity to a salad, but you can also pair meat or fish with bright fruits or briny quick pickled vegetables for even more contrast: steak with pear or quick pickled fennel, seared tuna with mango, salmon with grapefruit, or octopus with orange.

experiment with crunch

Endive, jicama, and sliced raw asparagus all give you crunch, as do plantain chips, crispy tofu, croutons, and tortilla strips. You can even consider doubling or tripling the crunch as we do in our Bibb and Frisée Salad with Apple and Celery (page 120), adding walnuts to the mix.

pan-fry (or microwave-fry) for crispy contrast

Pair a crispy fried item with fresh ingredients for textural and flavor variety. We combine pan-fried artichoke hearts with tender peas and mizuna, and we mix crispy fried eggplant and shallots with fresh herbs and tomatoes.

embrace herbs

Herbs can be more than a garnish. Use them in abundance like leafy greens, as we do in our Chicken Salad with Thai Basil and Mango (page 80); make pesto dressings with them; and when sprinkling herbs on a salad, do so lavishly so that they add flavor to every morsel.

finish with spice

Add a final flourish of flavor with flake Maldon or pink Himalayan salt, aromatic spice blends such as harissa and za'atar, or a drizzle of quick-bloomed spiced oils like Fennel Oil or Chipotle-Coriander Oil (page 39).

CREATE SENSATIONAL FLAVOR AND TEXTURE COMBOS

sweet-salty-crunchy

For sweetness in your salad, try raisins, cranberries, chopped dates, or dried cherries. Sprinkle them on greens and add a salty cheese such as Parmesan or feta and crunchy Spiced Nuts (page 50) or Black Pepper Candied Bacon (page 46).

sweet-spicy

Sweetness balances out spicy heat. Think cayenne, cumin, and salt with sliced pears or ripe mango. In Carrot Noodle Salad with Harissa and Honey (page 164), naturally sweet carrots, dried apricots, and honey make the heat of harissa, a Tunisian spice paste, tantalizingly warm and pleasant.

sweet-sour-soft

If sweet and sour is your thing, try chopped dates and sour cornichons with soft ripe avocados on spinach dressed with red wine vinegar and avocado oil. Or pair juicy oranges and cranberries with spicy greens in Citrus Salad with Watercress, Dried Cranberries, and Pecans (page 180).

sour-spicy-sweet

In Quinoa, Black Bean, and Mango Salad with Lime Dressing (page 300), we use tart limes and get heat from jalapeños, which are balanced by sweet mango, chewy black beans, and crunchy bell pepper. A hot sauce can give you both sour and spicy, so drizzle some on halloumi and bitter greens and add chewy elements such as chickpeas or dried fruit.

crunchy-soft-chewy

For textured bites of salad, throw on spiced nuts, ripe tomatoes, bits of jerky, or shrimp. In our Harvest Salad (page 314) we combine the crunch of apples with the softness of roasted sweet potatoes and the chewiness of wild rice.

bitter-mild

Toss bitter greens with mild lettuces or add soft cheese or chewy beans. In our Apple and Fennel Salad with Bitter Greens and Warm Pancetta Dressing (page 138), we pull out all the stops, balancing mild, sweet, bitter, and meaty flavors, with blue cheese to strongly round everything out.

six techniques to enhance your salads

Use these simple methods to get the most out of your salad ingredients, enhancing their flavor and visual appeal.

salt and sugar your vegetables and fruit

Salt and sugar draw out the excess moisture from vegetables and fruit that can dilute a dressing. Check individual recipes for specific amounts of salt, sugar, or both.

remove moisture To remove extra moisture from 12 ounces of tomatoes, toss the tomato pieces with ¼ teaspoon of table salt in a colander set in a large bowl. Drain for 30 minutes. Discard the juice and use the salted tomatoes. Cabbage can also be salted and drained to remove moisture.

use sugar To remove extra moisture from watermelon, toss 4 cups of watermelon cubes with 2 teaspoons of sugar in a colander set in a large bowl. Drain for 30 minutes, discard the juice, and use the sweetened watermelon.

vary your cutting technique

Cut vegetables, fruit, and herbs to maximize their flavor and appearance.

cut on bias Cut vegetables such as asparagus and celery on the bias to increase their surface area and crunch and to make them larger and more pleasing to the eye in a salad where small pieces would not be clearly visible.

enhance your garnish Slice scallions or chives on the bias to heighten their oniony aroma and taste and to enhance their look on salads.

keep flavors intact Coarsely chop fruit such as peaches or nectarines and cut apples or pears into slices to keep the juiciness or crispness intact.

shave, grate, or smash

To get more surface area for vegetables to be coated with dressing, we prep them in different ways.

shave vegetables Shave vegetables such as jicama, zucchini, and carrots thin for some salads.

grate vegetables Grate vegetables such as carrots for a subtle crunch.

smash vegetables Smash cucumbers into pieces with the bottom of a skillet to create jagged edges to hold on to more dressing. We use this technique for our Pai Huang Gua (page 186) or Chinese smashed cucumber salad.

toast nuts and seeds

Toasting nuts and seeds releases their oils and flavors and gives them an appealing golden color.

to toast less than 1 cup of nuts or seeds Place nuts or seeds in a dry skillet over medium heat. Toast the nuts until they are lightly browned and fragrant, 3 to 8 minutes, shaking the skillet occasionally to prevent scorching. Watch the nuts closely because they can go from golden to burnt very quickly.

to toast a large quantity of nuts Spread the nuts in a single layer on a rimmed baking sheet and toast in a 350-degree oven. Toast the nuts until they are lightly browned and fragrant, 5 to 10 minutes, shaking the baking sheet every few minutes for even toasting.

toast or bloom spices

Toasting spices makes them easier to grind. Toasted or bloomed whole spices enhance the taste and aroma of ingredients they are paired with.

to toast spices Place whole spices (2 tablespoons or less) in a dry skillet over medium heat. Toast until they are fragrant, 1 to 3 minutes, shaking the skillet occasionally to prevent scorching.

to bloom spices Heat oil in a seasoning wok (see page 19) or a small saucepan over medium-high heat until just smoking. Carefully add whole spices, such as mustard seeds, and reduce heat to low. The seeds should start to pop right away. Stir in remaining spices and cook until fragrant, about 5 seconds. Pour spices over prepped ingredients.

cook grains like pasta and overcook your pasta

Boiling grains in abundant salted water as you would pasta prevents the grains from clumping.

to cook grains for salad Add grains or rice to plentiful salted water so that the grains can stay separate.

ensure that grains don't clump Spreading out the grains on a baking sheet after cooking allows them to cool before dressing and also prevents them from clumping.

overcook your pasta For pasta salads that can be refrigerated for several days, cook pasta not to al dente but until tender. This way the pasta absorbs more dressing and doesn't dry out quickly.

what should I make?

the salad bowl

People love their wooden salad bowls, especially those that were wedding presents or have been handed down through generations.

A salad bowl is the perfect container for making a dressing and tossing salad greens with it before bringing the prepared salad to the table. But years of exposure to oily salad dressings can leave this beloved kitchen staple sticky with rancid residue, while frequent washing can leave a bowl looking dry and dull, with its patina worn off. Here's how to make your salad bowl look new again—and keep it that way.

keep it clean

On a daily basis, keeping your bowl clean and smooth between uses is easy. Never put a salad bowl in the dishwasher or let it soak in water, as that will not remove oil but instead make the bowl warp or crack.

1. Use mild dish soap and warm water to clean the bowl by hand.

2. Dry the bowl thoroughly immediately after cleaning.

season again

If your salad bowl looks dry or dull, its polish has likely worn off. It's easy to reseason. And if you use your bowl a lot, you should do so every three months.

1. Use a paper towel to liberally apply food-grade mineral oil to all surfaces of the bowl.

2. Let it stand for 15 minutes, and then wipe away any residue with clean paper towels.

removing sticky buildup

Gently heating a wooden salad bowl in a warm oven helps remove oil and other sticky residue.

1. Adjust the oven rack to the middle position and heat the oven to 275 degrees.

2. Line a rimmed baking sheet with aluminum foil or parchment paper and set a wire rack in the sheet. Place your wooden salad bowl upside down on the wire rack.

3. Turn off the oven. Carefully place the sheet with the bowl in the oven. Within minutes, oils will start to bead on the bowl's surface. After 1 to 2 hours, oils will run off the bowl and onto the sheet.

4. Once the bowl looks dry, remove the sheet from the oven. Wipe the bowl with paper towels to remove any residue. If the bowl is still oily or sticky, repeat the baking process once more. Reseason the dried bowl.

the salad kitchen

One of the great things about salad is that all the ingredients can be prepped ahead of time and brought together in different ways just before serving, giving you time to focus on other aspects of your meal. When you are ready to make a salad, all you need is a sharp chef's knife, a paring knife, mixing and serving bowls, and these helpful tools.

salad spinner

A salad spinner is great for more than just drying big batches of greens. We use the **OXO Good Grips Salad Spinner ($29.99)** for draining tomatoes of extra juice and cleaning sandy chopped leeks too.

mandoline

Many of our salads call for shaved vegetables. We use our **Swissmar Börner Original V-Slicer Plus Mandoline ($49.95)** to shave daikon, carrot, zucchini, and jicama evenly and effortlessly and to slice onion fine for pickles.

whisk

A good whisk like the **OXO Good Grips 11" Balloon Whisk ($9.99)** is great for making vinaigrettes and dressings quickly. It helps us emulsify oil and vinegar and is also great for whisking heavier ingredients such as sour cream or yogurt for dressings.

peeler

If you don't have a mandoline, a Y-shaped peeler or a swivel peeler is a great tool for shaving vegetables and Parmesan and for peeling. Both the **Kuhn Rikon Original Swiss Peeler ($3.50)** and the **Messermeister Pro-Touch Fine Edge Swivel Peeler ($10.00)** tackle papaya, potatoes, and beets equally easily.

kitchen tongs

Some people use their hands to toss a salad, but when you need tongs, you have two options: wooden salad tongs or metal kitchen tongs. The **OXO Good Grips 12-Inch Tongs ($12.95)** are light and perfect for tossing salads, turning meat or vegetables in a skillet, and delicately placing ingredients on a dressed salad.

rasp-style grater

Arguably our favorite tool ever, the **Microplane Premium Classic Zester/Grater ($14.95)** is superuseful for salad making because it does everything well: shredding cheese, zesting lemons, and grating garlic and ginger.

paddle grater

To quickly grate vegetables such as celery root for slaw or cheese to garnish a salad, we use a paddle-style grater like the **Rösle Coarse Grater ($35.93)**, which sits firmly on the counter.

box grater

If you prefer the greater security and shred containment of a box grater, you can comfortably shred vegetables and cheese on the **Cuisinart Box Grater ($11.95)**, keeping ingredients in place while doing so.

steamer basket

We use our steamer basket to make hard-cooked eggs. You can cook as few as two eggs or as many as 12 at one time. Taking the basket out of a hot pan and putting it in a bowl of ice is easy, thanks to the retractable, heatproof handle of the **OXO Good Grips Stainless Steel Steamer with Handle ($17.95)**.

blender

Blenders help make impressively silky dressings and mayonnaise. Our favorite inexpensive blender, the **KitchenAid 5-Speed Diamond Blender ($159.99)** also purees vegetables such as tomatoes and onions quickly and smoothly.

food processor

When we're short on time, the **Cuisinart Custom 14-Cup Food Processor ($229.95)** comes in handy for chopping, slicing, and shredding vegetables as well as making mayonnaise and pesto.

mortar and pestle

There's nothing like the aroma and flavor of freshly ground spices. The nicely sized **ImportFood.com Solid Granite Thai Mortar and Pestle ($25.95)** helps you grind spices in a jiffy. It's also great for making pesto and grinding toasted rice into powder for some of our Thai salads.

seasoning wok

To make hot oil and spice seasonings to pour on salads, as in Butternut Squash Raita (page 156), Indian cooks use a seasoning wok that looks like a large ladle. It gets oil or ghee hot quickly to bloom whole spices, green chiles, and curry leaves. You can use a small saucepan, too.

Dutch oven

We like to use a Dutch oven to make warm and wilted salads. Because it is large and retains heat after the burner is switched off, we can toss our prepared warm dressing and greens directly into our **Le Creuset 7¼ Quart Round Dutch Oven ($367.99)**. A large stockpot works well too, as does our Dutch oven Best Buy, the **Cuisinart Chef's Enameled Cast Iron Casserole ($83.70)**.

greens

Often considered the base of a salad, lettuces and other soft, leafy greens are among the most widely eaten vegetables in the United States today. Given the wide variety you have to choose from, we think it's smart to know how to choose, store, and wash them. Then mix and match them to build interesting salads with different textures, flavors, and colors.

Delicate lettuces such as iceberg, Boston, Bibb, and red and green leaf lettuce usually work best with simple, mild flavor combinations so that the subtle greens are highlighted rather than overpowered. Stronger-flavored leafy greens such as arugula and watercress can easily stand up to bigger flavors, while the ever-popular romaine lettuce, mild-flavored but sturdy in texture, is versatile, working with all kinds of flavors and toppings.

Apart from these more commonly known greens, we also like to use foraged greens such as purslane, mâche, and dandelion greens; earthy kale; mild but hearty red and green cabbage; mizuna, which is sharp and peppery but not as strong as arugula; and pretty little gem lettuce, often described as a flavorful mix between romaine and butter lettuce. These lettuces and greens star in our leafy salads, but they also add bulk and color to our meat, grain, rice, and vegetable salad recipes.

to buy or not to buy

Many lettuces and leafy greens are available year-round, and luckily for us, they are available as prewashed full heads in a bag, prewashed full or chopped heads in a clamshell, and prewashed and chopped in a bag. They can also be purchased loose (and not prewashed) in bulk bins.

How do you choose what to buy? We find whole lettuce heads or leaves, prewashed or not, preferable to bags or clamshells of chopped lettuces, which begin to spoil as soon as they are cut.

Romaine, which is crisp, is fine to buy prewashed and will keep well for up to a week. For tender lettuce, such as Bibb, the best choice is the nonprewashed heads. Leafy greens such as arugula, mâche, and watercress are often sold prewashed in cellophane bags. They offer great convenience, but be sure to turn the bags over at the store and inspect the greens closely. If you see moisture trapped in the bag or hints of blackened leaf edges, these greens are not for you. If you purchase greens in bunches (sometimes the roots will be attached), wash them well before using, as they can be sandy.

storing greens

To store crisp lettuce, such as iceberg or romaine, core the lettuce, wrap it in paper towels, and refrigerate it in a partially open plastic produce bag.

For tender lettuce, such as Boston or Bibb, if the lettuce comes with the roots attached, leave them attached and store them in the original plastic bag or container, making sure to remove twist ties and open the bag or container slightly, or use an open plastic produce bag. If the lettuce is without roots, wrap it in paper towels and refrigerate it in an open plastic produce bag.

Prewashed leafy greens, such as arugula, mesclun, and watercress, should be refrigerated in the original plastic container or bag. If the greens are not prewashed, lightly roll them in paper towels and store them in an open plastic produce bag in the refrigerator.

wash and dry before you dress

If salad greens aren't dry before you dress them, they will dilute the dressing and wilt before you can enjoy them, so make sure that you wash and dry them thoroughly using a salad spinner (see "Preparing Greens for Dressing"). Alternately, rinse the salad greens in a bowl of water, shake them dry in a colander, and then place the greens on a clean dish towel or paper towels to wick up any remaining moisture.

preparing greens for dressing

1. Fill salad spinner bowl with cool water, add greens, and gently swish them around. Let grit settle to bottom of bowl, then lift greens out and drain water. Repeat until greens no longer release any dirt.

2. Dry greens, stopping several times to dump out excess water.

3. Blot greens dry on paper towels or dish towels. To refrigerate greens for several days, roll them in paper towels and slip towels inside large plastic bag.

dressing up

We use high-quality oils and vinegars in our dressings because their flavor is so evident in salads. Here are some helpful buying and storage tips.

OIL

Extra-virgin olive oil is the first oil expressed and extracted from fresh olives. EVOO, as it is affectionately called, has fruity, grassy, buttery, and even spicy notes. Because of its low smoke point, it is best used uncooked, drizzled over salads, or in vinaigrettes where you can smell its aroma and taste its fresh flavor. That bottle of expensive EVOO that a friend just gave you? Bring it forth for a salad.

We also like avocado oil on salads. Rich in healthy fats and antioxidants, avocado oil has a nutritional profile and price tag similar to olive oil's (and is also sold as extra-virgin and refined). But its flavor is more neutral, so it's great for milder dressings, and its higher smoke point means that it can be used for frying. When buying avocado oil, remember that it is sometimes cut with other oils and that it can go rancid quickly. Buy avocado oil with the latest expiration date.

We like the nutty flavor of toasted sesame oil (also called Asian sesame oil) in some salads, especially when we use sesame seeds as a garnish. The aroma and flavor of toasted sesame oil fades quickly when exposed to heat, so we use this oil for drizzling or for whisking into dressing.

Another oil we use often is vegetable oil. It can be made from nuts, grains, beans, seeds, and olives, and many generically labeled vegetable oils contain soybean oil, so read the label to make sure that you are getting what you want. Also make sure that you buy good-quality oil since you will be eating it uncooked in salad dressings.

Since extra-virgin olive oil, which we typically use for dressings, can solidify when cold, we sometimes add vegetable oil to a dressing to prevent it from congealing in the refrigerator. Vegetable oil is also well suited for pan frying and deep frying because it has a higher smoke point than extra-virgin olive oil. We use it to fry artichokes, lentils, and other components of our salads. Grapeseed oil is another less expensive alternative to extra-virgin olive oil for both frying and vinaigrettes.

When buying high-end olive oil, check the harvest date printed on the label to ensure the freshest bottle possible. Don't buy olive oil in bulk if you can't use it quickly. Once you have invested in some good-quality oil, make sure that you store it properly. It doesn't belong on your counter or windowsill because strong sunlight will oxidize the chlorophyll in the oil, producing stale, harsh flavors. Keep all oils in a dark pantry or cupboard. Use a sticker to write the purchase date on bottles because oils have a very short shelf life once opened. Unopened oil will be good for one year. Once a bottle of any oil has been opened, its shelf life reduces to three months.

Store all oils in the pantry (toasted sesame oil belongs in the fridge). For optimal flavor, replace all oil six months after opening. To check if it is fresh, heat a little in a skillet. If it smells rancid once heated, throw out the bottle.

VINEGAR

Cider vinegar, made from fermented apple juice, is fruity, sweet, and slightly tart. Its round flavor and rich color evokes ripe apples, so it works well in salads tossed with apple or dried fruits. Italian balsamic vinegars are aged for years to have complex flavor, sweetness, and color. The expensive ones are stunning drizzled on fresh strawberries, but moderately priced ones are also delicious in vinaigrettes or drizzled with olive oil on fresh greens.

Slightly sweet, sharp red wine vinegar is delicious in bold vinaigrettes. Milder, more delicate white wine vinegar works for subtle dressings and in potato salad where the color of red wine vinegar would detract from the presentation. Rice vinegar, made from fermented rice, is light-colored and sweet, perfect for our noodle salads when mild acidity is called for. Spanish sherry vinegar, made from sherry wine, is like a mix between balsamic and cider vinegar. It has complex savory flavors and a sweetness that adds fruity depth to vegetable salads. If you would rather use fresh citrus juice and zest instead of vinegar in your salad dressing, you'll be adding bright, sweet-tart flavor to your salads.

simplest salad

serves 4

This salad makes an elegant pairing with just about any dish. The dressing requires no measuring, no whisking, and (virtually) no thought. For the salad, all you need is lettuce, good quality oil (infused if you like; see pages 38–39), vinegar, half a garlic clove, salt, and pepper. It's vital to use high-quality ingredients— you can't camouflage wilted lettuce, flavorless oil, or too-harsh vinegar. Try interesting and flavorful leafy greens, such as mesclun, arugula, or Bibb lettuce. Add toppings of your choice, if you wish.

½ garlic clove, peeled
8 ounces (8 cups) lettuce, torn into
bite-size pieces if necessary
Oil
Vinegar

Rub inside of salad bowl with garlic. Add lettuce. Slowly drizzle oil over lettuce, tossing greens very gently, until greens are lightly coated and just glistening. Season with vinegar, salt, and pepper to taste and toss gently to coat. Serve.

making a vinaigrette

A dressing is essentially the sauce that flavors salad. A vinaigrette is one kind of dressing—an emulsion of oil and vinegar, plus salt, pepper, and herbs or spices, with no creamy ingredients used. Still, a good vinaigrette is smooth and creamy in appearance, which is a result of emulsification. When you make an emulsion, using ingredients that are emulsifiers and stabilizers can speed up the process. Mustard or mayonnaise are effective short-term emulsifiers. For longer-term stabilization, use molasses or genuine aged balsamic vinegar, which contains similar compounds. Honey and garlic paste are great emulsifiers, too.

THE SCIENCE OF EMULSIFICATION

A well-emulsified vinaigrette clings to greens and vegetables, guaranteeing balanced flavor in every bite. You get a good emulsion by combining oil and vinegar strenuously enough that the oil breaks down into such tiny droplets that they remain separated and surrounded by the acid droplets, so the two liquids become one. Emulsifiers help speed up this process. Polysaccharides in mustard and lecithin in mayonnaise (from the egg yolks) have large molecules with one part that's attracted to oil and one part that's attracted to water. These act as bridges to link the oil and water (vinegar) together. The compounds in molasses, called melanoidins, forestall the oil droplets from their natural inclination to congregate back together, increasing the viscosity of the emulsion.

WHISKING AND SHAKING

Making a smooth vinaigrette requires strenuous mixing, either by whisking or shaking. To whisk, people often use a circular motion, but this only tires out your arms. What is needed is a brisk side-to-side motion that agitates the molecules of vinegar and oil. This causes "shear force" to be applied to the liquid. As the whisk moves in one direction across the bowl, the liquid starts to move with it; when the whisk is dragged in the opposite direction, it exerts force against the liquid still moving toward it. This helps break oil into tinier droplets that stay suspended in vinegar and creates an emulsion. When you don't have time to whisk or you want long-lasting dressing, use our shaking method for Make-Ahead Vinaigrette (page 29). It contains molasses, which is a powerful long-term emulsifier.

MASTERING THE VINAIGRETTE

use good vinegar Wine vinegars (white, red, balsamic, or sherry) are the first choice for us in the test kitchen.

use good oil Extra-virgin olive oil is the most flavorful choice.

know the right ratio For every tablespoon of vinegar, add 3 tablespoons of oil.

season well Salt and pepper are a must, and fresh herbs are better than dried.

whisk or shake Whisk ingredients vigorously or shake them up in a jar until emulsified.

BE ON TIME

Why does green salad wilt if you dress it way before serving? Both oil and vinegar lead to wilting. Oil dissolves the protective waxy cuticle on the lettuce leaves, allowing them to lose moisture and wilt, but this takes a very long time. Vinegar, however, can cause relatively rapid wilting. Vinegar, made up of water and molecules of acetic acid, breaks up the lettuce, causing it to wilt. Salt accelerates this process. So to prevent sad, wilted salad greens, dress them—tossing gently so that the greens are lightly and evenly coated—just before you want to serve your salad.

the
salad
bar

vinaigrettes and dressings

Vinaigrettes and dressings are the facade of a salad, the element that brings ingredients together cohesively, binding them with flavor, richness, and aroma, and showing them off with gloss.

They can be oil-and-vinegar-based, like our Foolproof Vinaigrette, or creamy like our Blue Cheese Dressing (page 35). Any of the recipes here can also bring brightness, acidity, and richness to other savory dishes when used as a marinade or dipping sauce.

To dress a salad, you will need about 1 tablespoon of any of our dressings or vinaigrettes per 2 cups of washed and dried greens. Generally speaking, bolder vinaigrettes with balsamic, garlic, and shallots work well to dress hearty or spicy greens such as arugula or watercress. Milder dressings marry well with delicate greens such as Bibb or iceberg lettuce.

foolproof vinaigrette

makes about ¼ cup

This master vinaigrette makes enough to dress 8 cups of greens and works with nearly any type of green. We use two emulsifiers to ensure that the vinaigrette doesn't separate. For a hint of garlic flavor, rub the inside of the salad bowl with a cut clove of garlic before adding the greens.

- 1 tablespoon red wine, white wine, or champagne vinegar
- 1½ teaspoons very finely minced shallot
- ½ teaspoon regular or light mayonnaise
- ½ teaspoon Dijon mustard
- ⅛ teaspoon table salt
- 3 tablespoons extra-virgin olive oil

1   Whisk vinegar, shallot, mayonnaise, mustard, and salt together in small bowl. Whisk until mixture is milky in appearance and no lumps of mayonnaise remain.

2   Whisking constantly, slowly drizzle in oil until emulsified. If pools of oil gather on surface as you whisk, stop adding oil and whisk mixture well to combine, then resume whisking in oil in slow stream. Vinaigrette should be glossy and lightly thickened, with no pools of oil on surface. Season with pepper to taste.

variations

foolproof lemon vinaigrette

This vinaigrette is best for dressing mild greens.

Substitute lemon juice for vinegar. Omit shallot. Add ¼ teaspoon grated lemon zest and pinch sugar along with salt.

foolproof balsamic-mustard vinaigrette

This vinaigrette is best for dressing assertive greens.

Substitute balsamic vinegar for wine vinegar, increase mustard to 2 teaspoons, and add ½ teaspoon chopped fresh thyme along with salt.

foolproof herb vinaigrette

Add 1 tablespoon minced fresh parsley or chives and ½ teaspoon minced fresh thyme, tarragon, marjoram, or oregano to vinaigrette just before using.

make-ahead vinaigrette

makes about 1 cup

A vinaigrette is so versatile that we wanted to create a really flavorful version to keep on hand for salads or any dish that needed a boost without relying on preservative-packed store-bought versions. To prevent the oil and vinegar from separating, we added mustard and mayonnaise, two natural emulsifiers, and a surprising ingredient—molasses—as a third stabilizer. Just a tablespoon worked wonders without imparting a strong flavor. Cutting the olive oil with some vegetable oil ensured that our refrigerated dressing was always pourable. Do not use blackstrap molasses. This vinaigrette pairs well with nearly any green.

- 1 tablespoon regular or light mayonnaise
- 1 tablespoon molasses
- 1 tablespoon Dijon mustard
- ½ teaspoon table salt
- ¼ cup white wine vinegar
- ½ cup extra-virgin olive oil, divided
- ¼ cup vegetable oil

1 Combine mayonnaise, molasses, mustard, and salt in 2-cup jar with tight-fitting lid. Stir with fork until mixture is milky in appearance and no lumps of mayonnaise or molasses remain. Add vinegar; seal jar; and shake until smooth, about 10 seconds.

2 Add ¼ cup olive oil; seal jar; and shake vigorously until combined, about 10 seconds. Repeat with remaining ¼ cup olive oil and vegetable oil in separate additions, shaking vigorously until combined after each addition. Vinaigrette should be glossy and lightly thickened after all oil has been added, with no pools of oil on surface. Season with salt and pepper to taste. (Vinaigrette can be refrigerated for up to 1 week; shake to recombine before using.)

variations

make-ahead sherry-shallot vinaigrette

Add 2 teaspoons minced shallot and 2 teaspoons minced fresh thyme to jar with mayonnaise. Substitute sherry vinegar for white wine vinegar.

make-ahead balsamic-fennel vinaigrette

Toast the fennel seeds in a skillet (page 13) and crack them in a mortar and pestle or on the counter using the bottom of a heavy skillet. Press firmly to crack them.

Add 2 teaspoons toasted and cracked fennel seeds to jar with mayonnaise. Substitute balsamic vinegar for white wine vinegar.

make-ahead cider-caraway vinaigrette

Toast the caraway seeds in a skillet (page 13) and crack them in a mortar and pestle or on the counter using the bottom of a heavy skillet. Press firmly to crack them.

Add 2 teaspoons toasted and cracked caraway seeds to jar with mayonnaise. Substitute cider vinegar for white wine vinegar.

tarragon-caper vinaigrette

makes about ½ cup

Delicate and light, herb vinaigrettes should showcase the flavors of fresh herbs and tangy vinegar. To help emulsification, we added mustard and mayonnaise to the mix. Pair this vinaigrette with mild greens.

- 2 tablespoons white wine vinegar
- 1 teaspoon regular or light mayonnaise
- 1 teaspoon Dijon mustard
- ¼ teaspoon table salt
- 6 tablespoons extra-virgin olive oil
- 2 tablespoons minced fresh tarragon or oregano
- 2 teaspoons minced shallot
- 2 teaspoons capers, rinsed and chopped

1   Whisk vinegar, mayonnaise, mustard, and salt in medium bowl until mixture is milky in appearance and no lumps of mayonnaise remain.

2   Whisking constantly, slowly drizzle in oil until emulsified. If pools of oil gather on surface as you whisk, stop adding oil and whisk mixture well to combine, then resume whisking in oil in slow stream. Vinaigrette should be glossy and lightly thickened, with no pools of oil on surface. Whisk in tarragon, shallot, and capers. Season with salt and pepper to taste. (Vinaigrette can be refrigerated for up to 2 days; whisk to recombine before using.)

maple-mustard vinaigrette

makes about ½ cup

Try this recipe for the flavors of autumn.

- 2 tablespoons cider vinegar
- 2 tablespoons maple syrup
- 1 teaspoon minced shallot
- 1 teaspoon Dijon mustard
- ¾ teaspoon table salt
- ½ teaspoon pepper
- 3 tablespoons extra-virgin olive oil

Whisk vinegar, maple syrup, shallot, mustard, salt, and pepper together in medium bowl. Whisking constantly, slowly drizzle in oil until emulsified. (Vinaigrette can be refrigerated for up to 3 days; whisk to recombine before using.)

raspberry vinaigrette

makes about ⅓ cup

This recipe works nicely for a slightly sweet vinaigrette. It pairs well with salads topped with berries or other fruit. Avoid chunky preserves and supersweet jams.

- 2 tablespoons seedless raspberry jam
- 2½ teaspoons red wine vinegar
- 1 teaspoon Dijon mustard
- ⅛ teaspoon table salt
- ⅛ teaspoon pepper
- 3 tablespoons extra-virgin olive oil

Whisk jam in medium bowl until smooth. Add vinegar, mustard, salt, and pepper, whisking until combined. Whisking constantly, slowly drizzle in oil until emulsified. (Vinaigrette can be refrigerated for up to 3 days; whisk to recombine before using.)

sriracha-lime vinaigrette

makes about ½ cup

This bright, spicy, fresh vinaigrette adds a burst of heat and citrus to salads. The sriracha packs a punch, but the sweetness of honey, the bold flavor of fresh ginger, the umami of fish sauce, and the freshness of lime juice balance out the heat for a unique and potent dressing to pair with robust salad ingredients such as steak, fish, and even cauliflower or sweet potato.

- 2 tablespoons lime juice
- 1 tablespoon honey
- 1 tablespoon fish sauce
- 1½ teaspoons grated fresh ginger
- 1½ teaspoons sriracha
- 2½ tablespoons extra-virgin olive oil

Whisk lime juice, honey, fish sauce, ginger, and sriracha together in small bowl. Whisking constantly, slowly drizzle in oil until emulsified. (Vinaigrette can be refrigerated for up to 3 days; whisk to recombine before using.)

Bring pomegranate juice and honey to boil in small saucepan over medium-high heat. Reduce heat to maintain simmer and cook until mixture is thickened and measures about ⅔ cup, 15 to 20 minutes. Transfer syrup to medium bowl and refrigerate until cool, about 15 minutes. Whisk in vinegar, shallot, salt, and pepper until combined. Whisking constantly, slowly drizzle in oil until emulsified. Season with salt and pepper to taste. (Vinaigrette can be refrigerated for up to 1 week; whisk to recombine before using.)

variations

orange-ginger vinaigrette

Substitute orange juice (4 oranges) for pomegranate juice and lime juice (2 limes) for red wine vinegar. Add 1 teaspoon grated fresh ginger to syrup with lime juice.

apple cider–sage vinaigrette

Substitute apple cider for pomegranate juice and cider vinegar for red wine vinegar. Add ½ teaspoon minced fresh sage to syrup with vinegar.

orange-lime vinaigrette

makes about 1 cup

Two citrus fruits shine in this easy dressing, with a touch of added sweetness coming from honey. Although fresh-squeezed orange juice will taste best, any store-bought orange juice will work here. To avoid off-flavors, make sure to reduce the orange juice in a nonreactive stainless-steel saucepan.

- 2 cups orange juice (4 oranges)
- 3 tablespoons lime juice (2 limes)
- 1 tablespoon honey
- 1 tablespoon minced shallot
- ½ teaspoon table salt
- ½ teaspoon pepper
- 2 tablespoons extra-virgin olive oil

Simmer orange juice in small saucepan over medium heat until slightly thickened and reduced to ⅔ cup, about 30 minutes. Transfer to medium bowl and refrigerate until cool, about 15 minutes. Whisk in lime juice, honey, shallot, salt, and pepper until combined. Whisking constantly, slowly drizzle in oil until emulsified. (Vinaigrette can be refrigerated for up to 1 week; whisk to recombine before using.)

pomegranate-honey vinaigrette

makes about 1 cup

Fruit juice makes a sweet-tart vinaigrette base. For a clingy, viscous texture, we reduced pomegranate juice to thicken it. (Usually, juices with residual tang work best; anything sweetened, such as cranberry cocktail, becomes cloying when reduced.) Reducing 2 cups of juice to ⅔ cup made for a pleasant glaze-like consistency, and we needed far less oil than usual to create a full-bodied vinaigrette. A little vinegar complemented the acidity of the juice, and honey enhanced its sweetness. Pair this dressing with sturdy or flavorful greens such as endive, kale, or arugula. To avoid off-flavors, reduce the juice in a nonreactive stainless-steel saucepan.

- 2 cups pomegranate juice
- 1 tablespoon honey
- 3 tablespoons red wine vinegar
- 1 tablespoon minced shallot
- ½ teaspoon table salt
- ½ teaspoon pepper
- 2 tablespoons extra-virgin olive oil

oregano–black olive vinaigrette

makes ½ cup

In this bold, savory dressing that works well on salads topped with Italian deli meats, fresh mozzarella, or burrata, we pair olives with olive oil and add oregano and garlic to bump up the flavor. Don't add the olives to the blender; they will turn the dressing black.

- 6 tablespoons extra-virgin olive oil, divided
- 1 tablespoon minced fresh oregano or marjoram, divided
- 2 tablespoons red wine vinegar
- ½ shallot, peeled
- 1½ teaspoons Dijon mustard
- 1 small garlic clove, peeled
- ¼ teaspoon table salt
- ⅛ teaspoon pepper
- 2 tablespoons pitted black olives, minced

1   Heat 2 tablespoons oil with 1½ teaspoons oregano in small saucepan over medium heat until oregano turns bright green and small bubbles appear, 2 to 3 minutes. Turn off heat and steep 5 minutes.

2   Process vinegar, shallot, mustard, garlic, salt, pepper, and remaining 1½ teaspoons oregano in blender until shallot and garlic are finely chopped, about 15 seconds. With blender running, slowly add oregano oil and remaining ¼ cup olive oil and continue to process until dressing is smooth and emulsified, about 15 seconds. Transfer to bowl and stir in olives. (Vinaigrette can be refrigerated for up to 3 days; whisk to recombine before using.)

creamless creamy herb dressing

makes 2 cups

For a creamy herb dressing inspired by vegan nut cream, we used soaked and pureed raw cashews instead of dairy or mayonnaise. Grinding the nuts before soaking allowed us to decrease the typical overnight soaking time to just 15 minutes. To further streamline the process, we hydrated the ground cashews with the other dressing ingredients rather than first soaking them in water and draining them. Using onion and garlic powders instead of fresh alliums prevented the dressing from tasting too sharp as it sat, thereby extending its shelf life. The dressing was initially warm from the friction of blending,

so we chilled it before adding minced herbs to prevent them from wilting. You'll need a conventional blender for this recipe; an immersion blender or food processor will produce dressing that is grainy and thin. If you use a high-powered blender such as a Vitamix or Blendtec, blending times may be shorter. Use unsalted raw cashews, not roasted, to ensure the proper flavor balance. This dressing works well drizzled over a hearty salad, but it can also be used as a dip for vegetables.

- 1 cup raw cashews
- ¾ cup water, plus extra as needed
- 3 tablespoons cider vinegar
- 1¼ teaspoons table salt
- 1 teaspoon onion powder
- ½ teaspoon sugar
- ¼ teaspoon garlic powder
- 2 tablespoons minced fresh chives or cilantro
- 1 tablespoon minced fresh parsley
- ½ teaspoon pepper

1 Process cashews in blender on low speed to consistency of fine gravel mixed with sand, 10 to 15 seconds. Add water, vinegar, salt, onion powder, sugar, and garlic powder and process on low speed until combined, about 5 seconds. Let mixture sit for 15 minutes.

2 Process on low speed until all ingredients are well blended, about 1 minute. Scrape down sides of blender jar. Process on high speed until dressing is smooth and creamy, 3 to 4 minutes. Transfer dressing to bowl. Cover and refrigerate until cold, about 15 minutes. Stir in chives, parsley, and pepper. Thin with extra water, adding 1 tablespoon at a time, if needed. (Dressing can be refrigerated for up to 1 week; whisk to recombine before using.)

variations
creamless creamy ginger-miso dressing
Omit salt, garlic powder, chives, and parsley. Decrease water to ⅔ cup. Substitute ¼ cup unseasoned rice vinegar for cider vinegar, 2 tablespoons white miso for onion powder, 2 tablespoons soy sauce for sugar, and 2 tablespoons grated fresh ginger for pepper. Add 1 teaspoon toasted sesame oil with water.

creamless creamy green goddess dressing
Decrease cashews to ¾ cup. Substitute lemon juice for cider vinegar, 1 tablespoon chopped fresh tarragon for onion powder, and 2 rinsed anchovy fillets for sugar. Increase chives and parsley to ⅓ cup chopped and add with water. Decrease salt to ¾ teaspoon and pepper to ¼ teaspoon.

creamless creamy roasted red pepper and tahini dressing
Omit chives and parsley. Decrease cashews to ½ cup. Substitute one 12-ounce jar roasted red peppers, drained and chopped coarse, for water; sherry vinegar for cider vinegar; 3 tablespoons tahini for onion powder; 2 teaspoons toasted sesame oil for sugar; and smoked paprika for pepper. Increase salt to 1½ teaspoons and garlic powder to ½ teaspoon and add pinch cayenne pepper.

tahini-lemon dressing
makes ⅓ cup
We balance the rich sesame flavor of tahini with lemon juice and garlic in a dressing that's best with mild greens.

2½ tablespoons lemon juice
 2 tablespoons tahini
 1 tablespoon water
 1 garlic clove, minced
 ½ teaspoon table salt
 ⅛ teaspoon pepper
 ¼ cup extra-virgin olive oil

Whisk lemon juice, tahini, water, garlic, salt, and pepper together in bowl. Whisking constantly, slowly drizzle in oil until emulsified. (Dressing can be refrigerated for up to 4 days; whisk to recombine before using.)

Remove garlic from oven and carefully open foil packets. When garlic is cool enough to handle, squeeze cloves from skins (you should have about 6 tablespoons); discard skins.

2   Process garlic, vinegar, water, honey, mustard, thyme, salt, and pepper in blender until smooth, about 45 seconds, scraping down sides of blender jar as needed. With blender running, slowly add oil until incorporated, about 1 minute. Season with salt and pepper to taste. (Dressing can be refrigerated for up to 1 week; whisk to recombine before using.)

yogurt-dill dressing
makes about ⅔ cup
Yogurt and dill are a match made in cucumber heaven. Pair this with a salad topped with cucumbers—or really any salad you enjoy in the summertime.

  ⅓   cup plain whole-milk yogurt
  2   tablespoons chopped fresh dill, parsley, or chives
1½   tablespoons whole-grain mustard
  ⅛   teaspoon table salt
  ⅛   teaspoon pepper
  1   tablespoon extra-virgin olive oil

Whisk yogurt, dill, mustard, salt, and pepper together in large bowl. Whisking constantly, slowly drizzle in oil until emulsified. (Dressing can be refrigerated for up to 4 days; whisk to recombine before using.)

poppy seed dressing
makes about ¾ cup
We toasted poppy seeds to enhance their sweet aroma and mixed them with red wine vinegar, sugar, and vegetable oil. This dressing pairs well with salads containing fruits such as strawberries or citrus. Poppy seeds are dark, so it's hard to see when they're fully toasted. Instead, use your nose: they should smell nutty.

  1   tablespoon poppy seeds
  ¼   cup red wine vinegar
2½   tablespoons sugar
  ½   teaspoon table salt
  1   teaspoon dry mustard
  ½   teaspoon pepper
  ¼   cup vegetable oil

creamy roasted garlic dressing
makes about 1 cup
Creating a thick, creamy dressing doesn't necessarily require dairy. Our recipe relies on three heads of roasted garlic for luscious, mellow sweet-savory flavor. Pair this dressing with sturdy greens.

  3   large garlic heads, outer papery skins removed and top third of head cut off and discarded
  ¼   cup white wine vinegar
  3   tablespoons water
  2   teaspoons honey
  1   teaspoon Dijon mustard
  1   teaspoon minced fresh thyme or rosemary
  ¼   teaspoon table salt
  ¼   teaspoon pepper
  ⅓   cup extra-virgin olive oil

1   Adjust oven rack to middle position and heat oven to 350 degrees. Wrap each garlic head in aluminum foil and roast until golden brown and very tender, 1 to 1¼ hours.

1   Toast poppy seeds in 8-inch skillet over medium heat until fragrant and slightly darkened, 1 to 2 minutes; transfer to bowl and set aside.

2   Whisk vinegar, sugar, and salt in bowl until sugar is dissolved. Whisk mustard, pepper, and poppy seeds into vinegar mixture. Whisking constantly, slowly drizzle in oil until emulsified. (Dressing can be refrigerated for up to 4 days; whisk to recombine before using.)

blue cheese dressing
makes about ¾ cup

Blue cheese in a dressing brings to mind a steakhouse iceberg wedge salad, but you can use this creamy, flavorful dressing on sturdy greens too. Look for a milder blue cheese such as Gorgonzola. If you don't have buttermilk, substitute milk and increase the vinegar to 2½ teaspoons.

2½   ounces mild blue cheese, crumbled (⅔ cup)
   3   tablespoons buttermilk
   3   tablespoons sour cream or Greek yogurt
   2   tablespoons mayonnaise
   2   teaspoons white wine vinegar
   ¼   teaspoon sugar
   ⅛   teaspoon garlic powder

Mash blue cheese and buttermilk in bowl with fork until mixture resembles cottage cheese with small curds. Stir in sour cream, mayonnaise, vinegar, sugar, and garlic powder until combined. Season with salt and pepper to taste. (Dressing can be refrigerated for up to 1 week; whisk to recombine before using.)

ranch dressing
makes about ¾ cup

The iconic ranch dressing works well as both a dressing and a dip and is also great on sandwiches and even leftover chicken. The key to a perfect creamy dressing is balance: It should be rich but not heavy, flavorful but not cloying. After testing myriad dairy mixtures, we landed on a base of mayonnaise, sour cream, and buttermilk for the right amount of body, tang, and silkiness. Pair this dressing with sturdy greens.

   ¼   cup buttermilk
   ¼   cup mayonnaise
   3   tablespoons sour cream or Greek yogurt
1½   teaspoons minced shallot or red onion
1½   teaspoons minced fresh parsley or chives
1½   teaspoons minced fresh dill
   1   small garlic clove, minced
   ½   teaspoon lemon juice
   ¾   teaspoon table salt
   ⅛   teaspoon pepper
      Pinch sugar

Whisk all ingredients in bowl until combined and smooth. (Dressing can be refrigerated for up to 4 days; whisk to recombine before using.)

vegan ranch dressing

makes about ½ cup

If you are vegan but recall the flavor of ranch dressing with nostalgia, try our version made with plant-based mayo and yogurt.

- ½ cup plant-based mayonnaise
- 2 tablespoons plain plant-based yogurt
- 1½ teaspoons minced fresh chives or parsley
- 1½ teaspoons minced fresh dill
- 1 teaspoon white wine vinegar
- ¼ teaspoon garlic powder
- ⅛ teaspoon table salt
- ⅛ teaspoon pepper

Whisk all ingredients in bowl until combined and smooth. (Dressing can be refrigerated for up to 4 days; whisk to recombine before using.)

green goddess dressing

makes about ¾ cup

A variety of herbs gives this boldly flavored dressing its name and green color; buttermilk, yogurt, and sour cream give it creamy power.

- 1½ teaspoons lemon juice
- 1½ teaspoons water
- 1 teaspoon dried tarragon
- ¼ cup buttermilk
- 2 tablespoons plain yogurt
- 2 tablespoons sour cream
- 2 tablespoons minced fresh parsley or cilantro
- 1 small garlic clove, minced
- ½ anchovy fillet, rinsed and minced (optional)
- 2 tablespoons minced fresh chives, scallions, or tarragon
- ⅛ teaspoon table salt
- ⅛ teaspoon pepper

1 Combine lemon juice, water, and tarragon in small bowl and let sit for 15 minutes.

2 Process tarragon mixture; buttermilk; yogurt; sour cream; parsley; garlic; and anchovy, if using, in blender until smooth, scraping down sides of blender jar as needed. Transfer dressing to clean bowl. Stir in chives, salt, and pepper. Cover and refrigerate until flavors meld, about 1 hour. Season with salt and pepper to taste. (Dressing can be refrigerated for up to 4 days; whisk to recombine before using.)

creamy peppercorn dressing

makes 1 cup

To make a creamy peppercorn dressing that actually tastes like pepper—but without the burn—we started with a blend of mayonnaise and sour cream, thinning this creamy base with buttermilk to give it the right consistency and tang. Red wine vinegar, garlic, and Dijon mustard rounded out the flavors. To tame the fiery intensity of the pepper while still ensuring that each spoonful of the dressing had a deep peppery taste, we used the technique of blooming by slowly simmering the pepper in olive oil. As a bonus, the peppery oil could simply be incorporated into the dressing. If you don't have buttermilk, substitute milk and increase the vinegar to 2½ teaspoons. Hardy, crisp iceberg and romaine work well with this creamy dressing.

- ¼ cup extra-virgin olive oil
- 1 tablespoon coarsely ground pepper
- ¼ cup sour cream or Greek yogurt
- ¼ cup mayonnaise
- 2 tablespoons buttermilk
- 2 teaspoons Dijon mustard
- 2 teaspoons red wine vinegar
- 1 garlic clove, minced

Heat oil and pepper in small saucepan over low heat until faint bubbles appear. Simmer gently, swirling saucepan occasionally, until pepper is fragrant, about 8 minutes. Remove from heat and let cool completely. Whisk sour cream, mayonnaise, buttermilk, mustard, vinegar, and garlic together in bowl. Whisking constantly, slowly drizzle in pepper oil until emulsified. Season with salt to taste. (Dressing can be refrigerated for up to 4 days; whisk to recombine before using.)

creamy avocado dressing

makes about 1 cup

Avocado lends this dressing a lovely pale-green color and a creamy mildness that works with sturdy greens.

- 1 avocado, halved, pitted, and cut into ½-inch pieces
- 2 tablespoons extra-virgin olive oil
- 1 teaspoon grated lemon zest plus 3 tablespoons juice
- 1 garlic clove, minced
- ¾ teaspoon table salt
- ¼ teaspoon pepper

Process all ingredients in food processor until smooth, about 30 seconds, scraping down sides of bowl as needed. Season with salt and pepper to taste. Use immediately.

creamy italian dressing

makes about ¾ cup

Oregano, basil, and sour cream or Greek yogurt flavor this creamy dressing to pair with sturdy greens.

- 1½ tablespoons red wine vinegar
- 1½ tablespoons grated Parmesan or Pecorino Romano cheese
- 1 small shallot, minced
- 1 small garlic clove, minced
- 1 teaspoon dried oregano
- ⅛ teaspoon red pepper flakes
- ¼ cup mayonnaise
- 2 tablespoons sour cream or Greek yogurt
- 1½ teaspoons chopped fresh basil
- ¼ cup extra-virgin olive oil

1   Combine vinegar, Parmesan, shallot, garlic, oregano, and pepper flakes in small bowl. Microwave until Parmesan is melted (vinegar will look cloudy) and mixture is fragrant, about 30 seconds; let cool slightly.

2   Process mayonnaise, sour cream, basil, and vinegar mixture in blender until smooth, scraping down sides of blender jar as needed. With blender running, slowly add oil and process until dressing is emulsified, about 1 minute. Season with salt and pepper to taste. (Dressing can be refrigerated for up to 4 days; whisk to recombine before using.)

caesar dressing

makes about 1 cup

Feel like Caesar salad for dinner but don't have time to make the whole dish from scratch? This dressing will evoke its flavor. Add the dressing to chopped romaine and store the rest in the refrigerator for your next craving.

- ⅔ cup mayonnaise
- 3 tablespoons lemon juice
- 1 tablespoon Dijon mustard
- 2 teaspoons Worcestershire sauce
- 2 garlic cloves, minced
- 3-4 anchovy fillets, rinsed, patted dry, and minced
- ½ teaspoon pepper
- ⅛ teaspoon table salt
- 1 tablespoon extra-virgin olive oil

Whisk mayonnaise, lemon juice, mustard, Worcestershire, garlic, anchovies, pepper, and salt together in medium bowl. Whisking constantly, slowly drizzle in oil until emulsified. (Dressing can be refrigerated for up to 4 days; whisk to recombine before using.)

flavored oils and vinegar

When we want to make salad on the fly and there's no time to whisk up a dressing, infused oil and flavorful vinegar save the day. Splash some on; add salt and pepper; and voilà, you've got a delicious dressed salad.

Our infused oils capture the essence of spices and herbs such as coriander, peppercorn, and rosemary to complement all manner of salads. The oils are easy to make, less expensive than store-bought, and last for up to one month in the refrigerator.

On the other hand, since you can buy a variety of good-quality vinegars—cider, sherry, balsamic—we offer only one infused version. Instead we focus on a project: homemade wine vinegar. Make it with a red or white wine that you enjoy drinking. The vinegar will reflect its flavor. Finally, we share a recipe for seasoned rice vinegar so that you can control the salt and sugar it contains.

OILS

In a salad, oil provides both flavor and fat. Olive oil is often the choice for salad dressings because of its lightness, natural fruitiness, and health benefits. But other oils work for salad dressings, too, such as corn, peanut, and vegetable oil. You can infuse any of these with spices or herbs to enhance their taste. For our simple spiced oils—an infusion of just one to two spices or herbs—we heated the flavorings in the oil over medium-low heat for a few minutes to extract their flavors (the process is efficient because the main flavor compounds in most spices are fat-soluble) and then let the oil steep off the heat for an additional 4 hours; this off-heat steeping was perfect for ensuring maximum flavor transfer (any more heated steeping made the oil taste harsh). For more strongly flavored ingredients such as peppercorn or ginger, we heated the oil with the ingredients for about 10 minutes and steeped them for a day to let the flavors meld.

rosemary oil

makes about 1 cup

You can strain the finished oil through a fine-mesh strainer just before serving, if desired.

1 cup extra-virgin olive oil
2 tablespoons dried rosemary

Heat oil and rosemary in small saucepan over medium-low heat until fragrant and starting to bubble, 2 to 3 minutes. Off heat, let sit until flavors meld, about 4 hours. Pour into clean glass jar, seal tightly, and refrigerate. (Oil can be refrigerated for up to 1 month.)

fennel oil

makes about 1 cup

You can strain the finished oil through a fine-mesh strainer just before serving, if desired.

1 cup extra-virgin olive oil
3 tablespoons fennel seeds, cracked

Heat oil and fennel in small saucepan over medium-low heat until fragrant and starting to bubble, 2 to 3 minutes. Off heat, let sit until flavors meld, about 4 hours. Pour into clean glass jar, seal tightly, and refrigerate. (Oil can be refrigerated for up to 1 month.)

chipotle-coriander oil

makes about 1 cup

You can strain the finished oil through a fine-mesh strainer just before serving, if desired.

1 cup extra-virgin olive oil
3 tablespoons coriander seeds, cracked
1 teaspoon chipotle chile powder

Heat oil, coriander, and chile powder in small saucepan over medium-low heat until fragrant and starting to bubble, 2 to 3 minutes. Off heat, let sit until flavors meld, about 4 hours. Pour into clean glass jar, seal tightly, and refrigerate. (Oil can be refrigerated for up to 1 month.)

ginger oil

makes about 1 cup

You can strain the finished oil through a fine-mesh strainer just before serving, if desired.

1 cup extra-virgin olive oil
⅓ cup grated fresh ginger

1　Combine oil and ginger in small saucepan. Over low heat, bring oil temperature to 140 degrees and maintain temperature for 10 minutes as oil weakly bubbles.

2　Carefully transfer oil to bowl and let cool completely. Let sit until flavors meld, at least 24 hours. Pour into clean glass jar, seal tightly, and refrigerate. (Oil can be refrigerated for up to 1 month.)

peppercorn oil

makes about 1 cup

You can strain the finished oil through a fine-mesh strainer just before serving, if desired.

1 cup extra-virgin olive oil
2 tablespoons cracked black peppercorns or mixture of green, white, black, and red peppercorns

1　Combine oil and peppercorns in small saucepan. Over low heat, bring oil temperature to 140 degrees and maintain temperature for 10 minutes as oil weakly bubbles.

2　Carefully transfer oil to bowl and let cool completely. Let sit until flavors meld, at least 24 hours. Pour into clean glass jar, seal tightly, and refrigerate. (Oil can be refrigerated for up to 1 month.)

VINEGAR

Though vinegar can be made from fruit, vegetables, sugar, or grain, arguably the word most often brings grapes to mind. This is only natural because vinegar comes from the French "vin aigre," which means "wine that has soured."

And yet vinegar brings so much more than tartness to food. Of course, we use a variety of vinegars in our vinaigrettes and dressings, but we also use them to pickle the vegetables and fruits that make crunchy salad toppers.

Balsamic vinegar, with its rich roundness, flavors meats, fall fruit, and root vegetables in salad; sherry vinegar brings aromatic savory notes and caramel sweetness; and unseasoned and seasoned rice vinegars pair well with soy sauce and complement salads inspired by East Asian cuisines. Red wine vinegar adds light color and a hint of red wine to vegetable salads, while more delicately flavored white wine vinegar is perfect with salads that showcase fruits such as raspberries, melon, and Cape gooseberries.

WINE VINEGAR

Most vinegars are not easy to make at home because of the equipment, space, and time needed. But wine vinegar is. While the process is often shrouded in mystery, with talk of "mothers," bacteria, and botched batches, all you really need to make wine vinegar is some wine and some patience. In theory, you could let wine turn to vinegar on its own. However, since the timeline is long and the results inconsistent, it's far better to start with a "vinegar mother," just as you would embark on sourdough bread making with a starter. A vinegar mother is a culture that helps acidify the wine. Buy some, add wine and water, and you're on your way. You can certainly use a fresh bottle of wine to make vinegar, but here's a neat tip: Every time you have red or white wine left over from a meal, pour it into a large, clean jar (using separate jars for red and white wines) with a tight-fitting lid. Collect wine this way for a month or so, and then use it to make our Wine Vinegar (recipe follows).

wine vinegar

makes 4 to 5 cups red wine vinegar or 2 to 3 cups white wine vinegar

If you have time, why not make your own wine vinegar? It's a fun project, the vinegar tastes great, and it lasts for up to six months. Use any wine you like; the vinegar will echo its flavor. Vinegars made with organic, low-sulfite wines ferment slightly faster, but the difference is negligible over a few months. Many wine vinegar recipes call for complicated steps such as feeding (with additional wine) or aerating. We found the simplest method was the most reliable and gave us the best vinegar. After mixing wine, water, and mother (culture) together, just wait. White wines take about a month longer than reds since they usually contain more sulfites that need to dissipate before the fermentation process can begin. Due to the lengthier process, white wine evaporates more and yields less vinegar. Start today and enjoy in three to four months.

> 2   (750-ml) bottles full-bodied red or white wine
> 3¼ cups filtered water
> 8   ounces red or white wine mother of vinegar

1   Combine wine, water, and mother of vinegar in sterilized 1-gallon ceramic crock. Cover top of crock with clean dish towel and secure with rubber band. Place in warm, dark space to ferment, undisturbed, until mixture no longer tastes alcoholic and has strong vinegar flavor, about 3 months for red wine or 4 months for white wine. After about 10 days for red wine and about 1 month for white wine, mother should be starting to form on surface of mixture (surface will look oily and wine will look cloudy). Oil slick will gradually transform into thick, gelatinous sheet; do not disturb crock during fermentation or mother will break up and become harder to remove.

2   Using your hands, gently transfer mother to separate bowl. Break off 2-inch piece and transfer to 4-ounce jar with tight-fitting lid; discard remaining mother.

3   Line fine-mesh strainer with double layer of coffee filters and set over 8-cup liquid measuring cup; pour vinegar through strainer. Pour enough strained vinegar over mother in jar to cover completely; cover jar and store at room temperature for up to 3 months for next batch of vinegar. Pour remaining vinegar into glass bottles with tight-fitting lids. (Vinegar and mother of vinegar can be stored in cool, dark place for at least 6 months.)

seasoned rice vinegar

makes ½ cup

Making seasoned rice vinegar at home means you know exactly how much salt and sugar it contains. Table salt dissolves most readily here, but if all you have is kosher salt, increase the amount to 2 tablespoons.

- ½ cup unseasoned rice vinegar
- ¼ cup sugar
- 1 tablespoon table salt

1   Combine all ingredients in bowl and let sit for 5 minutes.

2   Whisk constantly until sugar and salt dissolve, about 3 minutes. (Seasoned vinegar can be stored in airtight container at room temperature for up to 1 week.)

hot pepper vinegar

makes about 2 cups

Heating the pint jar with hot water and draining it before adding the hot brine ensures that the jar won't crack from an abrupt temperature change.

- ½ ounce (about 20) dried arbol chiles
- 2 cups distilled white vinegar
- 4 teaspoons sugar
- 1 teaspoon table salt
- ½ teaspoon black peppercorns

1   Prick chiles with fork and set aside. Combine vinegar, sugar, salt, and peppercorns in small saucepan and bring to boil over medium-high heat.

2   Fill 1-pint Mason jar with hot water to warm. Drain jar, then pack with chiles. Using ladle, pour hot brine over chiles to cover. Let cool completely, about 30 minutes. Cover and refrigerate until flavors meld, about 24 hours. (Vinegar can be refrigerated for up to 3 months; flavor will deepen over time.)

adding heft

Proteins such as nuts, tofu, meat, and fish are a great way to bulk up your salads and make them complete meals.

The recipes in this book feature a variety of proteins from squid to steak. In this section, you will find recipes for the proteins that are featured in more than one of our salad recipes, such as hard-cooked eggs, crispy tofu, or poached chicken (though this can be substituted with leftover chicken you have in the refrigerator).

These proteins are also great to keep on hand for when that sudden hearty salad craving strikes.

easy-peel hard-cooked eggs
makes 2 to 6 eggs
Be sure to use large eggs that have no cracks and are cold from the refrigerator.

　　2-6　large eggs

1　Bring 1 inch water to rolling boil in medium saucepan over high heat. Place eggs in steamer basket. Transfer basket to saucepan. Cover, reduce heat to medium-low, and cook eggs for 13 minutes.

2　When eggs are almost finished cooking, combine 2 cups ice cubes and 2 cups cold water in medium bowl. Using tongs or spoon, transfer eggs to ice bath; let sit for 15 minutes. Peel before serving. (Eggs can be refrigerated in their shells in airtight container for up to 5 days.)

perfect poached chicken
makes 4 cups

> 4 (6- to 8-ounce) boneless, skinless
> chicken breasts, trimmed
> Table salt for cooking chicken

1   Cover chicken breasts with plastic wrap and pound thick ends gently until ¾ inch thick. Whisk 4 quarts cool water with 2 tablespoons salt in Dutch oven.

2   Arrange chicken in steamer basket without over-lapping. Submerge basket in pot. Heat over medium heat, stirring occasionally, until water registers 175 degrees, 15 to 20 minutes.

3   Turn off heat, cover pot, remove from burner, and let sit until chicken registers 160 degrees, 17 to 22 minutes. Transfer chicken to cutting board and let cool for 10 to 15 minutes. Slice, chop, or shred as desired. Serve. (Chicken can be refrigerated for up to 2 days. Let come to room temperature before using in salads.)

crispy tofu
makes 5½ cups

Firm or extra-firm tofu will work here, but it will be drier. To halve the recipe, simply halve all the ingredients.

> 1¾ pounds soft or medium-firm tofu, halved
> lengthwise and sliced crosswise into
> 3-inch-long by ½-inch-thick slabs
> ½ teaspoon table salt
> ¼ teaspoon pepper
> ¾ cup cornstarch
> ¼ cup cornmeal
> ¾ cup vegetable oil for frying

1   Sprinkle tofu with salt and pepper. Combine cornstarch and cornmeal in shallow dish. Working with several tofu pieces at a time, coat thoroughly with cornstarch mixture, pressing gently to adhere; transfer to wire rack set in rimmed baking sheet.

2   Heat oil in 12-inch nonstick skillet over medium-high heat until shimmering. Working in 2 batches, cook tofu until crispy and golden on all sides, about 4 minutes. Gently lift tofu from oil, letting excess oil drip back into skillet, and transfer to paper towel-lined plate. Serve.

sautéed shrimp
makes 1½ cups

> 12 ounces extra-large shrimp (21 to 25 per pound),
> peeled, deveined, and tails removed
> ¼ teaspoon table salt
> ¼ teaspoon pepper
> 1 tablespoon extra-virgin olive oil

Pat shrimp dry with paper towels and sprinkle with salt and pepper. Heat oil in 12-inch nonstick skillet over medium-high heat until just smoking. Add shrimp in single layer and cook, without stirring, until spotty brown and edges turn pink on bottom, about 1 minute. Flip shrimp and continue to cook until all but very center is opaque, about 30 seconds; transfer shrimp to plate and let cool slightly. Serve. (Shrimp can be refrigerated for up to 2 days.)

croutons

When you think of salad toppings, croutons immediately come to mind. They are the ultimate finishing touch, lending that added bit of crunch and zip to a salad. Planning ahead and making a batch of croutons on the weekend can make packing salad for a workday lunch a walk in the park.

Our little bites of bready goodness—from classic to umami to herbed—work on any salad you choose to pair them with, allowing you to innovate and personalize your meal. And try our Parmesan croutons that use a little science to give you a texture that is crunchy and chewy all at once. It's simple: squeezing the croutons with water before pan frying gives you a crisp exterior while the interior stays pleasantly chewy.

Croutons can be stored in an airtight container at room temperature for up to three days.

classic croutons
makes about 3 cups
Either fresh or stale bread can be used in this recipe, although stale bread is easier to cut and crisps more quickly in the oven.

- 6 slices hearty white sandwich bread, crusts removed, cut into ½-inch pieces (about 3 cups)
- 3 tablespoons unsalted butter, melted, or extra-virgin olive oil

Adjust oven rack to middle position and heat oven to 350 degrees. Toss bread with melted butter in bowl, season with salt and pepper to taste, and spread onto rimmed baking sheet. Bake until golden brown and crisp, 20 to 25 minutes, stirring halfway through baking. Let cool and serve.

variation
garlic croutons
Whisk 1 minced garlic clove into melted butter before tossing with bread.

herbed croutons
makes about 2½ cups

- 1 tablespoon unsalted butter
- 1 teaspoon minced fresh parsley
- ½ teaspoon minced fresh thyme
- 4 slices hearty white sandwich bread, cut into ½-inch pieces (about 2½ cups)

Melt butter in 10-inch skillet over medium heat. Add parsley and thyme; cook, stirring constantly, for 20 seconds. Add bread and cook, stirring frequently, until light golden brown, 5 to 10 minutes. Transfer croutons to paper towel–lined plate and season with salt and pepper to taste. Serve.

buttery rye croutons
makes about 3 cups

- 6 tablespoons unsalted butter
- 2 tablespoons extra-virgin olive oil
- 4 slices light rye bread, cut into ½-inch pieces (about 3 cups)

Heat butter and oil in 12-inch skillet over medium heat until butter is melted. Add bread and cook, stirring frequently, until golden brown, about 10 minutes. Transfer croutons to paper towel-lined plate and season with salt to taste. Serve.

parmesan croutons
makes about 5 cups

If you can't find ciabatta, you can substitute a similar crusty, rustic loaf of bread. A rasp-style grater makes quick work of turning the garlic into a paste.

- 5 tablespoons extra-virgin olive oil, divided
- ½ teaspoon garlic, minced to paste
- ½–¾ loaf ciabatta, cut into ¾-inch pieces (about 5 cups)
- ¼ cup water
- ¼ teaspoon table salt
- 2 tablespoons finely grated Parmesan or Pecorino Romano cheese

1 Combine 1 tablespoon oil and garlic in small bowl; set aside. Place bread in large bowl. Sprinkle with water and salt. Toss, squeezing gently so bread absorbs water. Add remaining 4 tablespoons oil and bread to 12-inch nonstick skillet. Cook over medium-high heat, stirring frequently, until browned and crisp, 7 to 10 minutes.

2 Off heat, push croutons to sides of skillet to clear center; add garlic-oil mixture to clearing and cook with residual heat of skillet for 10 seconds. Sprinkle with Parmesan; toss until garlic and Parmesan are evenly distributed. Serve.

umami croutons
makes about 5 cups

- ¼ cup extra-virgin olive oil
- 3 tablespoons nutritional yeast
- 1 teaspoon white miso
- 1 teaspoon Dijon mustard
- ¼ teaspoon distilled white vinegar
- ⅛ teaspoon table salt
- 6 ounces baguette, cut into 1-inch pieces (about 5 cups)

Adjust oven rack to middle position and heat oven to 350 degrees. Whisk oil, nutritional yeast, miso, mustard, vinegar, and salt together in large bowl. Add bread and, using your hands, massage oil mixture into bread. Transfer to rimmed baking sheet and bake until golden brown and crisp, 13 to 15 minutes, stirring halfway through baking. Let cool and serve.

more crispy, crunchy things

Apart from croutons, there are other toppings that can add zest and crunch to your salads: microwave-fried aromatics, candied bacon, crispy lentils and chickpeas, savory brittle, and more. (You'll be tempted to just munch them on their own.)

These toppings are easy to make and store. If you have them in your pantry or refrigerator, you can use them on your simplest salad and make it a unique and beautiful thing.

Of course, some of these bites such as Black Pepper Candied Bacon and Crispy Chickpeas (recipes follow) work well as appetizers at cocktail parties, too.

black pepper candied bacon
makes 2 cups

It might seem hard to imagine improving on bacon, but crispy bacon can become a treat when layered with sweet-savory flavor. We sprinkled bacon strips with brown sugar and black pepper. The sugar contributed a lovely caramel-toffee background taste along with its sweetness, and the black pepper provided the spice punch. Baking the seasoned strips ensured even cooking and prevented the coating from burning. For this recipe, we prefer center-cut bacon, which is more uniform in thickness than traditional bacon. If your bacon slices range in thickness, place the thinner slices on one tray and the thicker pieces on the other for more-even cooking. Do not substitute dark brown sugar here.

¼ cup packed light brown sugar
1 teaspoon pepper
12 ounces center-cut bacon, halved crosswise

1 Adjust oven racks to upper-middle and lower-middle positions and heat oven to 350 degrees. Combine sugar and pepper in bowl. Arrange bacon on 2 aluminum foil-lined rimmed baking sheets and sprinkle with sugar mixture. Using your fingers, spread sugar mixture evenly over 1 side of slices so they are completely covered.

2 Bake until bacon is dark brown and sugar is bubbling, 20 to 25 minutes, switching and rotating sheets halfway through baking. Set wire rack over triple layer of paper towels. Remove sheets from oven as bacon finishes cooking and transfer bacon to prepared wire rack. Let cool for 5 minutes before serving.

crispy chickpeas
makes 1⅔ cups
Crispy chickpeas add outstanding texture and protein to a salad, and their mild flavor means that they can take on a variety of different spice combinations. This recipe calls for a metal baking pan; using glass or ceramic will result in unevenly cooked chickpeas.

2 (15-ounce) cans chickpeas
3 tablespoons extra-virgin olive oil
⅛ teaspoon table salt
  Pinch cayenne pepper

1 Adjust oven rack to middle position and heat oven to 350 degrees. Place chickpeas in colander and let drain for 10 minutes. Line large plate with double layer of paper towels. Spread chickpeas over plate in even layer. Microwave until exteriors of chickpeas are dry and many have split slightly at seams, 8 to 12 minutes.

2 Transfer chickpeas to 13 by 9-inch metal baking pan. Add oil and stir until evenly coated. Using spatula, spread chickpeas into single layer. Transfer to oven and bake for 30 minutes. While chickpeas bake, combine salt and cayenne in small bowl.

3 Stir chickpeas and crowd toward center of pan, avoiding edges of pan as much as possible. Continue to bake until chickpeas appear dry, slightly shriveled, and deep golden brown, 20 to 40 minutes. (To test for doneness, remove a few paler chickpeas and let cool briefly before tasting; if interiors are soft, return to oven for 5 minutes before testing again.)

4 Transfer chickpeas to large bowl and toss with spice mixture to coat. Season with salt to taste and let cool completely. Serve. (Chickpeas can be stored in airtight container at room temperature for up to 1 week.)

set over bowl; transfer lentils to paper towel–lined plate and discard oil. Sprinkle with cumin and ¼ teaspoon salt and toss to combine; let cool completely. Serve. (Cooled lentils can be stored in airtight container at room temperature for up to 24 hours.)

frico crumble

makes 1½ cups

This thin, crispy, crumbly topping adds cheesy flavor to any salad. We prefer aged Asiago for our frico, but aged Manchego or cheddar cheese are also good options. Use a rasp-style grater to grate the cheese.

    4 ounces aged Asiago cheese, grated fine
       (2 cups), divided

1   Sprinkle half of Asiago evenly over bottom of cold 10-inch nonstick skillet. Cook over medium heat until edges are lacy and light golden, 2 to 3 minutes. Remove skillet from heat and let sit for 1 minute.

2   Using 2 spatulas, carefully flip frico. Return to medium heat and cook until second side is golden, about 1 minute. Carefully slide frico onto plate and set aside until cooled, about 10 minutes.

3   Wipe skillet clean with paper towels and repeat with remaining Asiago. Let cool completely, then crumble into bite-size pieces. Serve. (Frico can be stored in airtight container at room temperature for up to 5 days.)

cumin-spiced crispy lentils

makes about 1 cup

You can use brown lentils in place of the lentilles du Puy if you prefer. Be sure to use a large saucepan to fry the lentils, as the oil mixture will bubble and steam.

    1 teaspoon table salt for brining
    ½ cup dried lentilles du Puy, picked over and rinsed
    ⅓ cup vegetable oil for frying
    ½ teaspoon ground cumin
    ¼ teaspoon table salt

1   Dissolve 1 teaspoon salt in 1 quart cold water in bowl. Add lentils and let sit at room temperature for at least 1 hour or up to 24 hours. Drain well and pat dry with paper towels.

2   Heat oil in large saucepan over medium heat until shimmering. Add lentils and cook, stirring constantly, until crisped and golden in spots, 8 to 12 minutes (oil should bubble vigorously throughout; adjust heat as needed). Carefully drain lentils in fine-mesh strainer

microwave-fried shallots

makes about ½ cup

Fried shallots deliver bursts of crunch and savory flavor, but they're easy to overcook and require constant stirring. To make the method foolproof and more hands-off, we fried three thinly sliced shallots in ½ cup of vegetable oil in a bowl in the microwave in decreasing increments of time (first 5 minutes, then 2 minutes, then 30 seconds), stirring them between increments.

    3 shallots, sliced thin
    ½ cup vegetable oil

Combine shallots and oil in medium bowl. Microwave for 5 minutes. Stir and continue to microwave for 2 minutes longer. Repeat stirring and microwaving in 2-minute increments until beginning to brown (4 to 6 minutes). Repeat stirring and microwaving in 30-second increments until deep golden brown (30 seconds to 2 minutes). Using slotted spoon, transfer shallots to paper towel–lined plate; season with salt to taste. Let drain and crisp for about 5 minutes. Serve.

variations

microwave-fried garlic

makes about ½ cup

Substitute ½ cup sliced or minced garlic cloves for shallots. After frying, dust garlic with 1 teaspoon confectioners' sugar (to offset any bitterness) before seasoning with salt.

microwave-fried leeks

makes about ¾ cup

Substitute 1 leek, white and light green parts only, halved lengthwise, sliced into very thin 2-inch-long strips, washed thoroughly, dried, and tossed with 2 tablespoons all-purpose flour (to accelerate browning) for shallots.

hazelnut-nigella dukkah

makes about ½ cup

A crunchy Egyptian condiment of pounded nuts, herbs, spices, and seeds, dukkah is traditionally eaten with bread or vegetables that have been dipped in olive oil, which helps the dukkah stick. We also like it as a delightfully crunchy salad topping, especially on salads with softer elements such as rice, grains, or fish. You can find nigella seeds at spice shops and Middle Eastern markets.

- 1 **teaspoon fennel seeds, toasted**
- 1 **teaspoon coriander seeds, toasted**
- 1½ **tablespoons raw sunflower seeds, toasted**
- 1 **tablespoon sesame seeds, toasted**
- 1½ **teaspoons nigella seeds**
- 3 **tablespoons hazelnuts, toasted, skinned, and chopped fine**
- 1½ **teaspoons paprika**
- ½ **teaspoon flake sea salt, such as Maldon**

Process fennel seeds and coriander seeds in spice grinder until finely ground, about 30 seconds. Add sunflower seeds, sesame seeds, and nigella seeds and pulse until coarsely ground, about 4 pulses; transfer to small bowl. Stir in hazelnuts, paprika, and salt. (Dukkah can be refrigerated for up to 3 months.)

za'atar

makes about ½ cup

Za'atar is an aromatic eastern Mediterranean spice blend that is used as both a seasoning and a condiment. The thyme gives it a round herbal flavor, the sumac lemony tartness, and the sesame seeds richness and subtle crunch. Earthy and citrusy, this irresistible spice mix can be sprinkled over anything that needs some oomph. We use it on meats and vegetables in our salads to add a finishing floral touch to the dish.

- ½ **cup dried thyme**
- 2 **tablespoons sesame seeds, toasted**
- 1½ **tablespoons ground sumac**

Working in batches, process thyme in spice grinder until finely ground, about 30 seconds; transfer to small bowl. Stir in sesame seeds and sumac. (Za'atar can be stored in airtight container at room temperature for up to 3 months.)

spiced pepitas or sunflower seeds
makes ½ cup

These salty, crunchy, spicy seeds are an easy, flavorful salad topping and make a great snack, too.

- 2 teaspoons extra-virgin olive oil
- ½ cup raw pepitas or sunflower seeds
- ½ teaspoon paprika
- ½ teaspoon ground coriander
- ¼ teaspoon table salt

Heat oil in 12-inch skillet over medium heat until shimmering. Add pepitas, paprika, coriander, and salt. Cook, stirring constantly, until pepitas are toasted, about 2 minutes; transfer to bowl and let cool. Serve. (Pepitas can be stored in airtight container at room temperature for up to 5 days.)

quick candied nuts
makes ½ cup

We like this recipe prepared with shelled pistachios, walnuts or pecans, roasted cashews, salted or unsalted peanuts, and sliced almonds. If you want to make a mixed batch, cook the nuts individually and then toss to combine.

- ½ cup nuts
- 1 tablespoon granulated sugar
- 1 tablespoon hot water
- ⅛ teaspoon table salt

1 Adjust oven rack to middle position and heat oven to 350 degrees. Spread nuts in single layer on rimmed baking sheet and toast until fragrant and slightly darkened, 8 to 12 minutes, shaking sheet halfway through toasting. Transfer nuts to plate and let cool for 10 to 15 minutes.

2 Line now-empty sheet with parchment paper. Whisk sugar, hot water, and salt in large bowl until sugar is mostly dissolved. Add nuts and stir to coat. Spread nuts on prepared sheet in single layer and bake until nuts are crisp and dry, 10 to 12 minutes. Let cool and serve.

spiced nuts
makes 2 cups

This method can be used with a variety of nuts to adapt to any salad's flavors.

- 1 tablespoon extra-virgin olive oil
- 2 cups skin-on whole almonds, walnuts, or shelled pistachios
- 2 teaspoons grated lemon zest
- 1 teaspoon ground coriander
- 1 teaspoon table salt
- ½ teaspoon hot paprika
- ¼ teaspoon pepper

Heat oil in 12-inch nonstick skillet over medium-high heat until shimmering. Add nuts, lemon zest, coriander, salt, paprika, and pepper and reduce heat to medium-low. Cook, stirring often, until nuts are fragrant and their color deepens slightly, about 8 minutes. Transfer nuts to paper towel–lined plate and let cool. Serve. (Nuts can be stored in airtight container at room temperature for up to 5 days.)

savory seed brittle

makes 2 cups

For a topping that can instantly take any salad to the next level, we developed a seed brittle packed with outstanding texture and savory flavor. To achieve the ideal crunchy, brittle texture that would break into bite-size pieces, we added an egg white and some maple syrup, which also contributed a bit of sweetness to balance all the savory flavors. Do not substitute quick or instant oats in this recipe.

1	large egg white
2	tablespoons maple syrup
1	tablespoon extra-virgin olive oil
1	tablespoon soy sauce
1	tablespoon caraway seeds, crushed
½	teaspoon table salt
¼	teaspoon pepper
½	cup old-fashioned rolled oats
⅓	cup raw sunflower seeds
⅓	cup raw pepitas
2	tablespoons sesame seeds
2	tablespoons nigella seeds

1   Adjust oven rack to upper-middle position and heat oven to 300 degrees. Line 8-inch square baking pan with parchment paper and spray parchment with vegetable oil spray. Whisk egg white, maple syrup, oil, soy sauce, caraway seeds, salt, and pepper together in large bowl. Stir in oats, sunflower seeds, pepitas, sesame seeds, and nigella seeds until well combined.

2   Transfer oat mixture to prepared pan and spread into even layer. Using stiff metal spatula, press oat mixture until very compact. Bake until golden brown and fragrant, 45 to 55 minutes, rotating pan halfway through baking.

3   Transfer pan to wire rack and let brittle cool completely, about 1 hour. Break cooled brittle into pieces of desired size, discarding parchment. Serve. (Brittle can be stored in airtight container at room temperature for up to 1 month.)

quick pickles

Making your own quick pickles is fun and easy. We tend to think of pickling as a slow process, but you can quick-pickle vegetables in vinegar in a matter of a few hours, or even less time in some cases. Most quick pickles begin with a brine of vinegar, salt, sugar, and seasonings and can be made with fruits as well as vegetables.

Pickles are not just accompaniments for burgers or sandwiches anymore. They make delicious salad toppers or can be mixed into bound salads such as crab, chicken, and tuna salad to add a refreshing tart crunch that is a counterpoint to the salad's creaminess.

quick pickled red onion
makes about 1 cup

Pickled onions are an absolute breeze to make and are a flavorful accompaniment to have on hand for salads, sandwiches, and more. Just a few minutes of hands-on preparation plus a 60-minute brine transform simple slices of red onion into a vibrant topping. Look for a firm, dry onion with thin, shiny skin and a deep-purple color.

- 1 cup red wine vinegar
- ⅓ cup sugar
- ¼ teaspoon table salt
- 1 red onion, halved and sliced thin through root end

Bring vinegar, sugar, and salt to simmer in small saucepan over medium-high heat, stirring occasionally, until sugar is dissolved. Off heat, stir in onion; cover; and let cool completely, about 1 hour. Serve. (Pickled onions can be refrigerated in airtight container for up to 1 week.)

quick giardiniera

makes 1 quart

For this mixed vegetable pickle, we bring the brine, flavored with garlic, peppercorns, and red pepper flakes, to a simmer; pour it over a mixture of cauliflower, celery, and carrot in a glass jar; and let the mixture cool completely. After a 3-hour refrigeration (or longer if possible), the pickles are ready to devour. We like to use our Seasoned Rice Vinegar (page 41) but you will need to make more than double the batch for this recipe. Any seasoned rice vinegar will work here.

- 1¼ cups 1-inch cauliflower florets
- 1 celery rib, sliced ¼ inch thick
- 1 carrot, peeled and sliced ¼ inch thick
- 1¾ cups seasoned rice vinegar
- ¼ cup water
- 2 garlic cloves, peeled and halved
- ½ teaspoon red pepper flakes
- ¼ teaspoon black peppercorns
- ¼ teaspoon yellow mustard seeds

Place cauliflower, celery, and carrot in 1-quart glass jar with tight-fitting lid. Combine vinegar, water, garlic, pepper flakes, peppercorns, and mustard seeds in small saucepan and bring to boil. Pour brine into jar, making sure all vegetables are submerged. Let cool completely. Affix jar lid and refrigerate for at least 3 hours before serving. (Pickles can be refrigerated for up to 1 week.)

pickled asparagus

makes 1 quart

For crunchy pickles that are delicious in salad or on a cheese plate, start with thick asparagus spears. Trimming the spears to the height of the jar was necessary to make sure that they fit properly. Cider vinegar tempered with sugar gave the pickles a balanced tang, and black peppercorns and mustard seeds added a pop of heat. Trim the asparagus spears so that they are no taller than the jar you're using. Depending on the size of your jar, you may have extra brine; the important thing is to make sure that the asparagus spears are fully submerged in it.

- 1 pound thick asparagus
- 6 sprigs fresh dill
- 1 bay leaf
- 1½ cups cider vinegar
- 1½ cups water
- ⅓ cup sugar
- ¼ cup kosher salt
- ½ teaspoon black peppercorns
- ½ teaspoon yellow mustard seeds

1 Trim asparagus spears to fit in wide-mouth 1-quart glass jar with tight-fitting lid. Place spears upright in jar. Add dill sprigs and bay leaf.

2 Combine vinegar, water, sugar, salt, peppercorns, and mustard seeds in small saucepan and bring to boil. Pour brine into jar, making sure spears are fully submerged. Let cool completely, about 1 hour.

3 Affix jar lid and refrigerate for at least 3 hours before serving. (Pickles can be refrigerated for up to 1 week.)

quick pickled daikon radish and carrot

makes about 2 cups

These citrusy pickles are delicious on our East Asian–inspired salads. They are ready to eat after just an hour in the brine. Be sure to drain the vegetables at that time or their texture will begin to soften rapidly. Try them on our Crab and Mizuna Salad (page 75).

- ½ teaspoon grated lime zest plus ¼ cup juice (2 limes)
- 1½ teaspoons fish sauce
- 1½ teaspoons sugar
- ¼ teaspoon table salt
- 8 ounces daikon radish, peeled and cut into 2-inch-long matchsticks
- 1 carrot, peeled and cut into 2-inch-long matchsticks

Whisk lime zest and juice, fish sauce, sugar, and salt in medium bowl until sugar and salt are dissolved. Add radish and carrot and toss to combine. Gently press on vegetables to submerge. Cover and let sit at room temperature for 1 hour; drain. Serve. (Drained vegetables can be refrigerated for up to 24 hours.)

quick pickled fennel

makes 2 cups

These pickles give any salad a burst of sweet anise and fresh citrus flavor but pair really well with meat salads.

- ¾ cup seasoned rice vinegar
- ¼ cup water
- 1 (1-inch) strip orange zest
- 1 garlic clove, peeled and halved
- ¼ teaspoon fennel seeds
- ⅛ teaspoon black peppercorns
- ⅛ teaspoon yellow mustard seeds
- 1 fennel bulb, stalks discarded, bulb halved, cored, and sliced thin

Combine vinegar, water, orange zest, garlic, fennel seeds, peppercorns, and mustard seeds in 4-cup liquid measuring cup. Microwave until boiling, about 3 minutes. Stir in fennel until completely submerged and let cool completely, about 30 minutes. Drain and serve. (Drained pickled fennel can be refrigerated for up to 6 weeks; fennel will soften significantly after 6 weeks.)

quick pickled cabbage with lemongrass

makes 2 cups

Crunchy, tender, and aromatic, this quick pickle evokes the freshness and vibrancy of Thai cuisine. We like it in our East Asian–inspired noodle salads. Ready in less than 2 hours, it gives texture and fragrance to any salad that needs tart crunch. We chose napa cabbage over other varieties for its supple juiciness and clean, fresh flavor. Before adding the cabbage to the brine, we tossed it in salt to help soften and season it while drawing out moisture that would otherwise dilute the brine. Rinsing the salted cabbage before tossing it with the vinegar helped extend the pickles' shelf life. Using unseasoned rice vinegar, rather than the seasoned rice vinegar we call for in our other quick pickles, prevented the pickled cabbage from tasting too salty. A little sugar in the brine balanced the vinegar's acidity and brought out the sweetness of the aromatics.

- ½ small head napa cabbage, quartered, cored, and cut into 1-inch pieces (3 cups)
- 2 teaspoons kosher salt
- ½ cup unseasoned rice vinegar
- 1 jalapeño chile, stemmed, seeded, and sliced thin
- 2 tablespoons shredded fresh Thai basil
- 2 teaspoons minced lemongrass
- 2 teaspoons sugar
- 1 garlic clove, minced
- 1 teaspoon grated fresh ginger

1 Toss cabbage and salt together in large bowl. Let cabbage sit at room temperature for 1 hour, stirring occasionally.

2 Transfer cabbage to colander and rinse with cold water. Drain cabbage well, gently squeeze to remove excess liquid, then pat dry with paper towels.

3 Whisk vinegar, jalapeño, basil, lemongrass, sugar, garlic, and ginger in large bowl until sugar is dissolved. Add cabbage, toss to combine, and let sit at room temperature for 30 minutes. Serve. (Pickled cabbage can be refrigerated for up to 3 days; cabbage will turn limp and gray after 3 days.)

quick pickled grapes

makes 1⅓ cups

Pickling adds vibrantly acidic flavor to grapes, rendering a perfect sweet-tart combination that works well on salads with crunchy or spicy greens.

- ⅓ cup white wine vinegar
- 1 tablespoon sugar
- ½ teaspoon table salt
- 8 ounces seedless grapes, halved (1⅓ cups)

Microwave vinegar, sugar, and salt in medium bowl until simmering, 1 to 2 minutes. Stir in grapes and let sit, stirring occasionally, for 45 minutes. Drain and serve. (Drained pickled grapes can be refrigerated for up to 1 week.)

leafy salads

purslane and watermelon salad

SERVES 4 TO 6

4 cups watermelon cut into
1-inch pieces

2 teaspoons sugar

2 tablespoons extra-virgin olive oil,
plus extra for drizzling

1 tablespoon cider vinegar

½ teaspoon grated lemon zest plus
1 tablespoon juice

½ teaspoon table salt

¼ teaspoon pepper

6 ounces purslane, trimmed and torn
into 1½-inch pieces (6 cups)

¼ cup fresh basil or parsley
leaves, torn

1 shallot, sliced thin

6 ounces fresh mozzarella cheese,
torn into 1-inch pieces

why this recipe works Purslane has crisp, juicy-sweet stems; tart, tangy, slightly peppery leaves; and the highest omega-3 fatty acid content of any plant, making it the perfect ingredient for salads. We paired it with watermelon because both watermelon and purslane are at their best in the summer. To start, we cubed watermelon into 1-inch pieces, tossed the pieces with sugar, and let them drain of any excess liquid. To gently balance the melon's sweetness and the purslane's tangy bite, we added thinly sliced shallot for delicate onion flavor. Tearing the fresh purslane into 1½-inch pieces ensured that every bite would have its flavor. Basil leaves brought freshness; torn fresh mozzarella added creamy substance; and a simple vinaigrette of olive oil, cider vinegar, and lemon married all the elements in delicate, savory harmony. This salad benefits from a liberal sprinkling of salt and pepper, so don't be shy when seasoning the salad at the end of step 2.

1 Toss watermelon with sugar in colander set over bowl; set aside and let sit for 30 minutes.

2 Whisk oil, vinegar, lemon zest and juice, salt, and pepper together in large bowl. Add purslane, basil, shallot, and drained watermelon and toss gently to combine. Transfer to serving platter and scatter mozzarella over top. Drizzle with extra oil and season with salt and pepper to taste. Serve.

purslane

In the height of summer, you've probably seen purslane growing all around—in open fields, in sidewalk cracks, or maybe even in your backyard—without realizing that this common foraged green is not only edible but also delicious. Native to India and Persia, purslane, or *Portulaca oleracea* (also called duckweed, pursley, and little hogweed), made its way across the world. It grows prolifically in the northeastern United States and a little less so in the Pacific Northwest. Apart from using the moisture-rich leaves of this easy-to-forage succulent in our purslane and watermelon salad, you can innovate by combining purslane with cucumber or avocado, drizzling it with oil and vinegar, and topping it with feta. Farmers' markets are likely to feature purslane from early summer to midsummer. Look for small, smooth, and dark-green oar-shaped leaves with a slight sheen. Store purslane in a plastic produce bag in the refrigerator for up to a week.

early growth of a pea plant

pea shoots Pea shoots, or pea sprouts, are the first growth of a pea plant. If you spot them, buy them; delicate, sweet, and mild, they're around only briefly and are delicious raw. Sprinkle them over a dressed salad like you would alfalfa sprouts or microgreens.

pea tendrils If you leave pea shoots alone, you'll soon have pea tendrils, the long, thin coils and leaves that spring out in every direction. Pea tendrils are more intense in flavor than pea shoots, but they add color and fresh spring flavor to salads and make a great garnish, too.

pea greens In the third stage of growth, you get pea greens, which you can harvest for use in our salad on the facing page. The rounded, bright-green, faintly bitter leaves taste of fresh peas but without their sweetness, and they are delicious in pesto, too.

pea green salad with warm apricot-pistachio vinaigrette

why this recipe works Both the delicate stems and leaves of pea greens are edible, making them the perfect choice for a light, unusual spring salad with a warm dressing made with dried apricots and pistachios. We complemented the grassy pea greens with sweet fresh peas and contrasted them with pleasantly bitter endive. The warm, slightly sweet vinaigrette both offset the faintly bitter quality of the endive and lightly wilted the greens. We steamed the peas in a skillet until they were just tender and then set them aside; in the same skillet, we toasted pistachios in olive oil. Meanwhile we warmed the rest of the dressing—shallot, apricots, mustard, and white wine vinegar—in the microwave and then added it to the skillet with the pistachios off the heat, since the hot oil would sizzle. Finally, we tossed the warmed vinaigrette with the pea greens, cooked peas, and endive. You can substitute thawed frozen peas for the fresh peas; if using frozen peas, skip step 1.

1 for the salad Bring peas and ¼ cup water to simmer in 10-inch skillet over medium-high heat. Cover; reduce heat to medium-low; and cook, stirring occasionally, until peas are tender, 5 to 7 minutes. Drain peas and set aside. Wipe skillet clean with paper towels.

2 for the vinaigrette Whisk vinegar, mustard, sugar, and salt together in medium bowl. Add apricots and shallot; cover; and microwave until steaming, 30 seconds to 1 minute. Stir to submerge shallot, then let cool completely, about 15 minutes.

3 Heat oil in now-empty skillet over medium heat until shimmering. Add pistachios and cook, stirring frequently, until toasted and fragrant, 1 to 2 minutes. Off heat, stir in shallot mixture and let sit until heated through, about 30 seconds.

4 Gently toss pea greens, endive, and peas with warm vinaigrette in large bowl until evenly coated and wilted slightly. Season with salt and pepper to taste. Serve.

SERVES 4 TO 6

salad

- 1 pound shell-on English peas, shelled (1¼ cups)
- 3 tablespoons extra-virgin olive oil
- ⅓ cup shelled pistachios, chopped
- 8 ounces (8 cups) pea greens or microgreens
- 2 heads Belgian endive (8 ounces), trimmed, halved lengthwise, and sliced ¼ inch thick

vinaigrette

- 3 tablespoons white wine vinegar
- 2 teaspoons whole-grain mustard
- ½ teaspoon sugar
- ¼ teaspoon table salt
- ½ cup dried apricots, chopped
- 1 small shallot, halved and sliced thin

spring pea salad

why this recipe works Spring is when peas are in season and at their sweetest, snappiest best. Here, we showcase the three types—English, snow, and sugar snap—in a knockout spring salad. First we briefly blanched the sugar snap and shelled English peas. Peas start converting their sugars into starch from the moment they're picked; a quick dip in boiling water dissolved their remaining sugars and made them more available to taste, and the moist heat evened out any toughness in their skins. The more-delicate snow peas lost too much of their crunch when blanched, so we left them raw. To add visual variety to the salad, we cut the snap peas into bite-size pieces and the snow peas on the bias into thin strips. This also helped them tangle with the other components: bright-red radishes cut into half-moons, handfuls of baby arugula, and lots of fresh mint. We tossed the salad with a little lemon juice and olive oil and plated it on top of a creamy yogurt-based dressing, which we tossed with the salad at the table as we served it. That way, the salad kept its vibrant, celebratory appearance. If you can't find fresh English peas, you can substitute ¾ cup of thawed frozen peas (there is no need to blanch them). The English peas and sugar snap peas can be blanched, shocked, patted dry, and refrigerated for up to 24 hours before serving.

1   Mince garlic and immediately combine with 2 tablespoons lemon juice in medium bowl; set aside. Fill large bowl halfway with ice and water. Nestle colander into ice bath. Line large plate with double layer of paper towels.

2   Bring 1 quart water to boil in medium saucepan over high heat. Add snap peas and 1 tablespoon salt and cook until snap peas are bright green and crisp-tender, about 1 minute. Using spider skimmer or slotted spoon, transfer snap peas to colander set in ice bath. Add English peas to boiling water and cook until bright green and tender, about 1½ minutes. Transfer to colander with snap peas. Once peas are chilled, lift colander from ice bath and transfer peas to prepared plate.

3   Whisk yogurt, mustard, pepper, and ½ teaspoon salt into garlic mixture until combined. Whisking constantly, slowly drizzle in ¼ cup oil until emulsified. Spread dressing evenly over bottom of large shallow bowl or serving platter.

4   In separate large bowl, toss arugula, snow peas, radishes, mint, and chilled peas with remaining 1 teaspoon lemon juice, remaining pinch salt, and remaining 1 tablespoon oil until evenly coated. Pile salad on top of dressing. Serve immediately, combining salad with dressing as you serve.

SERVES 4 TO 6

- 1   garlic clove, peeled
- 2   tablespoons plus 1 teaspoon lemon juice, divided
- 4   ounces sugar snap peas, strings removed, cut on bias into ½-inch pieces
- ½   teaspoon plus pinch table salt, divided, plus salt for blanching peas
- 9   ounces shell-on English peas, shelled (about ¾ cup)
- ¼   cup plain Greek yogurt
- 2   teaspoons Dijon mustard
- ¼   teaspoon pepper
- 5   tablespoons extra-virgin olive oil, divided
- 2   ounces (2 cups) baby arugula
- 4   ounces snow peas, strings removed, sliced thin on bias
- 4   radishes, trimmed, halved, and sliced into thin half-moons
- ⅓   cup fresh mint or cilantro leaves, torn if large

bitter greens and chickpea salad with warm vinaigrette

why this recipe works In this lightly wilted salad with a warm vinaigrette, we showcase unusual greens such as curly frisée, ruffled escarole, and frilly chicory. Alone or in combination, these greens make a robust, textured canvas for bold, flavorful ingredients. But drizzling a hot vinaigrette over the greens wasn't enough to wilt them. Instead, we warmed up a Dutch oven by sautéing the colorful salad mix-ins (carrots, raisins, and almonds), let it cool slightly, and then added the greens and lemon vinaigrette off the heat. A few turns of the tongs and the greens had just the right slightly softened texture. Nutty chickpeas and salty feta dotted the salad with savory heft. The volume measurement of the greens may vary depending on the variety or combination used.

1 for the vinaigrette Whisk lemon zest and juice, mustard, shallot, cumin, coriander, paprika, cayenne, salt, and pepper together in medium bowl. Whisking constantly, slowly drizzle in oil until emulsified.

2 for the salad Toss chickpeas with 1 tablespoon vinaigrette and pinch salt in bowl; set aside. Heat oil in Dutch oven over medium heat until shimmering. Add carrots, raisins, and almonds and cook, stirring frequently, until carrots are wilted, 4 to 5 minutes. Let cool off heat for 5 minutes.

3 Add half of remaining vinaigrette to pot, then add half of greens and toss for 1 minute to warm and wilt. Add mint and remaining greens, followed by remaining vinaigrette, and continue to toss until greens are evenly coated and warmed through, about 2 minutes longer. Season with salt and pepper to taste. Transfer greens to serving platter, top with feta and chickpeas, and serve.

SERVES 4

vinaigrette

- 1 tablespoon grated lemon zest plus 6 tablespoons juice (2 lemons)
- 1 tablespoon Dijon mustard
- 1 tablespoon minced shallot
- ½ teaspoon ground cumin
- ½ teaspoon ground coriander
- ¼ teaspoon smoked paprika
- ¼ teaspoon cayenne pepper
- ¼ teaspoon table salt
- ¼ teaspoon pepper
- 2 tablespoons extra-virgin olive oil

salad

- 1 (15-ounce) can chickpeas or white beans, rinsed
  Pinch table salt
- 1 tablespoon extra-virgin olive oil
- 3 carrots, peeled and shredded
- ¾ cup raisins or dried cranberries, chopped
- ½ cup slivered almonds or chopped hazelnuts
- 12 ounces (10–12 cups) bitter greens, such as escarole, chicory, and/or frisée, torn into bite-size pieces
- ⅓ cup mint or cilantro, chopped
- 1½ ounces feta or goat cheese, crumbled (⅓ cup)

salad with herbed baked goat cheese and vinaigrette

SERVES 4 TO 6

herbed baked goat cheese
- 3 ounces white Melba toasts (2 cups)
- 1 teaspoon pepper
- 3 large eggs
- 2 tablespoons Dijon mustard
- 1 tablespoon minced fresh thyme or rosemary
- 1 tablespoon minced fresh chives or scallions
- 12 ounces firm goat cheese
- Extra-virgin olive oil

salad and vinaigrette
- 2 tablespoons red wine vinegar
- 1 tablespoon Dijon mustard
- 1 teaspoon minced shallot
- ¼ teaspoon table salt
- 6 tablespoons extra-virgin olive oil
- 14 ounces (14 cups) mixed hearty salad greens such as arugula and frisée

why this recipe works Warm goat cheese salads on restaurant menus often feature artisanal cheeses, organic baby field greens, barrel-aged vinegars, and imported oils. But the descriptions are often more intriguing than the execution. We wanted warm, creamy cheese rounds infused with flavor and surrounded by crisp, golden breading, all cradled in lightly dressed greens. The first challenge was cutting the soft cheese. A knife quickly becomes covered with cheese, making it difficult to achieve clean, neat slices. Instead, we slid an 18-inch-long piece of kitchen twine or unwaxed dental floss under the log of goat cheese. We crossed the ends of the twine above the cheese and then pulled the twine through the cheese to cut it, moving the twine and cutting again to make slices. Our other challenge was coating and heating the cheese. Melba toast crumbs gave our cheese an exceptionally crisp crust; freezing the breaded goat cheese rounds for 30 minutes before baking them ensured a crunchy coating and a smooth, but not melted, interior. Mixed hearty salad greens, such as arugula and frisée, work best here. The baked goat cheese should be served warm. Prepare the salad components while the cheese is in the freezer and toss the greens and vinaigrette while the cheese cools a bit after baking.

1 for the herbed baked goat cheese Process Melba toasts in a food processor to fine even crumbs, about 1½ minutes; transfer crumbs to medium bowl and stir in pepper. Whisk eggs and mustard in second medium bowl until combined. Combine thyme and chives in small bowl.

2 Using kitchen twine or unwaxed dental floss, divide cheese into 12 even pieces. Roll each piece into a ball; roll each ball in herbs to coat lightly. Transfer 6 balls to egg mixture; turn each ball to coat. Transfer balls to Melba crumbs and turn each ball to coat, pressing crumbs into cheese. Flatten each ball into disk about 1½ inches wide and 1 inch thick and set on baking sheet. Repeat process with remaining 6 pieces. Freeze cheese disks until firm, about 30 minutes. (Disks can be wrapped tightly in plastic wrap and frozen for 1 week.)

3   Adjust oven rack to top position; heat oven to 475 degrees. Remove cheese from freezer and brush tops and sides of disks evenly with oil. Bake until crumbs are golden brown and cheese is slightly soft, 7 to 9 minutes (or 9 to 12 minutes if cheese is completely frozen). Using thin metal spatula, transfer cheese to paper towel-lined plate and let cool 3 minutes.

4   **for the salad and vinaigrette** Whisk vinegar, mustard, shallot, and salt together in large bowl. Whisking constantly, slowly drizzle in oil until emulsified. Season with pepper to taste. Add greens, toss gently to coat, then divide salad among individual plates. Serve, topping individual portions with warm goat cheese.

roasted cipollini and escarole salad

SERVES 4 TO 6

1½ pounds cipollini onions

6 tablespoons extra-virgin olive oil, divided

½ teaspoon table salt, divided

⅛ teaspoon pepper

4 ounces thin-sliced prosciutto

2 tablespoons cider vinegar

2 teaspoons Dijon mustard

1½ teaspoons caraway seeds, toasted and cracked

1 teaspoon honey

1 head escarole (1 pound), trimmed and cut into 1-inch pieces

½ head frisée (3 ounces), trimmed and cut into 1-inch pieces

2 ounces blue cheese, crumbled (½ cup)

why this recipe works Cipollini onions are gentler and sweeter in flavor and aroma than regular yellow, white, or red onions, making them perfect for use in salads. And, like Vidalia onions, cipollini have more residual sugars, so when they are roasted, these additional sugars caramelize beautifully, creating a melt-in-your-mouth texture that contrasts beautifully with the crunch of crisp, slightly bitter escarole and frisée. Halving the cipollini and roasting them on the middle oven rack ensured that they cooked through until they were buttery and tender at the same rate that they browned and caramelized. Crispy prosciutto and creamy blue cheese added saltiness and made the salad a textured meal. A tangy cracked caraway seed dressing balanced all the flavors. You can use prepeeled cipollini onions in this recipe; simply halve them through the root end and proceed with step 2.

1 Adjust oven rack to middle position and heat oven to 400 degrees. Bring 2 quarts water to boil in large saucepan. Add onions and cook for 30 seconds. Drain in colander and run under cold water until onions are cool enough to handle, about 1 minute. Transfer onions to paper towel–lined plate and pat dry. Trim root and stem ends, then peel and discard onion skins. Halve onions through root end and transfer to bowl.

2 Add 3 tablespoons oil, ¼ teaspoon salt, and pepper to bowl with onions and toss to coat. Arrange onions, cut side down, on parchment paper–lined rimmed baking sheet and roast until well browned and softened, 35 to 40 minutes, rotating sheet halfway through roasting. Let cool slightly, about 10 minutes.

3 Line plate with double layer of paper towels. Lay prosciutto slices in single layer on prepared plate and microwave until fat is rendered and prosciutto is beginning to crisp, 2 to 4 minutes. Set aside and let sit until cool enough to handle, then crumble into ½-inch pieces.

4 Whisk vinegar, mustard, caraway seeds, honey, and remaining ¼ teaspoon salt together in large bowl. Whisking constantly, slowly drizzle in remaining 3 tablespoons oil until emulsified. Add escarole, frisée, onions, and prosciutto and gently toss to combine. Season with salt and pepper to taste. Transfer to serving platter and sprinkle with blue cheese. Serve.

chopped winter salad with butternut squash

why this recipe works Winter cooking evokes roasted vegetables. But since we like to mix things up, we used roasted butternut squash in a salad. We topped romaine and red-hued, bitter-spicy radicchio with tender squash, crunchy apple, and toasted hazelnuts. We deepened the squash's flavor by cutting it into pieces and tossing the pieces with balsamic vinegar and olive oil before roasting them. The caramelized vinegar perfectly complemented the squash's earthiness. Feta cheese provided a richer, creamier element. Theres no need to peel the apple for this dish. We prefer Fuji, but any sweet apple will work here.

1 Adjust oven rack to lowest position and heat oven to 450 degrees. Toss squash with 1 tablespoon oil, 1½ teaspoons balsamic vinegar, ¼ teaspoon salt, and ¼ teaspoon pepper.

2 Spread squash in single layer on aluminum foil-lined rimmed baking sheet and roast until well browned and tender, 20 to 25 minutes, stirring halfway through roasting. Remove sheet from oven and let squash cool for 5 to 10 minutes.

3 Whisk mustard, remaining 2½ tablespoons balsamic vinegar, remaining ⅛ teaspoon salt, and remaining ⅛ teaspoon pepper together in large bowl. Whisking constantly, slowly drizzle in remaining 3 tablespoons oil until emulsified.

4 Add radicchio, romaine, and apple to bowl with dressing and toss to combine. Divide salad among individual plates. Season with salt and pepper to taste. Serve, topping individual portions with squash, hazelnuts, and feta.

SERVES 4

2 pounds butternut squash, peeled, seeded, and cut into ½-inch pieces (4½ cups)

¼ cup extra-virgin olive oil, divided

3 tablespoons balsamic vinegar, divided

¼ teaspoon plus ⅛ teaspoon table salt, divided

¼ teaspoon plus ⅛ teaspoon pepper, divided

1 tablespoon Dijon mustard

1 head radicchio (6 ounces), trimmed, cored, and sliced ½ inch thick

1 romaine lettuce heart (6 ounces), cored and cut into 1-inch pieces

1 Fuji, Macintosh, or Red Delicious apple, unpeeled, halved, cored, and cut into ½-inch pieces

½ cup skinned hazelnuts, almonds, or pecans, toasted and chopped

2 ounces feta cheese or goat cheese (½ cup), crumbled

chopped winter salad with
butternut squash, *page 69*

creamy chicken salad with fresh herbs

why this recipe works Recipes for chicken salad are only as good as the chicken in them. If it is dry or flavorless, no amount of dressing or add-ins can disguise it. To ensure silky, juicy, and flavorful chicken for this easy salad, we used tender poached chicken breasts. We cubed the breasts, rather than shredding them, which gave us satisfying bites of chicken that would hold on to fresh herbs and a creamy dressing, perfect for a picnic or a summer supper. For the homemade dressing, we combined mayonnaise with bright, fragrant lemon juice. Finely chopped celery provided crunch, and fresh chives, tarragon, and dill made the salad ultrarefreshing. We like using Perfect Poached Chicken (page 43) here, but any cooked chicken would work.

Combine chicken, mayonnaise, celery, chives, tarragon, dill, lemon juice, salt, and pepper in large bowl. Cover with plastic and refrigerate for at least 2 hours to allow flavors to meld. (Salad can be refrigerated for up to 2 days.) Serve with mesclun, spooning chicken mixture into leaves at table.

variations

curried chicken salad with dried apricots
Omit chives, tarragon, and dill. Add ½ cup finely chopped dried apricots, 6 tablespoons toasted slivered almonds, 4 thinly sliced scallions, and 2 teaspoons curry powder to bowl with chicken and mayonnaise.

creamy chicken salad with grapes and walnuts
Omit tarragon and dill. Add 1 cup halved seedless grapes; 6 tablespoons walnuts or pecans, toasted and chopped; and 3 tablespoons chopped fresh parsley to bowl with chicken and mayonnaise. Substitute Dijon mustard for lemon juice.

SERVES 4

- 4 cups cooked chicken, cut into ½-inch pieces
- ⅔ cup mayonnaise
- ¼ cup finely chopped celery
- 3 tablespoons chopped fresh chives or scallions
- 4 teaspoons chopped fresh tarragon or mint
- 1 tablespoon chopped fresh dill
- 1 tablespoon lemon juice
- ½ teaspoon table salt
- ¼ teaspoon pepper
- 10 ounces (10 cups) mesclun greens or 1 head Boston or Bibb Lettuce (8 ounces), leaves separated

mizuna

This gorgeous green with mild, sweet
stems and peppery leaves tastes like a mix
between arugula and mustard greens.
Also called Japanese mustard and California
peppergrass, mizuna makes a great salad
ingredient, both visually and in flavor.
If leaves are long, cut them into 2-inch
lengths for use. The green grows easily
year round, even in colder climates. In
fact, in Japan, where it originated, mizuna
is frequently grown in the winter. The
feathery, serrated leaves are flavorful on
their own and with other greens and are
eaten raw, lightly cooked, or pickled.

crab and mizuna salad

why this recipe works We wanted to add peppery heat to the sweet meat of a crab salad. We decided to collect some Japanese ingredients—mizuna, shiso, pickled ginger, and wasabi—that would bring bite and texture. Mayonnaise gave us the expected tangy richness, but we punched up its flavor with minced pickled ginger, a bit of wasabi paste, and scallion greens. Shiso leaves, whose bold, almost indescribable flavor combines hints of mint, cilantro, basil, and tarragon, completed our crab component. For our leafy greens, mizuna, a Japanese mustard green, was perfect. We stirred more wasabi into a simple vinaigrette of olive oil, scallion whites, and rice vinegar, and for a little more crunch, we turned to our recipe for pickled daikon and carrot. Note that this recipe uses unseasoned rice vinegar; we don't recommend using seasoned rice vinegar in its place.

Press crab dry with paper towels, then toss gently with mayonnaise, scallion greens, shiso, 2 teaspoons vinegar, pickled ginger, and ½ teaspoon wasabi in bowl; season with salt to taste. Whisk oil, salt, scallion whites, remaining 4 teaspoons vinegar, and remaining 1½ teaspoons wasabi together large bowl. Add mizuna and Quick Pickled Daikon Radish and Carrot and toss gently to combine, then divide among individual plates. Serve, topping individual portions with crab mixture.

SERVES 4

12 ounces lump crabmeat, picked over for shells

½ cup mayonnaise

2 scallions, white parts minced, green parts sliced thin

2 tablespoons minced fresh shiso

2 tablespoons unseasoned rice vinegar, divided

4 teaspoons minced pickled ginger

2 teaspoons wasabi paste, divided

¼ cup extra-virgin olive oil

¼ teaspoon table salt

8 ounces (8 cups) mizuna or baby arugula

1 cup Quick Pickled Daikon Radish and Carrot (page 54)

tuna salad with hard-cooked eggs, radishes, and capers

SERVES 4

¼   cup finely chopped onion

½   cup extra-virgin olive oil, divided

3   (6-ounce) cans solid white tuna in water

2   Easy-Peel Hard-Cooked Eggs (page 42), sliced thin

1   celery rib, minced

2   radishes, trimmed, halved, and sliced thin

¼   cup capers, minced

2   teaspoons lemon juice

½   teaspoon sugar

½   teaspoon table salt

½   teaspoon pepper

10 ounces (10 cups) mesclun or 1 head Boston or Bibb Lettuce (8 ounces), leaves separated

why this recipe works Tuna salad, so familiar, simple, and beloved, can often be watery, chalky, and/or bland. To achieve a version that would be moist and flavorful, we first thoroughly drained canned tuna and dried it with paper towels. We then used the microwave to quickly cook some onion in oil and added the onion mixture to the tuna along with some mayonnaise for texture and lemon juice for tang. The addition of hard-cooked eggs, radishes, and capers transformed this everyday tuna salad into a rich, peppery, briny avatar. Serve on mesclun or toast, or even make a sandwich. Be sure to use tuna packed in water for the most control over the flavor of your salad.

1   Combine onion and 2 tablespoons oil in small bowl and microwave until onion begins to soften, about 2 minutes. Let onion mixture cool for 5 minutes. Place tuna in fine-mesh strainer and press dry with paper towels. Transfer tuna to medium bowl and mash with fork until finely flaked.

2   Stir eggs, celery, radishes, capers, lemon juice, sugar, salt, pepper, onion mixture, and remaining 6 tablespoons oil into tuna until well combined. Season with salt and pepper to taste. (Salad can be refrigerated for up to 24 hours.) Serve with mesclun, spooning tuna mixture into leaves at table.

variations

tuna salad with apple, walnuts, and tarragon

Omit eggs, radishes, and capers. Add
1 apple, cored and cut into ½-inch pieces;
½ cup walnuts, toasted and chopped
coarse; and 1 tablespoon minced fresh
tarragon to salad.

curried tuna salad with grapes

Omit eggs, radishes, and capers. Add
1 teaspoon curry powder to bowl with
onion and oil before microwaving. Add
1 cup green grapes, halved, to salad.

chicken and arugula salad with figs and warm spices

why this recipe works We transformed this simple chicken salad with beautiful, deep-purple figs, added chickpeas for even more protein, and dressed it with a vinaigrette seasoned with cinnamon, citrusy ground coriander, and smoked paprika. We microwaved the spices to bloom their flavor and aroma, and then we whisked in lemon juice and honey. A bed of peppery baby arugula complemented our dressing and poached chicken for a salad full of warm, bright flavors. We just needed a bit of crunch to play against the soft figs, and we got that from toasted and chopped almonds. You can substitute dried figs for the fresh in this recipe. We like using Perfect Poached Chicken (page 43) here, but any cooked chicken would work.

1   Microwave 1 tablespoon oil, coriander, paprika, and cinnamon in large bowl until fragrant, about 30 seconds. Whisk lemon juice, honey, salt, and pepper into spice mixture. Whisking constantly, slowly drizzle in remaining 5 tablespoons oil until emulsified.

2   Add chicken, chickpeas, arugula, parsley, and shallot to dressing in bowl and gently toss to combine. Transfer salad to serving platter, arrange figs over top, and sprinkle with almonds. Serve.

SERVES 6

6   tablespoons extra-virgin olive oil, divided

1   teaspoon ground coriander

½   teaspoon smoked paprika

¼   teaspoon ground cinnamon

3   tablespoons lemon juice

1   teaspoon honey

½   teaspoon table salt

¼   teaspoon pepper

4   cups cooked chicken, shredded

1   (15-ounce) can chickpeas or white beans, rinsed

5   ounces (5 cups) baby arugula

½   cup fresh parsley or mint leaves

1   shallot, sliced thin

8   fresh figs, stemmed and quartered

½   cup whole almonds, pecans, or walnuts, toasted and chopped

chicken salad with thai basil and mango

SERVES 4

3 tablespoons lime juice (2 limes)

1 shallot, minced

2 tablespoons fish sauce, plus extra for serving

1 tablespoon palm sugar or packed brown sugar

1 garlic clove, minced

¼ teaspoon red pepper flakes

4 cups cooked chicken, shredded

1 mango, peeled, pitted, and cut into ¼-inch pieces

1½ cups chopped mint, cilantro, and Thai basil or basil

1 head Boston or Bibb lettuce (8 ounces), leaves separated

2 Thai chiles, sliced thin

why this recipe works This salad was inspired by the flavors of Thailand, which are reflected in our use of mango, fish sauce, garlic, Thai basil, and cilantro, and Thai chiles to provide heat. We found that shredding the chicken created more surface area that allowed for greater penetration of the pungent dressing. We like using Perfect Poached Chicken (page 43) here, but any cooked chicken would work. We like to serve this salad in leaves of Bibb lettuce to form lettuce cups, but it can also be served on a bed of greens. To serve over greens, toss 6 to 8 cups of greens with 2 teaspoons of lime juice, 1 teaspoon of toasted sesame oil, 1 teaspoon of vegetable oil, and a pinch of salt before spooning the chicken on top.

Whisk lime juice, shallot, fish sauce, sugar, garlic, and pepper flakes together in large bowl. Transfer chicken to bowl with dressing and toss to coat. Add mango, mint, cilantro, and basil to bowl with chicken and toss to coat. Season with salt to taste. Serve with lettuce, spooning chicken mixture into leaves at table, passing Thai chiles and extra fish sauce separately.

bibb lettuce and chicken salad with peanut dressing

SERVES 4

peanut dressing

¼ cup seasoned rice vinegar

3 tablespoons creamy peanut butter

1½ tablespoons fish sauce

¼ cup vegetable oil

salad

2 heads Boston or Bibb lettuce (1 pound), leaves separated and torn into pieces

1 English cucumber, cut into 2-inch-long matchsticks

¼ cup thinly sliced jarred hot cherry peppers

4 cups cooked chicken, sliced thin

¼ cup fresh mint or cilantro leaves, torn

why this recipe works For this salad, our inspiration was flavorings often seen in Thai cooking, from fish sauce and cilantro to rice vinegar and hot peppers. We tossed these with Bibb lettuce, cucumber, and chicken in a peanut dressing to create a flavorful salad. We like using Perfect Poached Chicken (page 43) here, but any cooked chicken would work. Note that this recipe uses seasoned rice vinegar; we don't recommend using unseasoned rice vinegar in its place.

1 **for the peanut dressing** Combine vinegar, peanut butter, and fish sauce in bowl. Microwave until peanut butter has just softened, about 15 seconds. Add oil and whisk until smooth and fully combined.

2 **for the salad** Toss lettuce, cucumber, cherry peppers, and 3 tablespoons vinaigrette together in large bowl. Divide salad among 4 individual plates. Serve, topping individual portions with chicken. Drizzle with remaining vinaigrette and sprinkle with mint.

steak salad with carrot-ginger vinaigrette

why this recipe works We decided to change things up and combine salad, steak, and vegetables in one satisfying dish. Seared steak, carrots, cucumbers, radish, and crisp greens are tossed in a bright, gingery dressing. Sesame oil enhanced the ginger and added hearty aroma and richness to the steak. But the real star was the carrots, which also made an appearance in the dressing, adding color and earthiness. We used a blender to make the vinaigrette quickly, gradually adding oil to help emulsify the dressing. We used our homemade Seasoned Rice Vinegar (page 41) here, but any store-bought variety will work. Note that this recipe uses seasoned rice vinegar; we don't recommend using unseasoned rice vinegar in its place.

1 **for the carrot-ginger vinaigrette** Process carrots, vinegar, water, ginger, sesame oil, and salt in blender until finely ground, about 30 seconds. With blender running, slowly add vegetable oil and process until incorporated and smooth, about 30 seconds; set aside vinaigrette. (The vinaigrette can be refrigerated for up to 1 week; whisk to recombine before using.)

2 **for the salad** Pat steak dry with paper towels and sprinkle with salt and pepper. Heat 1 tablespoon oil in 12-inch nonstick skillet over medium-high heat until just smoking. Add half of steak and cook until well browned and meat registers 125 degrees (for medium-rare), about 2 minutes per side. Transfer to carving board. Repeat with remaining 1 tablespoon vegetable oil and remaining steak. Let rest for 5 minutes.

3 Toss lettuce, cucumber, radishes, carrots, and ½ cup vinaigrette together in bowl. Divide salad among 4 individual plates. Slice steak thin against grain. Top individual portions with steak. Serve, passing remaining vinaigrette separately.

SERVES 4

carrot-ginger vinaigrette

- 2 carrots, peeled and chopped
- ¼ cup seasoned rice vinegar
- 2 tablespoons water
- 1 (1½-inch) piece ginger, peeled and chopped coarse
- 1 teaspoon toasted sesame oil
- ½ teaspoon table salt
- ¼ cup vegetable oil

salad

- 1½ pounds skirt steak, trimmed and cut with grain into approximate 4-inch lengths (about 8 pieces)
- ½ teaspoon table salt
- ¼ teaspoon pepper
- 2 tablespoons vegetable oil, divided
- 3 romaine lettuce hearts (18 ounces), quartered and sliced thin
- ½ English cucumber, halved lengthwise and sliced thin
- 4 radishes, trimmed and sliced thin
- 2 carrots, peeled and cut into 2-inch matchsticks

steak salad with pear and quick pickled fennel

SERVES 4

1 pound sirloin steak tips, trimmed and cut into 3-inch pieces

½ teaspoon table salt

½ teaspoon pepper

2 teaspoons extra-virgin olive oil

10 ounces (10 cups) baby arugula

¼ cup Apple Cider–Sage Vinaigrette (page 31)

1 ripe but firm pear or apple, cored and sliced thin

½ cup chopped Quick Pickled Fennel (page 54)

2 ounces Parmesan or Pecorino Romano cheese, shaved

why this recipe works For this luxurious, unusual salad, we paired juicy steak with pear and fennel and tossed the elements in an aromatic dressing. For our meat, we opted for steak tips, which are inexpensive but full of rich marbling. Thinly sliced fresh pear gave our salad subtle sweetness; quickly pickled fennel (steeped for a mere 30 minutes) brought acidity and a mild anise flavor. The pickled fennel keeps in the refrigerator so you'll have it on hand to use again. We reduced apple cider to concentrate its flavor for a sweet-savory vinaigrette flavored with sage. And a quick shaving of Parmesan brought the perfect saltiness to a mouthwatering dinner. Sirloin steak tips, also known as flap meat, can be sold as whole steaks, cubes, and strips. To ensure uniform pieces, we prefer to purchase whole steaks and cut them ourselves. For optimal tenderness, make sure to slice the cooked steak against the grain (perpendicular to the fibers). To avoid off-flavors, reduce the cider in a nonreactive stainless-steel saucepan. Microwave-fried shallots (page 48) make a great garnish.

1 Pat steak dry with paper towels and sprinkle with salt and pepper. Heat oil in 12-inch nonstick skillet over medium-high heat until just smoking. Add steak and cook until well browned all over and meat registers 125 degrees (for medium-rare), 8 to 10 minutes. Transfer to cutting board, tent with aluminum foil, and let rest for 5 minutes. Slice steak against grain ¼ inch thick.

2 Toss arugula with half of vinaigrette to coat, then season with salt and pepper to taste. Divide among individual plates. Serve, topping individual portions with steak, pear, fennel, and Parmesan. Drizzle with remaining vinaigrette.

arugula salad with steak tips and blue cheese

SERVES 4

1 pound sirloin steak tips, trimmed

¾ teaspoon table salt, divided

½ teaspoon pepper, divided

6 tablespoons extra-virgin olive oil, divided

1 shallot, minced

2 tablespoons cider vinegar

2 garlic cloves, minced

1 teaspoon Dijon mustard

1 teaspoon honey

12 ounces (12 cups) baby arugula

6 ounces blue cheese, crumbled (1½ cups)

why this recipe works For the allure of a steakhouse at home, make this quick salad of juicy steak, peppery arugula, and blue cheese. You'll get both a salad course and a steak course together. There's the freshness of greens with blue cheese, the hearty satisfaction of medium-rare steak, and Dijon mustard in the vinaigrette to amp up the arugula's spiciness. Sirloin steak tips, also known as flap meat, can be sold as whole steaks, cubes, and strips. To ensure uniform pieces, we prefer to purchase whole steaks and cut them ourselves after cooking. For optimal tenderness, make sure to slice the cooked steak against the grain (perpendicular to the fibers).

1 Pat steak dry with paper towels and sprinkle with ½ teaspoon salt and ¼ teaspoon pepper. Heat 2 tablespoons oil in 12-inch non-stick skillet over medium-high heat until just smoking. Add steak and cook until well browned all over and meat registers 125 degrees (for medium-rare), 8 to 10 minutes. Transfer to plate, tent with aluminum foil, and let rest for 5 minutes.

2 Whisk shallot, vinegar, garlic, mustard, honey, remaining ¼ teaspoon salt, and remaining ¼ teaspoon pepper together in large bowl. Whisking constantly, slowly drizzle in remaining ¼ cup oil until emulsified. Add arugula and blue cheese to vinaigrette and toss to combine. Season with salt and pepper to taste. Slice steak against grain ¼ inch thick. Divide salad among individual plates. Serve, topping individual portions with steak.

southwest beef salad with cornbread croutons

why this recipe works The beefy flavor of flank steak is the perfect choice for the Southwestern profile of this salad. For a bold yet easy-to-make dressing, we combined cilantro, jalapeño, garlic, and lime juice. Red bell pepper added sweetness and crunch to the mix, while mild Bibb lettuce allowed the strong flavors of the dressing to shine through. Corn is a familiar ingredient in Southwestern cooking, so we used convenient store-bought cornbread, cut into cubes and toasted to make croutons, to incorporate this flavor deliciously. To keep this recipe streamlined, we toasted the cornbread pieces while we cooked our steak and prepared the rest of the salad.

1   Adjust oven rack to middle position and heat oven to 375 degrees. Coat rimmed baking sheet with oil spray and spread cornbread pieces in even layer on sheet. Coat pieces with oil spray and bake until crisp and golden brown, 15 to 18 minutes, rotating sheet and stirring pieces halfway through baking.

2   Meanwhile, pat steak dry with paper towels and sprinkle with ½ teaspoon salt and pepper. Heat 1 tablespoon oil in 12-inch skillet over medium-high heat until just smoking. Cook steak until meat registers 125 degrees (for medium-rare), 3 to 5 minutes per side. Transfer to cutting board, tent with foil, and let rest for 5 minutes.

3   Process cilantro, lime juice, jalapeño, garlic, and remaining 1 teaspoon salt in food processor until finely chopped, about 10 seconds. With processor running, slowly drizzle in remaining 6 tablespoons oil until incorporated, about 15 seconds. Transfer ⅓ cup dressing to large bowl, toss with lettuce and bell pepper, and season with salt and pepper to taste. Slice steak thin against grain. Transfer lettuce mixture to serving platter or individual plates, top with steak and croutons, and drizzle with remaining dressing. Serve.

SERVES 4

Vegetable oil spray

10   ounces store-bought cornbread, cut into ¾-inch pieces

1   pound flank steak, trimmed

1½   teaspoons table salt, divided

¼   teaspoon pepper

7   tablespoons vegetable oil, divided

½   cup chopped fresh cilantro or parsley

¼   cup lime juice (2 limes)

1   jalapeño or serrano chile, stemmed, seeded, and chopped

1   garlic clove, minced

2   heads Boston or Bibb lettuce (1 pound), leaves separated and torn into bite-size pieces

1   red, orange, or yellow bell pepper, stemmed, seeded, and sliced thin

southwest beef salad with
cornbread croutons, *page 89*

chef's salad with fennel, asiago, and salami, *page 92*

chef's salad with fennel, asiago, and salami

SERVES 6 TO 8

6 tablespoons extra-virgin olive oil

3 tablespoons balsamic vinegar

1 garlic clove, minced

¼ teaspoon table salt

⅛ teaspoon pepper

2 heads romaine lettuce (1½ pounds), torn into bite-size pieces

4 ounces (4 cups) watercress, torn into 2-inch pieces

1 small fennel bulb, stalks discarded, halved, cored, and sliced thin

½ cup chopped fresh parsley or basil

1 cup jarred roasted red peppers, rinsed, patted dry, and cut crosswise into ½-inch-wide strips

1 (14-ounce) jar artichoke hearts, drained and halved

8 ounces hard salami, cut into 2-inch-long matchsticks

8 ounces deli turkey, cut into 2-inch-long matchsticks

8 ounces Asiago cheese, crumbled (2 cups)

1½ cups Garlic Croutons (page 44)

½ cup pitted kalamata olives, chopped

why this recipe works An American classic, the chef's salad is a composed dish of ham, turkey, chicken or roast beef, hard boiled eggs, and sliced yellow cheddar served on a bed of iceberg lettuce. For our version, we wanted distinctive flavor, so we chose sturdy but mild greens, such as Bibb, romaine, and red and green leaf lettuces, which held their shape under the weight of the other ingredients and stood up to the strong flavors of the meat and cheese. We also included a small amount of spicy greens, such as watercress or arugula, to add bite, and fennel for freshness. Thick slices of turkey, salami, and soft crumbled asiago complemented the greens, and an acidic vinaigrette worked with the rich components of the salad. While we prefer the flavor and texture of jarred whole baby artichoke hearts in this recipe, you can substitute 9 ounces of frozen artichoke hearts, thawed and patted dry, for the jarred. If you can't find water-packed artichoke hearts, use marinated artichoke hearts, but rinse and drain them before use. For this salad, opt for a mild, soft Asiago cheese that crumbles easily; avoid aged Asiago that has a hard, dry texture.

1 Whisk oil, vinegar, garlic, salt, and pepper together in medium bowl until combined.

2 Toss romaine, watercress, fennel, and parsley in large serving bowl. Add all but 1 tablespoon dressing and toss to combine. Season with salt and pepper to taste. Toss peppers and artichokes in remaining dressing, then arrange around perimeter of greens. Arrange salami, turkey, and cheese over center of greens; top with croutons and olives. Serve immediately.

romaine and watercress salad with asparagus and prosciutto

why this recipe works When you think of shaving, does asparagus come to mind? After you make this salad, it might. For this recipe, we shaved asparagus thinly so that we could use it raw. We then paired the crunchy shaved asparagus with spicy watercress and earthy romaine for a many-textured salad that would pleases anyone. Salty prosciutto and toasted pine nuts added richness. We picked sherry vinegar as the base of our vinaigrette; it best complemented the peppery watercress and salty pork. Use a vegetable peeler to shave the asparagus.

1   Whisk vinegar, shallot, mayonnaise, mustard, and salt in medium bowl and season with pepper to taste. Whisk until mixture is milky in appearance and no lumps of mayonnaise remain. Whisking constantly, slowly drizzle oil into vinegar mixture until emulsified and lightly thickened.

2   Place lettuce, watercress, asparagus, prosciutto, and half of pine nuts in large bowl. Toss to combine. Drizzle with dressing and toss until greens are evenly coated. Season with salt to taste. Sprinkle with remaining pine nuts. Serve immediately.

SERVES 4

1   tablespoon sherry vinegar

1½   teaspoons very finely minced shallot

½   teaspoon mayonnaise

¼   teaspoon Dijon mustard

⅛   teaspoon table salt

3   tablespoons extra-virgin olive oil

1   small head romaine lettuce, torn into bite-size pieces (7 cups)

3   ounces (3 cups) watercress, torn into bite-size pieces

8   ounces asparagus, trimmed and shaved lengthwise

1½   ounces thinly sliced prosciutto, cut into ½-inch pieces

3   tablespoons pine nuts, toasted, divided

larb

SERVES 4

- 1 (1-pound) pork tenderloin, trimmed and cut into 1-inch pieces
- 2½ tablespoons fish sauce, divided
- 1 tablespoon white rice
- ¼ cup chicken broth
- 2 shallots, sliced thin
- 3 tablespoons lime juice (2 limes)
- 6 tablespoons coarsely chopped fresh herbs, such as mint, cilantro, and Thai basil or basil
- 2 teaspoons sugar
- ¼ teaspoon red pepper flakes
- 1 head Boston or Bibb lettuce (8 ounces), leaves separated

why this recipe works Larb is a Thai and Laotian meat-based salad, often made with pork (though chicken, duck, beef, and fish are also used). Served slightly warm or at room temperature, this dish is made with finely chopped cooked meat tossed with fresh herbs and a light dressing that balances the signature sweet, sour, spicy, and salty flavors of Thailand and its neighbor, Laos. We like to eat it in lettuce cups. We prefer natural pork in this recipe. If the pork is enhanced (injected with a salt solution), do not marinate it in step 1, and reduce the amount of fish sauce to 2 tablespoons, adding it all in step 4. Don't skip the toasted rice; it's integral to the texture and flavor of the dish and is sometimes used in Thai cooking as a thickening agent (as it is here). Any style of white rice can be used. Prepared kao kua (toasted rice powder) can be found in Asian markets; you can substitute 1 tablespoon of the store-bought rice powder for homemade toasted white rice powder.

1 Place pork on large plate in single layer. Freeze until firm and starting to harden around edges but still pliable, 15 to 20 minutes. Pulse half of pork in food processor until coarsely chopped, 5 to 6 pulses. Transfer to medium bowl and repeat with remaining pork. Stir 1 tablespoon fish sauce into pork, cover with plastic wrap, and refrigerate for 15 minutes.

2 Toast rice in 8-inch skillet over medium-high heat, stirring constantly, until deep golden brown, about 5 minutes. Transfer to small bowl and let cool for 5 minutes. Grind rice using spice grinder, mini food processor, or mortar and pestle until it resembles fine meal (you should have about 1 tablespoon rice powder).

3 Bring broth to rapid simmer in 12-inch nonstick skillet over medium-high heat. Add pork mixture and cook, stirring frequently, until about half of pork is no longer pink, about 2 minutes. Sprinkle 1 teaspoon rice powder over pork mixture and continue to cook, stirring constantly, until remaining pork is no longer pink, 1 to 1½ minutes longer. Transfer pork mixture to large bowl and let cool for 10 minutes.

4 Add shallots, lime juice, herbs, sugar, pepper flakes, remaining 1½ tablespoons fish sauce, and remaining rice powder to pork mixture and toss to combine. Serve with lettuce, spooning pork mixture into leaves at table.

salade lyonnaise

SERVES 4

1 (½-inch-thick) slice pancetta (about 5 ounces)

2 tablespoons extra-virgin olive oil

1 tablespoon minced shallot

2 tablespoons red wine vinegar

4 teaspoons Dijon mustard

1 head frisée (6 ounces), torn into bite-size pieces

5 ounces chicory or escarole, torn into bite-size pieces (5 cups)

1 recipe Perfect Poached Eggs (recipe follows)

why this recipe works The iconic salade Lyonnaise originated in Lyons, France, and is a perfect mix of frisée, salty bacon, rich poached egg, and punchy vinaigrette. We added chicory or escarole to give this classic French salad more volume, structure, and flavor to stand up to its richer elements—bacon and egg. We called for pancetta in our recipe rather than American bacon, since it is unsmoked, salt cured, and rolled just like the traditionally used ventreche, also known as French pancetta. Making a bold, warm vinaigrette in the skillet not only infused the salad with richer bacon flavor but also allowed us to gently tenderize the frisée. Poached eggs delivered runny yolks and tender whites that easily melded into the salad, which was critical to its success. Order a ½-inch-thick slice of pancetta at the deli counter; presliced or diced pancetta is likely to dry out or become tough. If you can't find chicory or escarole, dandelion greens make a good substitute. If using escarole, strip away the first four or five outer leaves and reserve them for another use. Serve this salad with crusty bread as a light lunch or dinner.

1   Cut pancetta crosswise into thirds, then cut each third crosswise into ¼-inch-wide pieces. Combine pancetta and 2 cups water in 10-inch nonstick or carbon-steel skillet and bring to boil over medium-high heat. Boil for 5 minutes, then drain. Return pancetta to now-empty skillet. Add oil and cook over medium-low heat, stirring occasionally, until lightly browned but still chewy, 4 to 6 minutes.

2   Pour off all but 2 tablespoons fat from skillet, leaving pancetta in skillet. Add shallot and cook, stirring frequently, until slightly softened, about 30 seconds. Off heat, add vinegar and mustard and stir to combine.

3   Drizzle vinaigrette over frisée in large bowl and toss thoroughly to coat. Add chicory and toss again. Season with salt and pepper to taste. Divide salad among individual plates. Season with salt and pepper to taste. Serve immediately, topping individual portions with 1 egg.

perfect poached eggs

makes 4 eggs

Use the freshest eggs possible for this recipe.

> 4 large eggs
> 1 tablespoon distilled white vinegar for poaching
> 1 teaspoon table salt for poaching

1   Bring 6 cups water to boil in Dutch oven over high heat. Meanwhile, crack eggs, one at a time, into colander. Let stand until loose, watery whites drain away from eggs, 20 to 30 seconds. Gently transfer eggs to 2-cup liquid measuring cup.

2   Add vinegar and salt to boiling water. Remove pot from heat. With lip of measuring cup just above surface of water, gently tip eggs into water, one at a time, leaving space between them. Cover pot and let sit until whites closest to yolks are just set and opaque, about 3 minutes. If after 3 minutes whites are not set, let sit in water, checking every 30 seconds, until whites are set.

3   Using slotted spoon, carefully lift and drain each egg over Dutch oven. Season with salt and pepper to taste, and serve.

salmon, avocado, and watercress salad

SERVES 4

1 (2-pound) skin-on center-cut salmon fillet, 1 inch thick

1 teaspoon plus 3 tablespoons extra-virgin olive oil, divided

1 teaspoon table salt, divided

¼ teaspoon pepper

2 red grapefruits

1 tablespoon minced shallot

1 teaspoon white wine vinegar

1 teaspoon Dijon mustard

4 ounces (4 cups) watercress, torn into bite-size pieces

1 ripe avocado, halved, pitted, and sliced ¼ inch thick

¼ cup fresh mint or cilantro leaves, torn

¼ cup blanched hazelnuts or almonds, toasted and chopped

why this recipe works A composed salad should present an appealing mix of contrasting flavors, textures, and colors. The best examples are sometimes the simplest, like this beautiful pink-and-green salad. Watercress has a slight, pleasant bitterness; a peppery flavor punch; and a sturdy enough texture to act as the perfect bed for our rich toppings. We roasted the salmon only until it was just translucent before flaking it into large chunks. Thick slices of buttery avocado added creaminess and more richness. For a bright, light contrast, we cut up two sweet-tart red grapefruits; the segments mimicked the shape of the avocado. We reserved some grapefruit juice to whisk up a simple vinaigrette. Finally, we added a sprinkle of crunchy toasted hazelnuts and torn mint leaves over the top of this pretty dish. To ensure uniform pieces of fish that cooked at the same rate, we found it best to buy a whole center-cut fillet and cut it into four pieces ourselves.

1   Adjust oven rack to lowest position, place aluminum foil–lined rimmed baking sheet on rack, and heat oven to 500 degrees.

2   Cut salmon crosswise into 4 fillets. Pat salmon dry with paper towels, rub with 1 teaspoon oil, and sprinkle with ½ teaspoon salt and pepper. Reduce oven temperature to 275 degrees. Carefully place salmon skin side down on prepared sheet. Roast until center is still translucent when checked with tip of paring knife and registers 125 degrees (for medium-rare), 6 to 8 minutes. Let salmon cool completely, about 20 minutes. Using 2 forks, flake salmon into 2-inch pieces.

3   Cut away peel and pith from grapefruits. Holding fruit over bowl, use paring knife to slice between membranes to release segments. Measure out 2 tablespoons grapefruit juice and transfer to medium bowl.

4   Whisk shallot, vinegar, mustard, and remaining ½ teaspoon salt into grapefruit juice in bowl. Whisking constantly, slowly drizzle in remaining 3 tablespoons oil until emulsified. Arrange watercress in even layer on serving platter. Arrange salmon pieces, grapefruit segments, and avocado on top of watercress. Drizzle dressing over top, then sprinkle with mint and hazelnuts. Serve.

watercress

No green conjures up romantic notions of English teatimes and finger sandwiches quite like watercress (*Nasturtium officinale*). Also known as cress, watercress (not related to garden ornamental nasturtiums) is a semiaquatic perennial plant. It hails from Eurasia and grows along riverbanks and lakes, in hydroponic gardens, and in moist soil. Watercress is beloved for its tender shoots and delicate, peppery leaves that add oomph to both sandwiches and salads. In case you are wondering, upland cress is not the same as watercress. But it is a relative, one that makes its home in dry soil. Also known as early yellow rocket and land cress, upland cress retains its crispness for some time after being dressed, so it can make a great alternative to watercress, which bruises and wilts easily.

lemony salmon and roasted beet salad

why this recipe works The sweet, earthy flavor of roasted beets is especially nice when paired, as it is here, with rich salmon and a bright lemon-caper dressing. But roasting beets in the oven takes an hour or so, and canned beets are hardly a worthy substitute. So for this recipe, we found a faster way to cook beets: We peeled and cut them into cubes before cooking them in the microwave, which reduced their cooking time to just 4 minutes. Poaching the salmon fillets in barely simmering water ensured that the fish emerged moist and perfectly cooked. We took the time to dress each ingredient of this composed salad separately to make sure that it was properly seasoned. To ensure uniform pieces of fish that cooked at the same rate, we found it best to buy a whole center-cut fillot and cut it into three pieces ourselves.

1   Cut salmon crosswise into 3 fillets. Pat salmon dry with paper towels and sprinkle with ½ teaspoon salt and ¼ teaspoon pepper. Bring 4 cups water to boil in 12 inch skillet. Add ¼ cup lemon juice, reduce heat to medium-low, and gently slip salmon into water. Cover and simmer until center is still translucent when checked with tip of paring knife and salmon registers 125 degrees (for medium-rare), 4 to 6 minutes. Transfer salmon to plate. Using 2 forks, flake salmon into 1-inch pieces and transfer to medium bowl.

2   Place beets in second medium bowl and sprinkle with remaining ⅛ teaspoon salt and remaining pinch pepper. Microwave, covered, until tender, about 4 minutes.

3   Meanwhile, whisk oil, shallot, capers, 1 tablespoon dill, and lemon zest and remaining 3 tablespoons juice together in large bowl; set aside dressing.

4   Add 2 tablespoons dressing to bowl with beets, toss to combine, and let cool slightly. Add 2 tablespoons dressing to bowl with salmon and gently toss to combine. Add arugula to bowl with remaining dressing and toss to coat; season with salt and pepper to taste. Arrange arugula on serving platter or individual plates and top with eggs, salmon, beets, and remaining 2 tablespoons dill. Serve.

SERVES 4

- 1 (1¼-pound) skin-on center-cut salmon fillet, 1 inch thick
- ½ teaspoon plus ⅛ teaspoon table salt, divided
- ¼ teaspoon plus pinch pepper, divided
- 1 teaspoon grated lemon zest plus 7 tablespoons juice (3 lemons), divided
- ½ pound beets, trimmed, peeled, and cut into ½-inch pieces
- ⅓ cup extra-virgin olive oil
- 1 shallot, minced
- 2 tablespoons capers, rinsed
- 3 tablespoons minced fresh dill or parsley, divided
- 6 ounces (6 cups) baby arugula
- 2 Easy-Peel Hard-Cooked Eggs (page 42), grated

seared tuna poke salad

why this recipe works We were inspired by poke, a Hawaiian dish of superfresh, raw tuna, to make a salad featuring the fish. We seared the tuna to give it a crisp, browned exterior and deeper flavor and added delicate baby greens enlivened with finely chopped sweet onion. We also paired the tuna with the floral sweetness of fresh mango and the creaminess of ripe avocado and tossed the salad with a dressing of soy sauce, honey, and ginger. Most cooked proteins need time to rest before they are sliced, but cutting the tuna immediately prevented carryover cooking and maintained our preferred rare to medium-rare doneness. For tuna steaks cooked to medium, increase the cooking time in step 1 to about 4 minutes per side. Note that this recipe uses unseasoned rice vinegar; we don't recommend using seasoned rice vinegar in its place.

1   Pat tuna dry with paper towels; sprinkle with salt and pepper. Heat 2 teaspoons oil in 12-inch nonstick skillet over medium-high heat until just smoking. Add tuna and cook until opaque at perimeter and translucent red at center when checked with tip of paring knife and registering 110 degrees (for rare), 1 to 2 minutes per side. Transfer to cutting board and immediately cut into 1-inch pieces; set aside until ready to serve.

2   Whisk vinegar, soy sauce, ginger, and honey together in bowl. Whisking constantly, slowly drizzle in remaining ¼ cup oil until emulsified. Toss mesclun and onion with half of vinaigrette to coat, then season with salt and pepper to taste. Divide among individual plates. Serve, topping individual portions with tuna, mango, and avocado. Drizzle with remaining vinaigrette. Serve.

SERVES 4

- 4 (4- to 6-ounce) tuna steaks, 1 inch thick
- ½ teaspoon table salt
- ½ teaspoon pepper
- 2 teaspoons plus ¼ cup extra-virgin olive oil, divided
- 2 tablespoons unseasoned rice vinegar
- 2 tablespoons soy sauce
- 4 teaspoons grated fresh ginger
- 2 teaspoons honey
- 10 ounces (10 cups) mesclun
- 1 onion, chopped fine
- 1 mango, peeled and sliced thin
- 1 ripe avocado, sliced thin

summer dinner salad with scallops

SERVES 4

1½ tablespoons red wine vinegar

2½ teaspoons minced shallot

1 teaspoon Dijon mustard

½ teaspoon mayonnaise

¾ teaspoon table salt, divided

½ teaspoon pepper, divided

7 tablespoons extra-virgin olive oil, divided

10 ounces (10 cups) mesclun

4 carrots, peeled and sliced ⅛ inch thick

12 ounces snap peas or snow peas, strings removed, halved crosswise

1½ pounds large sea scallops, tendons removed

why this recipe works Sea scallops are one of our favorite types of seafood to cook and eat. They cook in minutes and add substance to a simple dish, turning salad into dinner. We like a simple pairing of sweet tender scallops with red wine vinegar and Dijon mustard. We showcase them on colorful mesclun with snap peas for crunch. We recommend buying "dry" scallops, which don't have chemical additives and taste better than "wet." Dry scallops will look ivory or pinkish; wet scallops are bright white.

1 Combine vinegar, shallot, mustard, mayonnaise, ¼ teaspoon salt, and ¼ teaspoon pepper in bowl. Whisking constantly, slowly drizzle in 5 tablespoons oil until emulsified. Toss mesclun, carrots, and snap peas with dressing. Divide salad among individual plates.

2 Place scallops on clean dish towel, then top with second clean dish towel and press gently to dry. Let scallops sit between towels at room temperature for 10 minutes. Line large plate with double layer of paper towels. Sprinkle scallops with remaining ½ teaspoon salt and remaining ¼ teaspoon pepper. Heat 1 tablespoon oil in 12-inch nonstick skillet over medium-high heat until just smoking. Add half of scallops flat side down in single layer and cook, without moving them, until well browned, 1½ to 2 minutes. Using tongs, flip scallops and continue to cook until sides of scallops are firm and centers are opaque, 30 to 90 seconds longer. Transfer scallops to prepared plate. Wipe out skillet with paper towels and repeat with remaining 1 tablespoon oil and remaining scallops. Serve, topping individual portions with scallops.

shrimp salad with avocado and grapefruit

SERVES 4

2 red grapefruits

1 large avocado, halved, pitted, and cut into ½-inch pieces

2 tablespoons lime juice

1½ teaspoons grated fresh ginger

½ teaspoon honey

¼ teaspoon table salt

¼ teaspoon pepper

2 ounces snow or snap peas, strings removed, cut lengthwise into ⅛-inch strips

1 tablespoon chopped fresh mint

2 cups Sautéed Shrimp (page 43)

2 heads Boston or Bibb lettuce (1 pound), torn into bite-size pieces

why this recipe works We set out to develop a satisfying yet healthy salad featuring tender shrimp and a complementary mix of fresh fruit and vegetables, without the usual mayo-based dressing. A combination of tart grapefruit; rich, buttery avocado; and a dressing made with grapefruit juice, more avocado, ginger, honey, and Dijon mustard offered our shrimp salad a balance of sweet, tart, and tangy flavors as well as a touch of welcome creaminess. If you can find ruby red grapefruit, its color and tangy sweetness work well in this dish. If you can't get enough juice from your grapefruit to equal ¼ cup, add water to make up the difference. If your grapefruit is especially tart, you can add ½ teaspoon more honey to the dressing.

1 Cut away peel and pith from grapefruit. Holding fruit over bowl, use paring knife to slice between membranes to release segments. Set aside ¼ cup grapefruit juice. Process reserved grapefruit juice, one-quarter of avocado, lime juice, ginger, honey, salt, and pepper in blender until smooth, about 30 seconds, scraping down sides of bowl as needed.

2 Toss snow peas, mint, grapefruit segments, dressing, and remaining avocado in large bowl with shrimp and toss to combine. Divide lettuce evenly among individual plates. Serve, topping individual portions with shrimp. Drizzle each salad with any remaining dressing left in bowl.

wilted spinach and shrimp salad with bacon-pecan vinaigrette

why this recipe works A warm bacon vinaigrette is a classic complement to a wilted spinach salad, but achieving perfection was a careful balancing act. We wanted the spinach leaves (here, tender baby spinach) to be just gently softened by the warm vinaigrette. Too much or too-hot dressing, and the spinach ended up overly wilted and lifeless. Too little or too-cool dressing, and the spinach stayed chewy, raw, and less pleasant to eat. We found that the trick for ensuring a properly wilted salad was to have everything at the ready—tongs and all—before we began and then to toss the spinach and crisp endive and serve the salad the moment the vinaigrette was at the right temperature. We used juicy shrimp and a particularly sweet, fragrant, and crisp apple variety to emphasize and offset the bacon-pecan dressing's smoky, salty, nutty richness.

1 Place endive in large bowl along with spinach. Whisk vinegar, mustard, sugar, and salt together in separate bowl. Measure out 2 tablespoons vinegar mixture and set aside in medium bowl. Add shallot to remaining vinegar mixture; cover; and microwave until steaming, 30 to 60 seconds. Stir briefly to submerge shallot; uncover and set aside to cool.

2 Transfer shrimp to bowl with reserved 2 tablespoons vinegar mixture and cover to keep warm.

3 Cook bacon and pecans in now-empty skillet over medium heat, stirring frequently, until bacon is crispy and fat is well rendered, 8 to 10 minutes.

4 Off heat, whisk shallot mixture into skillet until combined. Pour warm vinaigrette over spinach and endive and toss until spinach is wilted slightly. Add apple and gently toss to combine. Divide salad among individual serving plates. Season with salt and pepper to taste. Serve immediately, topping individual portions with shrimp.

SERVES 4

- 2 heads Belgian endive (8 ounces), halved, cored, and cut into ½-inch strips
- 10 ounces (10 cups) baby spinach
- 6 tablespoons red wine vinegar
- 2 tablespoons whole-grain mustard
- 1½ teaspoons sugar
- ¼ teaspoon table salt
- 1 shallot, thinly sliced
- 2 cups Sautéed Shrimp (page 43)
- 1 tablespoon extra-virgin olive oil
- 6 slices bacon, cut into ½-inch pieces
- ½ cup pecans or walnuts, chopped coarse
- 1 Fuji or Honeycrisp apple, halved, cored, and sliced thin

wilted spinach and shrimp salad with
bacon-pecan vinaigrette, *page 107*

grilled caesar salad

SERVES 6

dressing

- 1 tablespoon lemon juice
- 1 garlic clove, minced
- ½ cup mayonnaise
- ¼ cup grated Parmesan or Pecorino Romano cheese
- 1 tablespoon white wine vinegar
- 1 tablespoon Worcestershire sauce
- 1 tablespoon Dijon mustard
- 2 anchovy fillets, rinsed
- ½ teaspoon table salt
- ½ teaspoon pepper
- ¼ cup extra-virgin olive oil

salad

- 1 (12-inch) baguette, sliced on bias ½ inch thick
- 3 tablespoons extra-virgin olive oil
- 1 garlic clove, peeled
- 3 romaine lettuce hearts (18 ounces), halved lengthwise through cores
- ¼ cup grated Parmesan or Pecorino Romano cheese

why this recipe works With apologies to Shakespeare: It's not that we love Caesar less, but that we love grilled Caesar more. The smoky char of the grill brings a whole new dimension to classic Caesar salad. To develop good char and maintain crisp lettuce without any scorched, wilted, or even slimy leaves, we used sturdy, compact romaine hearts, which withstood the heat of the grill better than whole heads. Halving them lengthwise and grilling them on just one side gave them plenty of surface area for charring without turning limp. A hot fire meant that the heat didn't have time to penetrate and wilt the crunchy inner leaves before the exterior developed grill marks. Our boldly seasoned Caesar dressing replaced the traditional raw egg with mayonnaise. It was so good that we got the idea to brush it on the cut side of the uncooked lettuce instead of olive oil, allowing the dressing to pick up a mildly smoky flavor on the grill along with the lettuce. For the croutons, we brushed baguette slices with olive oil, toasted them over the coals, and then rubbed them with a garlic clove. Then we combined the lettuce and croutons, drizzled on extra dressing, and dusted everything with Parmesan. Your grilled Caesar will be gone in minutes.

1 for the dressing Combine lemon juice and garlic in bowl and let stand sit for 10 minutes. Process lemon-garlic mixture, mayonnaise, Parmesan, vinegar, Worcestershire, mustard, anchovies, salt, and pepper in blender until smooth, about 30 seconds. With blender running, slowly add oil until incorporated. Measure out and reserve 6 tablespoons dressing for brushing romaine.

2A for a charcoal grill Open bottom vent completely. Light large chimney starter filled with charcoal briquettes (6 quarts). When top coals are partially covered with ash, pour evenly over half of grill. Set cooking grate in place, cover, and open lid vent completely. Heat grill until hot, about 5 minutes.

2B for a gas grill Turn all burners to high; cover; and heat grill until hot, about 15 minutes. Leave all burners on high.

3 for the salad Clean and oil cooking grate. Brush bread with oil and grill (over coals if using charcoal), uncovered, until browned, about 1 minute per side. Transfer to serving platter and rub with garlic clove. Brush cut sides of half of lettuce with half of reserved dressing; place cut side down on grill (over coals if using charcoal). Grill, uncovered, until lightly charred, 1 to 2 minutes. Transfer to serving platter with bread. Repeat with remaining reserved dressing and remaining lettuce. Drizzle lettuce with remaining dressing. Sprinkle with Parmesan. Serve.

grilled chicken cobb salad

SERVES 4

- 2 ounces blue cheese, crumbled (½ cup)
- ¼ cup plus 2 tablespoons extra-virgin olive oil, divided
- 3 tablespoons red wine vinegar
- 1 teaspoon table salt, divided
- 1 teaspoon pepper, divided
- 3 romaine lettuce hearts (6 ounces each), halved lengthwise
- 2 avocados, halved and pitted
- 4 (6- to 8-ounce) boneless, skinless chicken breasts, trimmed
- 8 ounces cherry or grape tomatoes, halved
- 4 Easy-Peel Hard-Cooked Eggs (page 42), halved
- 1 recipe Crispy Bacon, crumbled (recipe follows)

why this recipe works It's nothing new to grill chicken for Cobb salad. But grilling the avocados and romaine too? How very Californian. Actually, grilling amps up the flavor of the avocado and the greens and gives this dinner salad a summertime twist. We like to use Crispy Bacon (recipe follows) here, but any cooked bacon would work. Serve this salad with a sprinkling of chopped fresh chives.

1 Combine blue cheese, ¼ cup oil, vinegar, ¼ teaspoon salt, and ¼ teaspoon pepper in bowl; set aside. Brush remaining 2 table-spoons oil onto cut sides of lettuce and avocados and sprinkle with ¼ teaspoon salt and ½ teaspoon pepper. Pat chicken dry with paper towels and sprinkle with remaining ½ teaspoon salt and remaining ¼ teaspoon pepper.

2A **for a charcoal grill** Open bottom vent completely. Light large chimney starter filled with charcoal briquettes (6 quarts). When top coals are partially covered with ash, pour evenly over half of grill. Set cooking grate in place, cover, and open lid vent completely. Heat grill until hot, about 5 minutes.

2B **for a gas grill** Turn all burners to high; cover; and heat grill until hot, about 15 minutes. Leave all burners on high.

3 Clean and oil cooking grate. Grill chicken until browned and chicken registers 160 degrees, about 5 minutes per side. Transfer to plate and tent with foil. Grill lettuce and avocados, cut sides down, until charred in spots, about 2 minutes. Using spoon, scoop avocado flesh from skin.

4 Cut lettuce in half lengthwise. Slice chicken ½ inch thick. Arrange lettuce, avocados, chicken, tomatoes, and eggs on serving platter and season with salt and pepper to taste. Top salad with bacon and drizzle with dressing. Serve.

crispy bacon

makes ½ cup

The addition of water keeps the initial cooking temperature low and gentle, so the bacon retains its moisture and turns out crispy and tender instead of dry and crumbly. You can use thin- or thick-cut bacon here, though the cooking times will vary.

6 slices bacon, halved crosswise

Place bacon in 12-inch skillet and add just enough water to cover (about ½ cup). Bring to simmer over medium-high heat and cook until water has evaporated, about 8 minutes. Lower heat to medium-low and cook bacon until crispy and well browned, 5 to 8 minutes. Transfer bacon to paper towel-lined plate to drain, and serve.

grilled radicchio salad with corn, cherry tomatoes, and pecorino romano

SERVES 4

½ cup extra-virgin olive oil

1 tablespoon ground coriander

3 garlic cloves, minced

1 teaspoon ground cumin

½ teaspoon chili powder

½ teaspoon table salt

½ teaspoon pepper

1½ tablespoons honey

1 head (10 ounces) radicchio, quartered through core

3 ears corn, husks and silk removed

2 limes, halved

8 ounces cherry tomatoes, halved

1 romaine lettuce heart (6 ounces), torn into bite-size pieces

1½ ounces Pecorino Romano cheese, shaved, divided

½ cup chopped fresh basil, divided

why this recipe works Grilled vegetables in a salad? Yes, please. They add smoky-sweet char and a hint of bitterness that contrasts nicely with the crisp greens. For this vibrant grilled salad, we used purple radicchio and yellow corn. When grilled, radicchio's leaves become lightly crisp and smoky, and the heat from the grill enhances corn's natural sweetness. For more flavor, before grilling we brushed both vegetables with some of our aromatic dressing base, which included coriander, cumin, and garlic. For optimal browning we flipped the radicchio so that both cut sides could be in direct contact with the heat. We also grilled lime halves to lighten their acidity and add brightness to our dressing. Cherry tomatoes gave an extra pop of bright sweetness, and the richness of shaved Pecorino Romano rounded out the salad. To keep the radicchio from falling apart on the grill, we left the core intact when cutting it into quarters. For extra crunch, top with Spiced Pepitas or Sunflower Seeds (page 50) or Crispy Chickpeas (page 47).

1 Microwave oil, coriander, garlic, cumin, chili powder, salt, and pepper in large bowl, stirring occasionally, until fragrant, about 1 minute. Set aside ¼ cup oil mixture for brushing radicchio and corn. Whisk honey into remaining oil mixture in bowl; set aside.

2 Place radicchio, corn, and lime halves on rimmed baking sheet. Whisk reserved ¼ cup oil mixture to recombine, then brush all over radicchio and corn on sheet.

3A for a charcoal grill Open bottom vent completely. Light large chimney starter filled with charcoal briquettes (6 quarts). When top coals are partially covered with ash, pour evenly over grill. Set cooking grate in place, cover, and open lid vent completely. Heat grill until hot, about 5 minutes.

3B for a gas grill Turn all burners to high; cover; and heat grill until hot, about 15 minutes. Leave all burners on high.

4   Clean and oil cooking grate. Place corn on grill and cook (covered if using gas), turning as needed, until lightly charred, 10 to 13 minutes. Return corn to sheet. Place radicchio and limes on grill and cook (covered if using gas), flipping radicchio as needed, until edges of radicchio are browned and wilted but centers are still slightly firm and lime halves are lightly charred, about 5 minutes. Return radicchio and limes to sheet with corn.

5   Once limes are cool enough to handle, squeeze limes to yield ¼ cup juice, then whisk into reserved honey-oil mixture in bowl until emulsified. Cut kernels from cobs and add to bowl with vinaigrette along with tomatoes, romaine, half of Pecorino, and half of basil. Toss gently to combine, then season with salt and pepper to taste. Transfer radicchio to serving platter and top with corn mixture, remaining Pecorino, and remaining basil. Serve.

arugula salad with fennel and shaved parmesan

SERVES 4 TO 6

- 6 ounces (6 cups) baby arugula
- 1 large fennel bulb, stalks discarded, bulb halved, cored, and sliced thin
- 1½ tablespoons lemon juice
- 1 small shallot, minced
- 1 teaspoon Dijon mustard
- 1 teaspoon minced fresh thyme or rosemary
- 1 small garlic clove, minced
- ⅛ teaspoon table salt
- Pinch pepper
- ¼ cup extra-virgin olive oil
- 1 ounce Parmesan or Pecorino Romano cheese, shaved

why this recipe works Arugula is a cruciferous green with a lively, peppery bite, so it's important to choose accompaniments that can stand up to its assertive character. In this salad, we used the sweet anise flavor of fresh fennel to temper the peppery sharpness of arugula, making for a delicate and flavorful summer salad that is quick and easy. Shaved Parmesan adds a pleasant salty note.

Gently toss arugula and fennel together in large bowl. Whisk lemon juice, shallot, mustard, thyme, garlic, salt, and pepper together in small bowl. Whisking constantly, slowly drizzle in oil until emulsified. Drizzle dressing over salad and gently toss to coat. Season with salt and pepper to taste. Serve, topping individual portions with Parmesan.

arugula salad with grapes, fennel, blue cheese, and pecans

why this recipe works In this salad, we found that the sweet and salty notes of fruits and cheeses worked well as supporting players to arugula for a simple, flavorful dish. Red grapes and bold blue cheese complemented the baby greens, thinly sliced fennel gave the salad more substance, and chopped pecans added crunch. As for the dressing, we started with oil, vinegar, and shallot, adding a spoonful of apricot jam for some fruity sweetness.

1 Whisk jam in large bowl until smooth. Add vinegar, shallot, salt, and pepper and whisk until combined. Whisking constantly, slowly drizzle in oil until emulsified. Stir in sliced fennel and let sit for 15 minutes.

2 Add arugula, grapes, and fennel fronds and toss gently to coat. Season with salt and pepper to taste and divide salad among individual plates. Serve, topping individual portions with blue cheese and pecans.

SERVES 6

4 teaspoons apricot jam

3 tablespoons white wine vinegar

1 small shallot, minced

¼ teaspoon table salt

¼ teaspoon pepper

3 tablespoons extra-virgin olive oil

½ small fennel bulb, fronds minced, stalks discarded, bulb halved, cored, and sliced thin

5 ounces (5 cups) baby arugula

6 ounces seedless grapes, halved lengthwise (1 cup)

3 ounces blue cheese, crumbled (¾ cup)

½ cup pecans or walnuts, toasted and chopped

arugula salad with grapes,
fennel, blue cheese,
and pecans, *page 117*

bibb and frisée salad with
apple and celery, *page 120*

bibb and frisée salad with apple and celery

SERVES 4 TO 6

1 tablespoon red wine vinegar

1½ teaspoons very finely minced shallot

½ teaspoon mayonnaise

½ teaspoon Dijon mustard

⅛ teaspoon table salt

3 tablespoons extra-virgin olive oil

1 head Bibb or Boston lettuce (8 ounces), torn into bite-size pieces

1 small head frisée, torn into bite-size pieces (4 cups)

1 Gala or Honeycrisp apple, cored, halved, and sliced thin

1 celery rib, sliced thin

⅓ cup walnuts, pecans, or almonds, toasted and chopped coarse, divided

why this recipe works An ideal salad should offer a mix of textures, flavors, and colors, and this salad exemplifies that notion. We found that frilly, crunchy frisée offered a welcome contrast to Bibb lettuce's soft, buttery texture. Thinly slicing the celery and apple allowed us to combine them cohesively with the salad greens. Walnuts added crunch and nuttiness. We chose red wine vinegar as a base for our vinaigrette here since the acid complemented (but didn't overpower) the apple's sweetness and the celery's subtle earthiness. Mayonnaise added creaminess to the dressing and helped emulsify it without imparting any mayonnaise flavor. Use a mandoline to thinly slice the celery and apple.

1 Combine vinegar, shallot, mayonnaise, mustard, and salt in medium bowl and season with pepper to taste. Whisk until mixture is milky in appearance and no lumps of mayonnaise remain. Whisking constantly, slowly in drizzle oil until emulsified and lightly thickened.

2 Place lettuce, frisée, apple, celery, and half of walnuts in large bowl. Toss to combine. Drizzle with dressing and toss until greens are evenly coated. Season with salt to taste. Sprinkle with remaining walnuts. Serve immediately.

green salad with artichokes and olives

why this recipe works There are as many ways to turn a green salad into something special as there are ingredients to add to it. Here we used baby artichoke hearts to give heft to the romaine and arugula, while kalamata or green olives added tangy bite. Fresh parsley and shaved Asiago finish the dish with salty, herby substance. While we prefer the flavor and texture of jarred whole baby artichoke hearts in this recipe, you can substitute 6 ounces frozen artichoke hearts, thawed and patted dry, for the jarred.

Gently toss romaine, arugula, artichoke hearts, parsley, and olives together in large bowl. Whisk oil, vinegar, garlic, salt, and pepper together in small bowl. Drizzle vinaigrette over salad and toss gently to combine. Season with salt and pepper to taste. Serve, topping individual portions with Asiago.

SERVES 4 TO 6

- 1 romaine lettuce heart (6 ounces), cut into 1-inch pieces
- 3 ounces (3 cups) baby arugula
- 1 cup jarred whole baby artichoke hearts packed in water, quartered, rinsed, and patted dry
- ⅓ cup fresh parsley leaves
- ⅓ cup pitted olives, halved
- 3 tablespoons extra-virgin olive oil
- 2 tablespoons white wine vinegar or white balsamic vinegar
- 1 small garlic clove, minced
- ¼ teaspoon table salt

    Pinch pepper

- 1 ounce Asiago or Parmesan cheese, shaved

green salad with marcona almonds and manchego cheese

SERVES 4 TO 6

6 ounces (6 cups) mesclun

5 teaspoons sherry vinegar

1 shallot, minced

1 teaspoon Dijon mustard

¼ teaspoon table salt

¼ teaspoon pepper

¼ cup extra-virgin olive oil

⅓ cup Marcona almonds, chopped coarse

2 ounces Manchego cheese, shaved

why this recipe works Can you take a green salad from ordinary to extraordinary quickly and simply? With two Spanish specialties—salty Manchego cheese and sweet Marcona almonds—the answer is yes. The sweetness of Marconas and the briny Manchego are enhanced by greens dressed with sherry vinegar. If you use unsalted Marconas, adjust the seasoning. We prefer the flavor of sherry vinegar here; however, red wine vinegar can be substituted. If you can't find Marcona almonds, substitute regular blanched almonds, toasted.

Place mesclun in large bowl. Whisk vinegar, shallot, mustard, salt, and pepper together in small bowl. Whisking constantly, slowly drizzle in oil until emulsified. Drizzle vinaigrette over mesclun and toss gently to coat. Season with salt and pepper to taste. Serve, topping individual portions with almonds and Manchego.

marcona almonds

Spain, the second-largest producer of almonds in the world after the United States, is home to the Marcona variety of almonds. Marcona almonds are shorter and rounder than conventional ones, with a texture that sets them apart. Softer and more tender to the bite than California almonds, the Spanish variety also have a satisfying, slightly oily quality due to their higher fat content. Marconas are sold roasted and salted or blanched, and they work well as a savory snack; on a cheese plate; with fruits like figs; and as delicate toppers for a variety of salad greens, from arugula to radicchio.

mâche

Mâche (French for lamb's lettuce, also called lamb's tongue, corn lettuce, and field lettuce), like purslane, was long considered a weed. It grew in French wheat, corn, and rye fields and was weeded and discarded until farmers realized it was edible, delicious, and versatile. The soft, tender green, which has leaves that grow in a pretty rosette pattern, is now beloved in French kitchens for its sweet, nutty flavor. Mâche is too tender to withstand heat and cooking, but it makes the perfect salad ingredient. It pairs well with a range of toppings, from eggs, bacon, and anchovies to new potatoes, asparagus, and avocado. We use the delicate green on its own in salads or pair it with sharper greens such as arugula and watercress for contrast. Delicious with green garlic, fennel fronds, and spring onions, mâche also offers a subtle canvas for the fragrance of herbs such as mint and parsley.

mâche salad with cucumber and mint

why this recipe works This pretty lettuce makes an elegant summer salad with its rosette-like leaves and nutty taste. We paired the mâche with the crisp, fresh flavor of thinly sliced cucumber and added brightness with chopped mint. Crunchy pine nuts reinforced the mâche's buttery notes. A simple dressing of lemon juice, fresh parsley, fresh thyme, and minced garlic was all that was needed, but we added capers for some briny contrast. Mâche is a very delicate green, so be sure to handle it gently and make sure that it is thoroughly dry before tossing it with the vinaigrette. If you can't find mâche, you can substitute either baby spinach or mesclun.

Gently toss mâche, cucumber, mint, and pine nuts together in large bowl. Whisk oil, lemon juice, parsley, capers, thyme, garlic, salt, and pepper together in small bowl. Drizzle dressing over salad and toss gently to coat. Season with salt and pepper to taste. Serve.

SERVES 6 TO 8

- 12 ounces (12 cups) mâche
- 1 cucumber, sliced thin
- ½ cup chopped fresh mint or parsley
- ⅓ cup pine nuts, toasted
- ¼ cup extra-virgin olive oil
- 1 tablespoon lemon juice
- 1 tablespoon minced fresh parsley or cilantro
- 1 tablespoon capers, rinsed and minced
- 1 teaspoon minced fresh thyme or rosemary
- 1 garlic clove, minced
- ¼ teaspoon table salt
- ¼ teaspoon pepper

spinach salad with egg and red onion

why this recipe works In this salad of spinach, eggs, and bread, the dressing serves three purposes. To make it, we whisked olive oil, salt, red wine vinegar, mustard, minced thyme, and garlic until the dressing was emulsified. We then used a little dressing to sauté the onion, taking the bite out of the raw slices. We tossed the croutons in some dressing to add flavor before we baked them. And we also tossed the salad with the remaining dressing. Grating the eggs, rather than slicing or quartering them, created a pretty visual effect. This salad makes a great meal or a hearty side. The dressing, croutons, and hard-cooked eggs can be prepared one day before you plan to serve the salad.

1 **for the vinaigrette** Whisk vinegar, mustard, garlic, thyme, salt, and pepper together in small bowl. Whisking constantly, slowly drizzle in oil until creamy and emulsified. (Dressing can be refrigerated for up to 1 day; whisk to recombine before using.)

2 **for the salad** Adjust oven rack to middle position and heat oven to 400 degrees. Toss bread pieces with 2 tablespoons dressing in medium bowl until thoroughly coated. Spread cubes in even layer on rimmed baking sheet and bake until golden, 10 to 15 minutes, stirring halfway through. Set aside. (Croutons can be stored in an airtight container for up to 1 day.)

3 Heat 2 tablespoons dressing in 12-inch nonstick skillet over medium heat. Add onion, sugar, and salt and cook, covered, until softened and lightly browned, 5 to 7 minutes. Separately grate egg whites and yolks using small holes of box grater. Toss spinach, croutons, onion, and remaining dressing together in large bowl. Divide among individual plates. Serve, topping individual portions with grated eggs.

SERVES 4 TO 6

vinaigrette

- 3 tablespoons red wine vinegar
- 2 tablespoons Dijon mustard
- 2 garlic cloves, minced
- ½ teaspoon minced fresh thyme or rosemary
- ¼ teaspoon table salt
- ¼ teaspoon pepper
- ¼ cup extra-virgin olive oil

salad

- 3 slices hearty white bread, cut into ½-inch pieces
- 1 red onion, halved and sliced thin
- 1 teaspoon sugar
- ½ teaspoon table salt
- 4 Easy-Peel Hard-Cooked Eggs (page 42), peeled, yolks and whites separated
- 10 ounces (10 cups) baby spinach

spinach salad with raspberry vinaigrette

SERVES 4 TO 6

8 ounces (8 cups) baby spinach

⅓ cup Raspberry Vinaigrette (page 30)

1 cup fresh raspberries

¾ cup shredded Gouda cheese

½ cup thinly sliced radishes

⅓ cup pistachios, toasted

why this recipe works A salad can be a canvas for playing with colors. Fresh raspberries gleam red on bright-green, crisp spinach (used fresh rather than wilted). This makes for a pretty plate, but the simple summer salad is also easy and fresh. Seedless raspberry jam in the dressing echoed the flavors of the fresh fruit and enhanced the caramel sweet notes of the Gouda and spicy red-edged radishes.

Toss spinach and dressing in large bowl. Add raspberries, Gouda, radishes, and pistachios and toss to combine. Season with salt and pepper to taste. Serve.

wilted spinach salad with strawberries, goat cheese, and almonds

why this recipe works Of course, a wilted spinach salad tastes great with a warm bacon dressing, but we wondered if there was a fresher, lighter way to make and dress this typically rich salad, losing the bacon but keeping the dressing warm. We replaced traditional bacon and bacon fat with extra-virgin olive oil. Tender flat-leaf and baby spinach became soft and mushy when tossed with the warm dressing, but heartier curly-leaf spinach stood up to the heat just fine and became deliciously tender. We added freshness by swapping out the sharp vinegar of many wilted spinach salad recipes for fresh grapefruit juice. A strip of zest infused the hot oil for the warm dressing with even more citrus flavor. And soft crumbled cheese, instead of bacon, gave richness to our salad. We briefly froze the cheese to prevent it from melting in the dressing's heat. Preparing the dressing in a Dutch oven and allowing the spinach to cook off the heat, covered with the dressing, for just 30 seconds produced a perfect, evenly wilted spinach salad. Almonds and strawberries added freshness and crunch. We recommend slightly sweet Ruby Red grapefruit for this salad.

1 Place goat cheese on plate and freeze until slightly firm, about 15 minutes.

2 Heat oil, grapefruit zest, shallot, and sugar in Dutch oven over medium-low heat until shallot is softened, about 5 minutes. Off heat, discard zest, stir in grapefruit juice, and add spinach; cover, allowing spinach to steam until just beginning to wilt, about 30 seconds.

3 Transfer spinach mixture to large bowl. Add strawberries, almonds, and goat cheese and toss to combine. Season with salt and pepper to taste. Serve.

SERVES 4 TO 6

1½ ounces goat cheese or feta, crumbled (⅓ cup)

¼ cup extra-virgin olive oil

1 (3-inch) strip grapefruit zest plus 1½ tablespoons juice

1 shallot, minced

2 teaspoons sugar

10 ounces curly-leaf spinach, stemmed and torn into bite-size pieces

6 strawberries, hulled and sliced ¼ inch thick

¼ cup sliced almonds or chopped hazelnuts, toasted

wilted spinach salad with
strawberries, goat cheese,
and almonds, *page 129*

radicchio, endive, and arugula salad

SERVES 4 TO 6

1 small head radicchio (6 ounces), cored and cut into 1-inch pieces

1 head Belgian endive (4 ounces), cut into 2-inch pieces

3 ounces (3 cups) baby arugula

3 tablespoons extra-virgin olive oil

1 tablespoon plus 1 teaspoon balsamic vinegar

1 teaspoon red wine vinegar

⅛ teaspoon table salt

Pinch pepper

why this recipe works This simple salad refreshes the eyes with its red, white, and green hues. It also offers the bitter and spicy tastes of different greens contrasted with the slight sweetness of balsamic in the vinaigrette. Not only is this an easy salad to assemble, but it also tingles the palate with the clean flavor of its punchy dressing. By definition, a vinaigrette contains oil, vinegar, and salt and pepper. This is an ultravinaigrette, balancing the sweet complexity of balsamic vinegar with the tartness of red wine vinegar. To keep the greens fresh, toss them with the bold dressing just before serving.

Gently toss radicchio, endive, and arugula together in large bowl. Whisk oil, balsamic vinegar, red wine vinegar, salt, and pepper together in small bowl. Drizzle vinaigrette over salad and gently toss to coat. Season with salt and pepper to taste. Serve.

pan-roasted pear salad with watercress, parmesan, and pecans

SERVES 6

1½ pounds pears, quartered lengthwise and cored

¼ teaspoon table salt

⅛ teaspoon pepper

2 tablespoons extra-virgin olive oil, divided

3 tablespoons plus 1 teaspoon balsamic vinegar, divided

1 small shallot, minced

½ teaspoon sugar

½ small head green leaf lettuce (4 ounces), torn into 1-inch pieces

4 ounces (4 cups) watercress

1 cup shaved Parmesan or Pecorino Romano cheese

3 tablespoons chopped pecans, walnuts, or almonds, toasted

why this recipe works We aren't limited to eating our favorite fruits fresh or in desserts. They can add sweetness, texture, and heft to salads too. For this aromatic, inviting dish, we gently caramelized pears and paired them with peppery watercress. We wanted a simple technique for caramelizing that wouldn't overcook the fruit. We tossed the quartered pears with sugar to encourage better browning and cooked them briefly on the stove. Since we were already using balsamic vinegar in the vinaigrette (its fruity flavor accentuates pear flavor), we tried also adding a couple tablespoons of balsamic vinegar to the hot pan while cooking the pears. The vinegar formed a glaze on the pears and perfectly matched the flavor of the salad dressing. To maximize caramelization, arrange the pear quarters so that one of the cut sides is flush with the hot skillet. Once the first side is lightly browned, simply use a fork or small spatula to tip each pear quarter onto its uncooked cut side. We prefer Bartlett pears here, but Bosc pears can also be used. The pears should be ripe but firm. Check the flesh at the neck of the pear—it should give slightly when pressed with your finger. Romaine lettuce can be substituted for the green leaf.

1 Toss pears with salt and pepper. Heat 2 teaspoons oil in 12-inch skillet over medium-high heat until just smoking. Add pears in single layer, cut side down, and cook until golden brown, 6 to 8 minutes, flipping them halfway through cooking.

2 Turn off heat, leaving skillet on burner, and add 2 tablespoons balsamic vinegar to skillet. Gently stir until vinegar becomes glazy and coats pears, about 30 seconds. Transfer pears to large plate and let cool completely, about 45 minutes. Cut each pear quarter crosswise into ½-inch pieces.

3 Whisk shallot, sugar, remaining 4 teaspoons oil, and remaining 4 teaspoons balsamic vinegar in large bowl until well combined. Add lettuce, watercress, and cooled pears and toss to combine. Season with salt and pepper to taste, sprinkle with Parmesan and pecans, and serve.

variations

pan-roasted pear salad with frisée, goat cheese, and almonds

Substitute 1 head frisée, torn into 1-inch pieces, for watercress; crumbled goat cheese or feta for Parmesan; and ¾ cup toasted sliced almonds for pecans.

pan-roasted pear salad with radicchio, blue cheese, and walnuts

Substitute 1 large head radicchio, quartered, cored, and cut crosswise into ½-inch pieces, for watercress; crumbled blue cheese for Parmesan; and ¾ cup toasted and chopped walnuts for pecans.

fruit & vegetable salads

apple and fennel salad with bitter greens and warm pancetta dressing

SERVES 4

vinaigrette

- ¼ cup red wine vinegar
- 1 tablespoon Dijon mustard
- 1 tablespoon minced shallot
- 1 teaspoon minced fresh thyme
- ¼ teaspoon table salt
- ¼ teaspoon pepper
- 2 tablespoons extra-virgin olive oil

salad

- 3 ounces pancetta, cut into ¼-inch pieces
- 1 small fennel bulb (8 ounces), stalks discarded, bulb halved, cored, and sliced thin
- 1 cup walnuts, chopped coarse
- 12 ounces (10-12 cups) bitter greens, such as escarole, chicory, and/or frisée, torn into bite-size pieces, divided
- 1 Fuji apple, cored, halved, and sliced thin
- 2 ounces blue cheese, crumbled (½ cup)

why this recipe works In this salad, the contrast between the sweetness of apples, the anise flavor of fennel, and the sharpness of bitter greens is highlighted by an unctuous warm pancetta dressing. Using a preheated Dutch oven provided just the right amount of heat to wilt hearty bitter greens without actually cooking them. We started by sautéing fennel in the pot and then pulled the pot off the heat to let it cool slightly. When we added the greens, the warm fennel softened them slightly and helped the entire salad retain heat longer. Finally, carefully choosing mix-ins that delivered a wide range of flavors and textures—apple, walnuts, and blue cheese—made this salad truly satisfying. The volume measurement of the greens may vary depending on the variety or combination used.

1 for the vinaigrette Whisk vinegar, mustard, shallot, thyme, salt, and pepper together in bowl. Whisking constantly, slowly drizzle in oil until emulsified.

2 for the salad Cook pancetta in large Dutch oven over medium heat until browned and fat is rendered, 7 to 8 minutes. Using slotted spoon, transfer pancetta to paper towel-lined plate. Pour off all but 1 tablespoon fat from pot. Add fennel and walnuts to fat left in pot and cook over medium heat, stirring occasionally, until fennel is crisp-tender, 5 to 7 minutes. Remove pot from heat and let cool for 5 minutes.

3 Add half of vinaigrette to pot, then add half of greens and toss for 1 minute to warm and wilt. Add remaining greens followed by remaining vinaigrette and continue to toss until greens are evenly coated and warmed through, about 2 minutes. Season with salt and pepper to taste. Transfer greens to serving platter, top with apple, sprinkle with blue cheese and pancetta, and serve.

apple-fennel rémoulade

SERVES 6 TO 8

¼ cup mayonnaise

2 tablespoons whole-grain mustard

2 tablespoons lemon juice

2 tablespoons capers, rinsed,
plus 1 tablespoon brine

4 celery ribs, sliced thin on bias

1 fennel bulb, 1 tablespoon fronds
minced, stalks discarded,
bulb halved, cored, and sliced
thin crosswise

1 apple, cored and cut into
2-inch-long matchsticks

why this recipe works A rémoulade, which gets its name from the Italian word "remolata" (or "gremolata"), is essentially a variation of mayonnaise that has been made in France since at least the 17th century. The cold sauce, often flavored with anchovies, pickles, and capers, is used for seafood, but here we pair it with apple and fennel. This great alternative to coleslaw is perfect to serve with barbecue. The tangy, rich dressing also makes a great dipping sauce for anything fried. Slicing the fennel and celery thin and cutting the apple into matchsticks made the pieces easy to spear with a fork. Whole-grain mustard, caper brine, and lemon juice gave brightness to the mayonnaise. Any variety of apple can be used here, but we recommend a crisp-sweet variety such as Fuji, Gala, or Honeycrisp.

Whisk mayonnaise, mustard, lemon juice, and caper brine together in large bowl. Add celery, fennel bulb, apple, and capers and toss to combine. Season with salt and pepper to taste. Top with fennel fronds and serve.

crispy artichoke salad with lemon vinaigrette

why this recipe works We wanted to feature artichokes in a salad, but we wanted the dish to be easy. So we went straight to the heart of the matter. Raw or braised artichokes required too much prep for a quick meal, but jarred artichoke hearts have been processed already. For textural interest, we tossed the artichoke hearts in cornstarch and fried them till crispy but juicy. Then we placed the fried artichokes on a bed of peas and spicy-sweet mizuna leaves. Tossed in a lemony dressing, the mizuna complemented the richness of the artichokes and a hint of za'atar added more tartness and some needed crunch. We prefer the flavor and texture of jarred whole baby artichoke hearts here, but you can substitute 18 ounces of frozen artichoke hearts, thawed and patted dry, for the jarred.

SERVES 4

- 3 cups jarred whole baby artichoke hearts packed in water, halved, rinsed, and patted dry
- 3 tablespoons cornstarch
- 1 cup plus 4 teaspoons extra-virgin olive oil, divided
- 1 tablespoon lemon juice
- ¾ teaspoon Dijon mustard
- ¾ teaspoon minced shallot

  Pinch table salt
- 2 ounces (2 cups) mizuna or baby arugula
- ¾ cup frozen peas, thawed
- 1 teaspoon Za'atar (page 49)

1   Toss artichokes with cornstarch in bowl to coat. Heat 1 cup oil in 12-inch skillet over medium heat until shimmering. Shake excess cornstarch from artichokes and add artichokes to skillet. Cook, stirring occasionally, until crispy and golden, 5 to 7 minutes. Transfer to paper towel–lined plate and let cool slightly.

2   Whisk lemon juice, mustard, shallot, and salt together in bowl. Whisking constantly, slowly drizzle in remaining 4 teaspoons oil until emulsified.

3   Toss mizuna, peas, and 2 tablespoons vinaigrette together in large bowl and transfer to platter. Top with artichokes, drizzle with remaining vinaigrette, and sprinkle with za'atar. Serve.

crispy artichoke salad with lemon vinaigrette, *page 141*

asparagus salad with radishes, pecorino romano, and croutons

why this recipe works We all look forward to freshly steamed in-season asparagus. But did you know that raw asparagus is just as delicious as cooked? Mildly sweet and nutty, it has a delicate crunch and none of the sulfurous flavors cooked asparagus can sometimes have. As long as we chose the right spears (bright green, firm, and crisp, with tightly closed tips) and sliced them very thin on the bias, we could avoid woodiness and keep things crunchy. To complement the asparagus, we wanted a summery dressing; inspired by the herb garden, we devised a pesto-style dressing with mint and basil. A high ratio of herbs to oil made the dressing potent enough to enhance but not mask the vegetable's flavor. A food processor made it easy to chop the herbs together with Pecorino Romano cheese, garlic, lemon, and salt before stirring in extra-virgin olive oil. Fresh radishes, more Pecorino, and buttery croutons rounded out the dish. Look for asparagus spears between ½ and ¾ inch in diameter. Grate the cheese for the dressing with a rasp-style grater or use the small holes of a box grater; shave the cheese for the salad with a vegetable peeler.

1 for the pesto dressing Process mint, basil, Pecorino, lemon zest and juice, garlic, and salt in food processor until smooth, about 20 seconds, scraping down sides of bowl as needed. With processor running, slowly add oil until incorporated; transfer to large bowl and season with salt and pepper to taste.

2 for the salad Cut asparagus tips from spears and set aside. Slice spears on bias ⅛ inch thick. Add asparagus tips and spears, radishes, and Pecorino to dressing and toss to combine. Season with salt and pepper to taste. Transfer salad to serving platter and top with croutons. Serve.

SERVES 4 TO 6

pesto dressing

- 2 cups fresh mint or cilantro leaves
- ¼ cup fresh basil leaves
- ¼ cup grated Pecorino Romano or Parmesan cheese
- 1 teaspoon grated lemon zest plus 2 teaspoons juice
- 1 garlic clove, minced
- ¾ teaspoon table salt
- ⅓ cup extra-virgin olive oil

salad

- 2 pounds thick asparagus, trimmed
- 5 radishes, trimmed and sliced thin
- 2 ounces Pecorino Romano or Parmesan cheese, shaved
- 1 cup Classic Croutons (page 44)

beet salad with spiced yogurt and watercress

why this recipe works Beets often get short shrift, maybe because cooking them takes time. But beets are pretty and sweet, and a beet salad is always a treat. For a version we could make often, we wanted to avoid hours-long roasting. We peeled the beets, cut them into small chunks, and microwaved them in a covered bowl with some water. Cutting the beets into pieces exposed more surface area so that they cooked faster, and using the microwave caused water molecules inside the beets to boil rapidly and intensely, so they were done in about 30 minutes. We thinned yogurt with lime juice and water; spread it on a platter; and topped it with the lightly dressed beets and watercress, adding toasted pistachios for crunch. Be sure to wear gloves when peeling and cutting the beets to prevent your hands from becoming stained. The moisture content of Greek yogurt varies, so add the water slowly in step 2. We like to make this salad with watercress, but you can substitute baby arugula, if desired. For the best presentation, use red beets here, not golden or Chioggia beets.

1 In largest bowl your microwave will accommodate, stir together beets, ⅓ cup water, and ½ teaspoon salt. Cover with plate and microwave until beets can be easily pierced with paring knife, 25 to 30 minutes, stirring halfway through microwaving. Drain beets in colander and let cool.

2 In medium bowl, whisk yogurt, 3 tablespoons cilantro, 2 tablespoons oil, ginger, lime zest and 1 tablespoon juice, garlic, cumin, coriander, pepper, and ½ teaspoon salt together. Slowly stir in up to 3 tablespoons water until mixture has consistency of regular yogurt. Season with salt, pepper, and extra lime juice to taste. Spread yogurt mixture over serving platter.

3 In large bowl, combine watercress, 2 tablespoons pistachios, 2 teaspoons oil, 1 teaspoon lime juice, and pinch salt and toss to coat. Arrange watercress mixture on top of yogurt mixture, leaving 1-inch border of yogurt mixture. Add beets to now-empty bowl and toss with remaining pinch salt, remaining 1 teaspoon oil, and remaining 2 teaspoons lime juice. Place beet mixture on top of watercress mixture. Sprinkle salad with remaining 2 tablespoons pistachios and remaining 1 tablespoon cilantro and serve.

SERVES 4 TO 6

- 2 pounds beets, trimmed, peeled, and cut into ¾-inch pieces
- 1 teaspoon plus 2 pinches table salt, divided
- 1¼ cups plain Greek yogurt
- ¼ cup minced fresh cilantro or mint, divided
- 3 tablespoons extra-virgin olive oil, divided
- 2 teaspoons grated fresh ginger
- 1 teaspoon grated lime zest, plus 2 tablespoons juice, divided, plus extra juice for seasoning (2 limes)
- 1 garlic clove, minced
- ½ teaspoon ground cumin
- ½ teaspoon ground coriander
- ¼ teaspoon pepper
- 5 ounces (5 cups) watercress, torn into bite-size pieces
- ¼ cup shelled pistachios or almonds, toasted and chopped, divided

grilled panzanella

SERVES 4

dressing

- 1 cup extra-virgin olive oil
- 3 garlic cloves, minced
- ⅓ cup white wine vinegar
- 2 tablespoons capers, rinsed and minced, plus 1 tablespoon brine
- 1 teaspoon Dijon mustard
- ½ teaspoon table salt
- ½ teaspoon pepper

salad

- 1 red onion, halved and cut through root end into ½-inch-thick wedges
- 1 red, orange, or yellow bell pepper, stemmed, seeded, and cut into 2-inch-long planks
- 1 zucchini or summer squash, trimmed and quartered lengthwise
- 1 (12-inch) baguette, cut on bias into 4-inch-long, 1-inch-thick slices
- ½ teaspoon table salt
- ½ teaspoon pepper
- ½ English cucumber, cut into ½-inch pieces
- 1 cup cherry or grape tomatoes, halved
- ½ cup chopped fresh basil or parsley
- 1½ ounces Parmesan or Pecorino Romano cheese, shredded (½ cup)

why this recipe works Panzanella, a Tuscan salad, is traditionally a marriage of stale bread and vegetables at their peak, tossed with a vinaigrette for a colorful, multitextured side dish or a light lunch or supper. It's important that the bread be stale so that it doesn't go completely soggy when dressed. The problem is that you don't always have stale bread on hand. The answer? The grill. By slicing a fresh baguette 1 inch thick, brushing the slices with a mixture of extra-virgin olive oil and minced garlic, and grilling them, we had bread that could stand up to dressing and had a bonus layer of smoky, grill-marked flavor. We also grilled onion, bell pepper, and zucchini before tossing them and the bread in a tangy dressing along with tomatoes and cucumbers. The result was crunchy, chewy, and delightful.

1   for the dressing Whisk oil and garlic together in small bowl. Set aside ⅓ cup garlic oil for brushing vegetables and bread. Whisk vinegar, capers and brine, mustard, salt, and pepper together in medium bowl. Whisking constantly, slowly drizzle in remaining ⅔ cup garlic oil until emulsified. (Dressing can be refrigerated for up to 24 hours; whisk to recombine before using.)

2   for the salad Place onion, bell pepper, zucchini, and bread on rimmed baking sheet and brush all over with reserved ⅓ cup garlic oil. Sprinkle with salt and pepper.

3A   for a charcoal grill Open bottom vent completely. Light large chimney starter mounded with charcoal briquettes (7 quarts). When top coals are partially covered with ash, pour evenly over grill. Set cooking grate in place, cover, and open lid vent completely. Heat grill until hot, about 5 minutes.

3B   for a gas grill Turn all burners to high; cover; and heat grill until hot, about 15 minutes. Turn all burners to medium.

4   Clean and oil cooking grate. Transfer onion, bell pepper, and zucchini to grill and cook (covered if using gas) until well browned and tender, 6 to 12 minutes, flipping and turning as needed for even cooking. Return vegetables to sheet as they finish grilling.

5 Arrange bread on grill and cook, uncovered, until golden brown and lightly charred, 1 to 2 minutes per side. Return to sheet.

6 Cut grilled vegetables and bread into ¾-inch pieces and transfer to large bowl. Add cucumber, tomatoes, basil, and ¾ cup dressing and toss to combine. Let sit for 10 minutes until flavors meld, then season with salt and pepper to taste. Transfer salad to serving platter and sprinkle with Parmesan. Serve, passing remaining ¼ cup dressing separately.

duck salad with blackberries and quick pickled fennel

SERVES 4

2 (8- to 10-ounce) boneless split duck breasts, trimmed

¼ teaspoon table salt

¼ teaspoon pepper

2 oranges

6 ounces (1¼ cups) blackberries, halved

½ head frisée (3 ounces), torn into bite-size pieces

2 ounces (2 cups) baby watercress or baby arugula

1 cup Quick Pickled Fennel (page 54)

6 tablespoons Orange-Ginger Vinaigrette (page 31), divided

why this recipe works Some pairings are so perfect that they become classics. Duck and orange is one such pairing, and we updated this classic by creating a salad worthy of a dinner party. We cooked two duck breasts slowly in a skillet skin side down to render the fat and create a perfectly crispy cap of skin covering succulent, rosy meat. Lacy, delicately bitter frisée and soft and peppery baby watercress stood up to the duck's substantial presence. Then, to complement duck's affinity for oranges and to cut through its richness, we sliced oranges into sweet, juicy triangles as well as juiced them for a punchy orange-ginger vinaigrette. We also added blackberries for visual interest and pops of sweetness. Lastly, quick pickled fennel was an easy yet complexly flavored addition that added crunch, subtle anise notes, and vinegary tartness. If you use mature watercress, trim its thicker, woodier stems before using and tear leaves into bite-sized piece.

1 Using sharp knife, cut slits ½ inch apart in crosshatch pattern in duck skin and fat cap, being careful not to cut into meat. Pat breasts dry with paper towels and sprinkle with salt and pepper.

2 Heat 12-inch skillet over medium heat for 3 minutes. Reduce heat to low; carefully place breasts skin side down in skillet; and cook until fat begins to render, about 5 minutes. Continue to cook, adjusting heat as needed for fat to maintain constant but gentle sizzle, until most of fat has rendered and skin is deep golden and crispy, 10 to 15 minutes.

3 Flip breasts skin side up and continue to cook until duck registers 120 to 125 degrees (for medium-rare), 2 to 5 minutes. Transfer breasts to cutting board and let rest while finishing salad.

4 Meanwhile, cut away peel and pith from oranges. Quarter oranges, then slice crosswise ¼ inch thick. Slice breasts ¼ inch thick. Gently toss blackberries, frisée, watercress, fennel, oranges, and ¼ cup vinaigrette in large bowl to combine. Divide among individual plates. Serve, topping individual portions with duck and drizzling with remaining 2 tablespoons vinaigrette.

broccoli salad with creamy avocado dressing

why this recipe works When we think of avocado, we usually think of eating fresh slices. But avocado's texture makes it a great ingredient to use in creamless creamy dressings. So we updated the classic picnic salad of crisp broccoli, dried fruit, and nuts with an avocado dressing instead of a mayo-based one. We devised a method to cook the broccoli stalks and florets concurrently, so we wasted nothing. We got the best texture and flavor out of broccoli by quickly steaming it and then shocking it in ice water. The tougher broccoli stalks cooked in the water below so we wasted nothing. By placing the chopped stalks in the boiling water and perching the florets on top to steam, we ensured that both became tender at the same time. Toasted almonds added crunch, dried cranberries gave brightness, and fresh tarragon contributed a hint of anise.

1 Bring 1 cup water and ½ teaspoon salt to boil in large saucepan over high heat. Add broccoli stalks, then place florets on top of stalks so they sit just above water. Cover and cook until broccoli is bright green and crisp-tender, about 3 minutes. Meanwhile, fill large bowl halfway with ice and water. Drain broccoli well; transfer to ice bath; and let sit until just cool, about 2 minutes. Transfer broccoli to plate lined with triple layer of paper towels and dry well.

2 Gently toss broccoli with dressing, cranberries, almonds, shallot, and tarragon in separate large bowl until evenly coated. Season with salt and pepper to taste. Serve.

SERVES 4 TO 6

Table salt for cooking broccoli

1½ pounds broccoli, stalks peeled, halved lengthwise, and sliced ¼ inch thick, florets cut into 1-inch pieces

1 recipe Creamy Avocado Dressing (page 37)

½ cup dried cranberries or raisins

½ cup sliced almonds or chopped walnuts, toasted

1 shallot, sliced thin

1 tablespoon minced fresh tarragon or chives

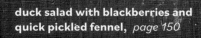

duck salad with blackberries and
quick pickled fennel, *page 150*

red cabbage

Red cabbage is often cooked, but with its deep purple color, it is stunning when raw. Thinly sliced or shredded, it adds fresh brightness and crunch to salads and slaws and is a great substitute for green cabbage. But both cabbages have a delicate, almost sweet, flavor when uncooked or even just charred for our salads. The quick cooking doesn't release their characteristic sulfurous odor.

brussels sprout, red cabbage, and pomegranate slaw

why this recipe works Green cabbage is a coleslaw standby, but we flip things around and use red cabbage here instead. Thinly sliced brussels sprouts and red cabbage created a vibrant color contrast, pomegranate seeds provided bright sweetness, and toasted sliced almonds added crunch. Instead of the traditional mayonnaise dressing, we used a vinaigrette of cider vinegar, pomegranate molasses, and olive oil, so our salad tasted lighter but still had the sweet-tart notes we like. You can substitute 2 teaspoons of lemon juice plus 2 teaspoons of molasses for the pomegranate molasses. The brussels sprouts and cabbage can be sliced with a knife or the slicing disk of a food processor. Either way, slice them as thin as possible.

1   Whisk vinegar, pomegranate molasses, salt, and pepper together in large bowl. Whisking constantly, slowly drizzle in oil until emulsified.

2   Add brussels sprouts, cabbage, pomegranate seeds, almonds, and mint and toss well to coat. Season with salt and pepper to taste. Serve.

SERVES 8

- ¼ cup cider vinegar
- 1 tablespoon pomegranate molasses
- ¾ teaspoon table salt
- ¼ teaspoon pepper
- 3 tablespoons extra-virgin olive oil
- 1 pound brussels sprouts, trimmed, halved, and sliced very thin
- 3 cups thinly sliced red cabbage
- 1½ cups pomegranate seeds
- ½ cup sliced almonds or chopped pecans, toasted
- 2 tablespoons minced fresh mint or cilantro

butternut squash raita

SERVES 4 TO 6

raita

- 1 pound butternut squash, peeled, seeded, and shredded
- 2 cups plain whole-milk yogurt
- ¼ cup chopped fresh cilantro leaves and stems, divided
- 1 shallot, minced
- 2 tablespoons milk, plus extra as needed
- 1 teaspoon ground cumin
- 1 teaspoon packed brown sugar
- ½ teaspoon table salt
- ¼ teaspoon cayenne pepper

spiced seasoning oil

- 1 tablespoon vegetable oil
- 1 teaspoon black mustard seeds
- ¼ teaspoon ground turmeric
- ⅛ teaspoon ground asafetida
- 10 fresh curry leaves

why this recipe works Many people think that raita, an Indian "salad" with a yogurt "dressing," is always cucumbers in yogurt. Actually, raitas are made with various vegetables, raw or cooked (think spinach, beets, onion, bitter melon, potato, and okra), and served as part of a complete meal with lentils, vegetables, bread, and rice. They contribute a delicious cooling element (not necessarily cooling against heat but inwardly cooling in a holistic health sense). In western India, raita is sometimes made with pumpkin, similar in flavor to butternut squash, which we used. We grated the squash, using the large holes of a box grater, then microwaved it. We flavored yogurt with ground cumin, brown sugar, shallot, and cayenne and stirred in the cooled squash. The raita can be eaten as is or flavored further with a spice seasoning of black mustard seeds, turmeric, asafetida, and fresh curry leaves (available at Indian markets, spice purveyors, and online) bloomed in hot oil, a technique called phodni, tadka, chonk, or vagar. Curry leaves are best used fresh but can be refrigerated for longer storage. Blooming spices progresses very quickly so it's important to have ingredients measured out before you start. Mustard seeds jump out of the pan when added to hot oil; covering the pan with a splatter screen or lid can be helpful to keep them contained. This dish should be eaten within 24 hours of making it.

1 for the raita Microwave squash in covered bowl until tender, about 6 minutes, stirring halfway through microwaving. Drain if necessary, then set aside to cool completely, about 30 minutes.

2 Meanwhile, whisk yogurt, 2 tablespoons cilantro, shallot, milk, cumin, sugar, salt, and cayenne together in bowl. Stir in squash. (Raita can be refrigerated for up to 24 hours. Let come to room temperature and thin with extra milk as needed before serving; raita should have consistency of regular yogurt.)

3 for the spiced seasoning oil Heat oil in small saucepan or seasoning wok over medium-high heat until just smoking. (Test temperature of oil by adding 1 mustard seed; mustard seed should sizzle and pop immediately; if it does not, continue to heat oil and repeat testing.) Carefully add mustard seeds, then reduce heat to low. Stir in turmeric and asafetida and cook until fragrant, about 5 seconds. Off heat, carefully stir in curry leaves and cook until leaves sizzle and are translucent in spots, 5 to 10 seconds.

4 Pour hot oil mixture over raita and stir in until combined. Sprinkle with remaining 2 tablespoons cilantro and serve.

roasted butternut squash salad with za'atar and parsley

SERVES 4 TO 6

3 pounds butternut squash, peeled, seeded, and cut into ½-inch pieces (8 cups)

¼ cup extra-virgin olive oil, divided

1¼ teaspoons table salt, divided

½ teaspoon pepper

1 teaspoon Za'atar (page 49)

2 tablespoons lemon juice

2 tablespoons honey

1 small shallot, minced

¾ cup fresh parsley or cilantro leaves

⅓ cup roasted pepitas or sunflower seeds

½ cup pomegranate seeds

why this recipe works The sweet nuttiness of a roasted winter squash such as butternut pairs best with flavors bold enough to balance it. In this hearty salad, that boldness comes from a traditional eastern Mediterranean spice blend, za'atar (a pungent combination of toasted sesame seeds, thyme, and sumac). We found that using high heat and placing the oven rack in the lowest position produced perfectly browned, tender squash in about 30 minutes. Dusting the za'atar over the hot squash worked much like toasting the spice blend, boosting its flavor. For a foil to the tender squash, we considered many nuts and seeds before landing on toasted pepitas. They provided the textural accent the dish needed and reinforced the squash's flavor. Pomegranate seeds added a burst of tartness and color. We prefer to use our homemade Za'atar here (page 49), but you can substitute store-bought za'atar. You can substitute chopped red grapes or small blueberries for the pomegranate seeds.

1 Adjust oven rack to lowest position and heat oven to 450 degrees. Toss squash with 1 tablespoon oil and sprinkle with 1 teaspoon salt and pepper. Arrange squash in single layer on rimmed baking sheet and roast until well browned and tender, 30 to 35 minutes, stirring halfway through roasting. Sprinkle squash with za'atar and let cool for 15 minutes.

2 Whisk lemon juice, honey, shallot, and remaining ¼ teaspoon salt together in large bowl. Whisking constantly, slowly drizzle in remaining 3 tablespoons oil until emulsified. Add squash, parsley, and pepitas and toss gently to coat. Transfer salad to serving platter and sprinkle with pomegranate seeds. Serve.

charred cabbage salad with torn tofu and plantain chips

why this recipe works We used Southeast Asian flavors for this showstopping salad, first coating wedges of red cabbage with oil, Thai red curry paste, and turmeric and then roasting them in the oven. The spice paste gave flavor; the roasting brought out the cabbage's natural sweetness. We marinated tofu in lime juice, honey, rice vinegar, fish sauce, and ginger, taking it from neutral to sweet and sour. Scallions and bean sprouts added pleasant crispness to the dish. For our warm dressing, we bloomed more curry paste, turmeric, and ginger in the microwave and then added rice vinegar. Plantain chips gave a sweet-salty crunch. If you don't have plantain chips, chopped macadamia nuts or cashews work fine. The tofu can be marinated for up to 24 hours. Note that this recipe uses seasoned rice vinegar; we don't recommend using unseasoned rice vinegar in its place.

1 Adjust oven rack to lowest position and heat oven to 500 degrees. Gently press tofu dry with paper towels. Whisk 1 tablespoon vinegar, lime juice, 2 teaspoons ginger, honey, and fish sauce together in medium bowl. Add tofu and toss gently to coat; set aside for 20 minutes. (Tofu can be refrigerated for up to 24 hours.)

2 Halve cabbage through core and cut each half into 4 approximately 2-inch-wide wedges, leaving core intact (you will have 8 wedges). Whisk ¼ cup oil, 1 teaspoon curry paste, 2 teaspoons turmeric, and salt together in bowl. Arrange cabbage wedges in single layer on aluminum foil–lined rimmed baking sheet, then brush cabbage all over with oil mixture. Cover tightly with foil and roast for 10 minutes. Remove foil and drizzle 2 tablespoons oil evenly over wedges. Return sheet to oven and roast, uncovered, until cabbage is tender and sides touching sheet are well browned, 10 to 15 minutes. Let cool slightly, about 15 minutes.

3 Whisk remaining 2 teaspoons ginger, remaining 1 tablespoon oil, remaining 1 tablespoon curry paste, and remaining 1 teaspoon turmeric together in bowl. Microwave until fragrant, about 30 seconds. Whisk water and remaining 2 tablespoons vinegar into ginger mixture.

4 Chop cabbage coarse and divide among individual plates. Serve, topping individual portions with bean sprouts, basil, scallions, and tofu. Drizzle with vinaigrette and sprinkle with plantain chips.

SERVES 4

- 14 ounces firm tofu, torn into bite-size pieces
- 3 tablespoons seasoned rice vinegar, divided
- 2 tablespoons lime juice
- 4 teaspoons grated fresh ginger, divided
- 1 tablespoon honey
- 1 tablespoon fish sauce
- 1 head red cabbage (2 pounds)
- 7 tablespoons vegetable oil, divided
- 4 teaspoons Thai red curry paste, divided
- 1 tablespoon ground turmeric, divided
- ½ teaspoon table salt
- 1 tablespoon water
- 1 cup bean sprouts
- ¼ cup chopped fresh basil
- 2 scallions, sliced thin on bias
- ¼ cup plantain or banana chips, crushed

charred cabbage salad with torn
tofu and plantain chips, *page 159*

tangy cabbage-apple slaw

why this recipe works What's the secret to a flavorful Southern slaw to eat with barbecue? A mix of sweetness, tartness, and crunch. This salad exemplifies the best of those flavors, with tender cabbage and crunchy Granny Smith apples in a warm, sweet, and spicy vinegary dressing. We salted the chopped cabbage to draw out excess moisture before dressing it, preventing the dressing from being diluted later. Warming the dressing enabled the cabbage and apples to absorb it more readily, and they absorbed even more flavor when left to rest for an hour. Cider vinegar gave the dressing a fruity flavor while red pepper flakes, sliced scallions, and mustard packed some punch. To prep the apples, cut the cored fruit into ¼-inch-thick planks, then stack the planks and cut them into matchsticks.

1 Toss cabbage and salt in colander set over medium bowl. Let sit until wilted, about 1 hour. Rinse cabbage under cold water, drain, dry well with paper towels, and transfer to large bowl. (Salted, rinsed, and dried cabbage can be refrigerated in zipper-lock bag for up to 24 hours.) Add apples and scallions and toss to combine.

2 Bring vinegar, sugar, oil, mustard, and pepper flakes to boil in small saucepan over medium heat. Pour over cabbage mixture and toss to coat. Cover with plastic wrap and refrigerate for at least 1 hour or up to 24 hours. Serve.

SERVES 6 TO 8

- 1 head green cabbage (2 pounds), cored and chopped fine
- 2 teaspoons table salt
- 2 Granny Smith apples, cored and cut into matchsticks
- 2 scallions, sliced thin
- ½ cup cider vinegar
- ½ cup sugar
- 6 tablespoons vegetable oil
- 1 tablespoon Dijon mustard
- ¼ teaspoon red pepper flakes

carrot noodle salad with harissa and honey

SERVES 4

¼ cup harissa

¼ cup lemon juice (2 lemons)

2 tablespoons water

4 teaspoons honey

¼ teaspoon table salt

¼ teaspoon pepper

1½ pounds carrot noodles, cut into 6-inch lengths

4 ounces (4 cups) baby arugula

¼ cup chopped fresh mint or cilantro, divided

4 ounces goat or feta cheese, crumbled (1 cup)

½ cup dried apricots, sliced thin

½ cup shelled pistachios, toasted and chopped

why this recipe works Spiralized vegetable noodles are a low-carb, fresh alternative to pasta, and their shape also works well in salads. Here we used naturally sweet carrot noodles, smoky-hot harissa, and peppery arugula for a salad with vibrant visual appeal and flavor. Chopped mint gave cool freshness, and jammy bites of dried apricots echoed the carrots' sweetness. Topping our jewel-colored salad with goat cheese added creamy tang. We prefer our homemade Harissa (recipe follows) here, but you can substitute store-bought harissa; spiciness can vary greatly by brand. You will need 2 pounds of carrots to get 1½ pounds of noodles. We prefer to spiralize the carrots ourselves for the best flavor, but you can use store-bought carrot noodles.

1   Whisk harissa, lemon juice, water, honey, salt, and pepper together in large bowl. Measure out and reserve 1 tablespoon vinaigrette for serving.

2   Add carrot noodles, arugula, and 3 tablespoons mint to bowl with vinaigrette and toss to coat; season with salt and pepper to taste. Divide among individual plates. Serve, topping individual portions with goat cheese, apricots, pistachios, and remaining 1 tablespoon mint. Drizzle with reserved 1 tablespoon vinaigrette. Serve.

harissa

makes ½ cup

Harissa is a Tunisian chile paste that is popular all over North Africa and parts of the Middle East. Traditionally made with roasted chiles, coriander, and cumin, our simplified take is made with paprika and dried Aleppo pepper. Harissa is great for flavoring soups, sauces, and dressings and even for spreading on a turkey sandwich if you want a spicy condiment instead of mayo. If you can't find Aleppo pepper, you can substitute ¾ teaspoon of paprika and ¾ teaspoon of finely chopped red pepper flakes.

6	tablespoons extra-virgin olive oil
6	garlic cloves, minced
2	tablespoons paprika
1	tablespoon ground coriander
1	tablespoon ground dried Aleppo pepper
1	teaspoon ground cumin
¾	teaspoon caraway seeds
½	teaspoon table salt

Combine all ingredients in bowl and microwave until bubbling and very fragrant, about 1 minute, stirring halfway through microwaving. Let cool completely. (Harissa can be refrigerated for up to 4 days.)

gajarachi koshimbir

SERVES 4 TO 6

salad

- 12 ounces carrot noodles, cut into 3-inch lengths
- 3 tablespoons sugar
- ¾ teaspoon table salt
- ½ onion, chopped fine (optional)
- 2 tablespoons lime juice
- 6 tablespoons dry-roasted peanuts, chopped fine
- ¼ cup chopped fresh cilantro leaves and stems
- ¼ cup shredded fresh coconut

spiced seasoning oil

- 1 tablespoon vegetable oil
- 2 teaspoons black mustard seeds
- 1 Thai chile, halved lengthwise
- ⅛ teaspoon ground turmeric
- ⅛ teaspoon ground asafetida
- 10 fresh curry leaves

why this recipe works Sweet, spicy, acidic, crunchy, and aromatic, this traditional salad from the state of Maharashtra in western India combines carrots with coconut, peanuts, cilantro, and a finishing spiced oil. The traditional salad ("koshimbir" is "salad" in Maharashtra's official language, Marathi) uses spices and aromatics that, if they aren't there already, will soon be in your pantry. We found that spiralized carrots were the right thickness to pair with the spiced dressing. Salting and sugaring the carrots first intensified their flavor and sweetness. We prefer to spiralize the carrots ourselves for the best flavor, but you can use store-bought carrot noodles or matchstick carrots. You will need 1 pound of carrots to get 12 ounces of noodles. Black mustard seeds, turmeric, asafetida, and curry leaves can be found at Indian markets, spice purveyors, or online. We prefer to shred fresh coconut on the large holes of a box grater. You can also use frozen unsweetened, shredded coconut from Indian or Asian markets. Curry leaves are best used fresh but can be refrigerated for longer storage. Mustard seeds will jump out of the pan and curry leaves will spatter when added to hot oil; consider topping the saucepan with either a splatter screen or a lid during cooking. Blooming spices in hot oil will progress very quickly, so it's important to have all your ingredients measured out before you start. If you prefer, you can add ¼ teaspoon of cayenne pepper to the carrot mixture with the lime juice in step 1 in place of the Thai chile used in step 2.

1 for the salad Toss carrot noodles with sugar and salt in salad spinner and let sit until partially wilted and reduced in volume by one-third, about 15 minutes. Spin carrots until excess liquid is removed, 10 to 20 seconds. Transfer carrots to large bowl and toss with onion, if using, and lime juice.

2 for the spiced seasoning oil Heat oil in small saucepan or seasoning wok over medium-high heat until just smoking. (Test temperature of oil by adding 1 mustard seed; mustard seed should sizzle and pop immediately; if it does not, continue to heat oil and repeat testing.) Carefully add mustard seeds, then reduce heat to low. Stir in Thai chile, turmeric, and asafetida and cook until fragrant, about 5 seconds. Off heat, carefully stir in curry leaves and cook until leaves sizzle and are translucent in spots, 5 to 10 seconds.

3 Pour hot oil mixture into carrot mixture and let sit for 15 minutes. (Carrot mixture can be refrigerated for up to 6 hours.) Stir in peanuts, then sprinkle with cilantro and coconut. Serve.

curry leaves

The curry leaf tree (*Murraya koenigii*) is native to southern India and unwittingly gave its name to a spice blend called curry powder, which is used everywhere but in real Indian cooking. The tree can grow up to 20 feet high and has white flowers; small green, bitter fruit; and pungently scented leaves. These iron-rich leaves are used in Indian chutney powders and hot oil-and-spice seasonings for lentils and vegetables. They are best used fresh rather than dried; they can be refrigerated for up to three weeks and frozen for longer. Quickly rinsed and wiped dry, they can be stripped off a branch like rosemary and bloomed in a seasoning for a salad such as Gajarachi Koshimbir or Butternut Squash Raita (page 156). Before cooking with them, rub a curry leaf between your fingers to breathe in its strong fragrance. That's the unique flavor you will taste in your dish. Curry leaves are edible, but you can easily remove them from a dish as you might cinnamon sticks or chiles.

carrots

Carrots likely originated in central Asia and were first cultivated for their greens and seeds. The root, which we now relish, was really just the root. Today, a variety of carrots—white, orange, yellow, red, black, or purple—offer us sweet, crunchy flavor that is suited to salads but is also a perfect snack to bite into raw. The "baby carrots" that you see in supermarkets are actually full-grown carrots mechanically cut into smaller pieces and sculpted into small rounded batons. True baby carrots that have not fully matured are usually available at summer farmers' markets. The perky-looking greens still attached to carrots are a sign of freshness. Twist off the greens when you get home and store them separately. After rinsing them well and patting them dry, use the greens as a salad garnish, like parsley, or make them into a pesto to dress pasta or vegetables.

carrot and smoked salmon salad

why this recipe works In this dinner salad, we use all of the carrot—greens and root—for a beautifully bright orange and green dish. To make it a filling meal, we also add silky, rich smoked salmon, which happens to also be a lovely shade of orange. First, we chose carrots with their greens attached because they taste sweeter than bagged carrots, and the feathery greens are fresh and slightly bitter like parsley. We pickled some of the carrots, shaved into ribbons, for a sweet and punchy bite. We roasted the remaining carrots, keeping the baking sheet close to the heat source for good browning. Tossing the roasted carrots with a Dijon-dill vinaigrette while slightly warm allowed them to absorb a lot of flavor. Finally, we added raw endive for its crisp bite and color contrast and grapefruit for sweet-tart flavor. To finish, we chopped up the carrot greens and tossed them into the salad. Parsley can be substituted for the carrot greens. You should have about 1½ pounds of carrots after trimming the carrot greens.

1 Adjust oven rack to lowest position and heat oven to 450 degrees. Peel and shave 4 ounces carrots into thin ribbons with vegetable peeler; set aside. Peel and slice remaining carrots on bias ¼ inch thick; set aside.

2 Microwave ¼ cup vinegar, sugar, and ⅛ teaspoon salt in medium bowl until simmering, 1 to 2 minutes. Add shaved carrots and stir to combine. Let sit, stirring occasionally, for 45 minutes. (Drained pickled carrots can be refrigerated for up to 5 days.)

3 Toss sliced carrots, 1 tablespoon oil, pepper, and ½ teaspoon salt together in bowl to coat. Spread carrots in single layer on rimmed baking sheet, cut side down. Roast until tender and bottoms are well browned, 15 to 25 minutes. Let cool slightly, about 15 minutes.

4 Meanwhile, cut away peel and pith from grapefruit. Quarter grapefruit, then slice crosswise into ¼-inch-thick pieces.

5 Whisk dill, mustard, remaining 1 tablespoon vinegar, and remaining ¼ teaspoon salt together in large bowl. Whisking constantly, slowly drizzle in remaining 3 tablespoons oil until emulsified. Add endive, carrot greens, roasted carrots, pickled carrots, and grapefruit and toss to combine; season with salt and pepper to taste. Arrange salmon around edge of serving platter, then transfer salad to center of platter. Serve.

SERVES 4 TO 6

- 2 pounds carrots with greens attached, divided, ¼ cup greens chopped
- 5 tablespoons cider vinegar, divided
- 1 tablespoon sugar
- ⅛ teaspoon plus ¾ teaspoon table salt, divided
- ¼ cup extra-virgin olive oil, divided
- ¼ teaspoon pepper
- 1 red grapefruit
- 2 tablespoons chopped fresh dill
- 2 teaspoons Dijon mustard
- 2 heads Belgian endive (4 ounces each), halved, cored, and sliced ½ inch thick
- 8 ounces smoked salmon

chopped carrot salad with mint, pistachios, and pomegranate seeds

SERVES 4 TO 6

¾ cup shelled pistachios or almonds, toasted

3 tablespoons lemon juice

1 tablespoon honey

1 teaspoon table salt

½ teaspoon pepper

½ teaspoon smoked paprika

⅛ teaspoon cayenne pepper

¼ cup extra-virgin olive oil

1 pound carrots, trimmed and cut into 1-inch pieces

1 cup pomegranate seeds, divided

½ cup minced fresh mint or cilantro

why this recipe works It is a little known fact that carrots originated in central Asia, so pairing them with pistachios and pomegranate seeds, beloved in that part of the world, seemed apropos. We saved time on prep by not peeling the carrots; scrubbing them was sufficient. For contrasting flavor, brightness, and crunch, we used lots of fresh mint along with the pomegranate seeds and toasted pistachios. A bright dressing bound the ingredients together. For East Asian flavors, try our variation. We prefer the convenience of leaving the carrots unpeeled and the hint of bitterness that it lends to the salad; just be sure to scrub the carrots well before using them.

1 Pulse pistachios in food processor until coarsely chopped, 10 to 12 pulses; transfer to small bowl. Whisk lemon juice, honey, salt, pepper, paprika, and cayenne together in large bowl. Whisking constantly, slowly drizzle in oil until emulsified.

2 Process carrots in now-empty processor until finely chopped, 10 to 20 seconds, scraping down sides of bowl as needed. Transfer carrots to bowl with dressing; add ½ cup pomegranate seeds, mint, and half of pistachios and toss to combine. Season with salt to taste. Transfer to serving platter, sprinkle with remaining ½ cup pomegranate seeds and remaining pistachios, and serve.

variation

chopped carrot salad with radishes and sesame seeds

Omit pistachios. Substitute unseasoned rice vinegar for lemon juice and 1½ teaspoons gochugaru (Korean red pepper flakes) for pepper, paprika, and cayenne. Increase honey to 2 tablespoons and salt to 1¼ teaspoons. Substitute 2 teaspoons toasted sesame oil for 1 tablespoon extra-virgin olive oil. Before processing carrots, pulse 10 radishes, trimmed and halved, in food processor until coarsely but evenly chopped, 10 to 12 pulses; add to dressing. Substitute ¼ cup toasted sesame seeds for pomegranate seeds and cilantro for mint.

Fruit & Vegetable Salads   **171**

roasted grape and cauliflower salad with chermoula

why this recipe works Cauliflower's delicate flavor makes it an ideal canvas on which to paint other flavors and textures. Here those "paints" come from grapes, cilantro, and red onion. We started by roasting florets from one head of cauliflower until they were caramelized. Instead of discarding the core, we blitzed it in the food processor and added it to the salad for a contrasting rice-like texture. In the empty food processor we made a quick chermoula, a North African sauce made with hefty amounts of cilantro, lemon, and garlic. While chermoula is traditionally used as a marinade for meat and fish, we liked it as a dressing to brighten the cauliflower. To balance the chermoula, we added sliced red onion and whole red grapes to the same baking sheet as the cauliflower to roast together. The grapes and onion caramelized and sweetened while roasting, creating complex flavor. Fresh cilantro leaves and crunchy walnuts were the finishing touch.

1 for the salad Adjust oven rack to lowest position and heat oven to 475 degrees. Toss cauliflower florets, grapes, onion, oil, salt, and pepper together in bowl. Transfer to rimmed baking sheet and roast until vegetables are tender, florets are deep golden, and onion slices are charred at edges, 12 to 15 minutes, stirring halfway through roasting. Let cool slightly, about 15 minutes.

2 Meanwhile, pulse cauliflower core in food processor until finely ground into ⅛-inch pieces, 6 to 8 pulses, scraping down sides of bowl as needed; transfer to large bowl.

3 for the chermoula Process all ingredients in now-empty processor until smooth, about 1 minute, scraping down sides of bowl as needed. (Chermoula can be refrigerated for up to 2 days.) Transfer to bowl with cauliflower core.

4 Add roasted cauliflower mixture to chermoula mixture in bowl and toss to combine. Season with salt and pepper to taste. Sprinkle with cilantro and walnuts. Serve.

SERVES 4 TO 6

salad

- 1 head cauliflower (2 pounds), core chopped coarse, florets cut into 1-inch pieces (6 cups)
- 1 cup seedless red grapes
- ½ small red onion, sliced thin
- 2 tablespoons extra-virgin olive oil
- ½ teaspoon table salt
- ¼ teaspoon pepper
- 2 tablespoons fresh cilantro or parsley leaves
- 2 tablespoons walnuts or sliced almonds, toasted and chopped coarse

chermoula

- 1 cup fresh cilantro or parsley leaves
- 5 tablespoons extra-virgin olive oil
- 2 tablespoons lemon juice
- 4 garlic cloves, minced
- ½ teaspoon ground cumin
- ½ teaspoon paprika
- ¼ teaspoon table salt
- ⅛ teaspoon cayenne pepper

celery root, celery, and apple slaw

SERVES 4 TO 6

1½ pounds celery root, peeled and shredded

¼ cup sugar, plus extra for seasoning

1½ teaspoons table salt, divided

3 tablespoons cider vinegar, plus extra for seasoning

2 tablespoons Dijon mustard

½ teaspoon pepper

½ cup extra-virgin olive oil

5 celery ribs, sliced thin on bias

2 Honeycrisp or Fuji apples, peeled, cored, and cut into 2-inch-long matchsticks

½ cup chopped fresh parsley, cilantro, or mint

why this recipe works The word "slaw" brings cabbage to mind, but it can be delicious with other vegetables, too. Celery root stays just as crisp as cabbage and brings distinctive texture and flavor to a slaw. Both salt and sugar help remove excess moisture from vegetables, with the added benefit of flavoring them, so we tossed shredded celery root with salt and sugar before draining it. Then we complemented its flavor with its aboveground celery ribs and apples. A vinaigrette made with cider vinegar (to echo the apples) and Dijon mustard was a fresher, more flavorful alternative to a mayonnaise-based slaw dressing. To save time, we recommend treating the celery root before prepping the other ingredients. Use the large holes of a box grater or the shredding disk of a food processor to shred the celery root.

1 Toss celery root, sugar, and 1 teaspoon salt together in large bowl and let sit until partially wilted and reduced in volume by one-third, about 15 minutes.

2 Meanwhile, whisk vinegar, mustard, pepper, and remaining ½ teaspoon salt together in large bowl. Whisking constantly, slowly drizzle in oil until emulsified.

3 Transfer celery root to salad spinner and spin until excess water is removed, 10 to 20 seconds. Transfer celery root to bowl with dressing. Add celery, apples, and parsley to bowl with celery root and toss to combine. Season with salt, pepper, extra sugar, and extra vinegar to taste. Serve immediately.

variation
kohlrabi, radicchio, and apple slaw
Shred the kohlrabi on the large holes of a box grater or with the shredding disk of a food processor.

Substitute kohlrabi for celery root. Substitute 1 small head radicchio, halved, cored, and sliced ½ inch thick, for celery; Granny Smith apples for Honeycrisp; and ½ cup coarsely chopped fresh mint for parsley.

radishes

This pretty root vegetable with bite and crunch comes in many varieties, shapes, and colors. The small size; red, purple, pink, or white skin; crisp bite; and slightly peppery flavor of small European radishes make them a great choice to use raw in salads. Long white daikon radish varieties from East Asia are milder in flavor than red radishes. Often pickled with carrots, they are used to top salads and sandwiches, such as the Vietnamese banh mi.

california
chicken salad

why this recipe works You can put avocado on just about anything and call it "Californian," but we wanted to earn our West Coast cred with a healthy, hearty salad that paid respect to the Golden State in every bite. Instead of just throwing on diced avocado, we prepared our luscious, dairy-free dressing with avocado, pureeing the ripe fruit with lemon, garlic, and olive oil. Of course, a California salad should burst with fresh flavors, so we went heavy on green vegetables such as spinach and sugar snap peas. Thinly sliced radishes offered a pop of color, then we added sweet grapes (think Napa Valley). And then we realized we were missing something quintessentially West Coast: a light, fluffy mound of alfalfa sprouts. Sprinkle on chopped California almonds too, if you like. We like using Perfect Poached Chicken (page 43) here, but any cooked chicken would work.

Toss spinach, scallions, and half of dressing together in bowl to coat, then season with salt and pepper to taste. Divide among individual plates. Serve, topping individual portions with chicken, grapes, snap peas, and radishes. Drizzle with remaining dressing, add alfalfa sprouts, and top with chopped almonds. Serve.

SERVES 4

- 8 ounces (8 cups) baby spinach
- 2 scallions, sliced thin
- 1 cup Creamy Avocado Dressing (page 37), divided
- 4 cups cooked chicken, chopped
- 9 ounces seedless grapes, halved (1½ cups)
- 4 ounces sugar snap peas or snow peas, strings removed, halved
- 8 radishes, trimmed, halved, and sliced thin
- 2 ounces (1 cup) alfalfa sprouts or microgreens
- ¼ cup chopped almonds

mexican street corn salad with shrimp

why this recipe works Mexican street cart vendors sell a snack or antojito called esquites or "corn off the cob" ("toasted corn" in the Nahuatl language from which it derives), unlike elote or "corn on the cob." To make a hearty salad, we add romaine and shrimp to the corn. The sweet, charred corn kernels also play off traditional flavorings such as cotija cheese, garlic, chile, and lime. We toasted corn on the stovetop and then used the hot skillet to bloom chili powder and lightly cook minced garlic to temper its bite. We added lettuce and dressed the salad with a creamy and tangy mixture of sour cream and lime juice. Letting the corn cool before adding chopped cilantro and lettuce preserved their bright colors and fresh flavors. You will need a 12-inch nonstick skillet with a tight-fitting lid for this recipe. For more spice, reserve, mince, and add the ribs and seeds from the jalapeño.

1   Combine lime zest and juice; sour cream; jalapeño, if using; and ¼ teaspoon salt in medium bowl. Set aside. Heat 2 tablespoons oil in 12-inch nonstick skillet over medium-high heat until shimmering. Add corn and remaining ¼ teaspoon salt; cover; and cook, without stirring, until corn is charred, 3 to 4 minutes. Remove skillet from heat and let sit, covered, until any popping subsides, about 1 minute. Transfer corn to bowl with lime mixture and wipe skillet clean with paper towels.

2   Add remaining 2 teaspoons oil, garlic, and chili powder to now-empty skillet and cook over medium heat until fragrant, about 30 seconds; transfer to bowl with corn mixture and toss to combine. Let cool completely, about 10 minutes. (Corn-dressing mixture can be refrigerated separately for up to 2 days.)

3   Add lettuce, ⅔ cup cotija, and ½ cup cilantro to corn mixture; toss to combine; and season with salt and pepper to taste. Transfer to individual plates. Sprinkle with radishes, remaining ⅓ cup cotija, and remaining cilantro and top with shrimp. Serve with lime wedges.

SERVES 4

- 2 teaspoons grated lime zest plus 2 tablespoons juice, plus lime wedges for serving
- 2 tablespoons sour cream or Greek yogurt
- 1 jalapeño or serrano chile, stemmed, seeded, and sliced thin (optional)
- ½ teaspoon table salt, divided
- 2 tablespoons plus 2 teaspoons extra-virgin olive oil, divided
- 6 ears corn, kernels cut from cobs, or 4½ cups frozen
- 2 garlic cloves, minced
- 1 teaspoon chili powder
- 2 romaine lettuce hearts (12 ounces), chopped
- 4 ounces cotija cheese, queso fresco, or feta cheese, crumbled (1 cup), divided
- ⅔ cup coarsely chopped fresh cilantro or parsley, divided
- 2 radishes, trimmed and sliced thin
- 1½ cups Sautéed Shrimp (page 43)

citrus salad with watercress, dried cranberries, and pecans

SERVES 4 TO 6

2 red grapefruits

3 oranges

1 teaspoon sugar

1 teaspoon table salt, divided

1 teaspoon unsalted butter

½ cup pecans or walnuts, chopped coarse

3 tablespoons extra-virgin olive oil

1 small shallot, minced

1 teaspoon Dijon mustard

4 ounces (4 cups) watercress, torn into bite-size pieces

⅔ cup dried cranberries or cherries, divided

why this recipe works Salads made with orange and grapefruit are a way to showcase winter fruit and present a mix of sweet and savory flavors. But you need to tame the grapefruit's bitterness and prevent its ample juice from drowning the other components. We started by treating the fruit with salt and sugar to counter the grapefruits' bitter notes. Draining the seasoned fruit helped us remove excess juice, which we reserved to use in the dressing. Finally, we placed the greens on top of the fruit to prevent the greens from getting soggy. Toasted, salted pecans added richness while dried cranberries provided more texture and sweetness to the salad. We prefer to use navel oranges, tangelos, or Cara Caras here. Blood oranges can also be used, but because they are smaller you'll need four of them.

1 Cut away peel and pith from grapefruits and oranges. Cut each fruit in half from pole to pole, then slice crosswise into ¼-inch-thick pieces. Transfer fruit to bowl, toss with sugar and ½ teaspoon salt, and let sit for 15 minutes.

2 Melt butter in 8-inch skillet over medium heat. Add pecans and remaining ½ teaspoon salt and cook, stirring often, until pecans are lightly browned and fragrant, 2 to 4 minutes; transfer to paper towel–lined plate.

3 Drain fruit in colander set over bowl, reserving 2 tablespoons juice. Arrange fruit on platter and drizzle with oil. Whisk reserved 2 tablespoons juice, shallot, and mustard together in medium bowl. Add watercress, ⅓ cup cranberries, and ¼ cup pecans and toss to coat. Arrange watercress mixture over fruit, leaving 1-inch border of fruit. Sprinkle with remaining ⅓ cup cranberries and remaining ¼ cup pecans. Season with salt and pepper to taste, and serve.

citrus

Native to Asia, citrus is a genus of flowering and fruiting trees—lemons, limes, oranges, grapefruit, and citrons—from the Rutaceae family. Interestingly, this is the same family that Sichuan peppercorns and curry leaves belong to. Citrus is now grown in warm climates the world over and eaten as fruit, drunk as juice, made into desserts, and squeezed on savory foods to add a welcome tang. We like to use a variety of oranges and grapefruits in our salads. We also use their juice and zest (as well as those of lemons and limes) in our vinaigrettes and dressings. Unlike bananas or peaches, which ripen at room temperature, citrus fruits stop ripening the moment they are picked, so they are best stored in the refrigerator. Allow them to come to room temperature before slicing, juicing, or zesting them.

nam tok

SERVES 4

1 teaspoon paprika

1 teaspoon cayenne pepper

1 tablespoon white rice

3 tablespoons lime juice (2 limes)

2 tablespoons fish sauce

2 tablespoons water

½ teaspoon sugar

1 (1½-pound) flank steak, trimmed

½ teaspoon table salt

¼ teaspoon white pepper

1 English cucumber, sliced on bias ¼ inch thick

1½ cups fresh mint or Thai basil leaves, torn

1½ cups fresh cilantro or mint leaves

4 shallots, sliced thin

1 Thai chile, stemmed, seeded, and sliced into thin rings

why this recipe works In nam tok (a Thai grilled-beef salad), the cuisine's five signature flavor elements—hot, sour, salty, sweet, and bitter—come together in a light but satisfying dish perfectly suited for a special-occasion summer dinner. We prepared a standard half-grill fire to get a perfect medium-rare steak with a nicely charred crust. The five flavors came together in the dressing of fish sauce, lime juice, sugar, and hot spices, creating a counterpoint to the subtle bitter char of the meat. Kao kua (toasted rice powder) ground in a spice grinder added extra body to the dressing. If fresh Thai chiles are unavailable, substitute half a serrano chile. Don't skip the toasted rice; it's integral to the texture and flavor of the dish. Any variety of white rice can be used. Toasted rice powder can also be found in many Asian markets; substitute 1 tablespoon of rice powder for the white rice.

1   Combine paprika and cayenne in 8-inch skillet and cook over medium heat, shaking skillet, until fragrant, about 1 minute. Transfer to small bowl. Return skillet to medium-high heat; add rice and toast, stirring constantly, until deep golden brown, about 5 minutes. Transfer to second small bowl and let cool for 5 minutes. Grind rice using spice grinder, mini food processor, or mortar and pestle until it resembles fine meal, 10 to 30 seconds (you should have about 1 tablespoon rice powder).

2   Whisk lime juice, fish sauce, water, sugar, and ¼ teaspoon paprika mixture in large bowl and set aside.

3A   **for a charcoal grill** Open bottom vent completely. Light large chimney starter filled with charcoal briquettes (6 quarts). When top coals are partially covered with ash, pour evenly over half of grill. Set cooking grate in place, cover, and open lid vent completely. Heat grill until hot, about 5 minutes.

3B   **for a gas grill** Turn all burners to high; cover; and heat grill until hot, about 15 minutes. Leave primary burner on high and turn off other burner(s).

4   Clean and oil cooking grate. Pat steak dry with paper towels and sprinkle with salt and white pepper. Place steak on hotter side of grill and cook until beginning to char and beads of moisture appear on edges of meat, 5 to 6 minutes. Flip steak and continue to cook on second side until meat registers 120 to 125 degrees (for medium-rare), about 5 minutes. Transfer to cutting board, tent with aluminum foil, and let rest for 10 minutes (or let cool completely, about 1 hour).

5   Line large platter with cucumber slices. Slice steak against grain on bias ¼ inch thick. Transfer steak to bowl with lime juice mixture. Add mint, cilantro, shallots, Thai chile, and half of rice powder and toss to combine. Arrange steak over cucumber-lined platter. Serve, passing remaining rice powder and remaining paprika mixture separately.

horiatiki salata

why this recipe works Imagine bites of sweet tomatoes, briny olives, savory onion, crunchy cucumber, and tangy feta—without any lettuce filler—and you've got horiatiki salata, the traditional Greek salad. For optimum flavor, sourcing high-quality components and bringing out their best was a must. Since ripe tomatoes are loaded with juice that can flood the salad, we tossed halved wedges (which allowed for chunky but manageable bites) with salt and set them in a colander to drain for 30 minutes. Soaking onion slices in ice water lessened their hot bite by washing away the thiosulfinates alliin and allicin (also present in garlic) while maintaining a fresh, crisp texture. A creamy Greek feta brought richness to the lean vegetables. When we tried subbing in fresh oregano for the traditional dried, we understood why the dried herb is preferred: Its more delicate flavor complemented—but didn't upstage—the vegetables. Vinaigrette is never used to dress horiatiki salata, but we tweaked the custom of drizzling the salad separately with oil and vinegar by tossing the vegetables with each component, ensuring that the mixture was lightly but evenly dressed. Use only large, round tomatoes here, not Roma or cherry varieties, and choose the ripest in-season tomatoes you can find. A fresh, fruity, peppery olive oil works well here if you have it.

1 Cut tomatoes into ½-inch-thick wedges. Cut wedges in half crosswise. Toss tomatoes and ½ teaspoon salt together in colander set in large bowl. Let drain for 30 minutes. Place onion in small bowl, cover with ice water, and let sit for 15 minutes. Whisk vinegar, oregano, pepper, and remaining ¾ teaspoon salt together in second small bowl.

2 Discard tomato juice and transfer tomatoes to now-empty bowl. Drain onion and add to bowl with tomatoes. Add vinegar mixture, cucumber, bell pepper, olives, and capers and toss to combine. Drizzle with ¼ cup oil and toss gently to coat. Season with salt and pepper to taste. Transfer to serving platter and top with feta. Season each slice of feta with extra oregano to taste. Drizzle feta with remaining 1 tablespoon oil. Serve.

SERVES 4 TO 6

1¾ pounds tomatoes, cored

1¼ teaspoons table salt, divided

½ red onion, sliced thin

2 tablespoons red wine vinegar

1 teaspoon dried oregano, plus extra for seasoning

½ teaspoon pepper

1 English cucumber, quartered lengthwise and cut into ¾-inch pieces

1 green bell pepper, stemmed, seeded, and cut into 2 by ½-inch strips

1 cup pitted olives

2 tablespoons capers, rinsed

5 tablespoons extra-virgin olive oil, divided

1 (8-ounce) block feta cheese, sliced into ½-inch-thick triangles

pai huang gua

SERVES 4

2 English cucumbers

1½ teaspoons kosher salt

4 teaspoons Chinese black vinegar

1 teaspoon garlic, minced to paste

1 tablespoon soy sauce

2 teaspoons toasted sesame oil

1 teaspoon sugar

1 teaspoon sesame seeds, toasted

why this recipe works In the Chinese province of Sichuan, pai huang gua (smashed cucumbers) is traditionally served as a cooling salad with rich, spicy food. It's delicious with beef, chili, or barbecued meats, too. Traditionally, cucumbers are smashed with the side of a cleaver, an all-purpose tool in Chinese kitchens. We used the bottom of a skillet. We placed chunks of English cucumbers, which are nearly seedless and have a thin, crisp skin, in a zipper-lock bag and smashed them into large, irregular pieces, which allowed them to soak up salt quickly and release more liquid, too. The craggy pieces also did a better job of holding on to the dressing than slices would. Black vinegar, an aged rice-based vinegar, added complexity to the soy sauce and sesame dressing. We recommend using Chinese Chinkiang (or Zhenjiang) black vinegar for this dish. If you can't find it, you can substitute 2 teaspoons of unseasoned rice vinegar and 1 teaspoon of balsamic vinegar. A rasp-style grater makes quick work of turning the garlic into a paste. When serving pai huang gua with milder dishes such as grilled fish or chicken, we like to drizzle the cucumbers with Sichuan Chili Oil (recipe follows).

1 Trim and discard ends from cucumbers. Cut cucumbers crosswise into 3 equal lengths. Place pieces in large zipper-lock bag and seal bag. Using small skillet or rolling pin, firmly but gently smash cucumber pieces until flattened and split lengthwise into 3 to 4 spears each. Tear spears into rough 1- to 1½-inch pieces and transfer to colander set in large bowl. Toss pieces with salt and let sit for at least 15 minutes or up to 30 minutes.

2 While cucumbers sit, whisk vinegar and garlic together in small bowl; let sit for at least 5 minutes or up to 15 minutes.

3 Whisk soy sauce, oil, and sugar into vinegar mixture until sugar has dissolved. Transfer cucumbers to medium bowl and discard any extracted liquid. Add dressing and sesame seeds to cucumbers and toss to combine. Serve immediately.

sichuan chili oil
makes about 1½ cups

The hallmark of Sichuan chili oil is a balance between là—the concentrated heat from dried chiles—and má—the numbing effect of Sichuan peppercorns. Blooming the aromatics (ginger, bay leaves, star anise, and cardamom) in vegetable oil brought out their flavors and built a pungent base. We poured this hot oil over the chili powder, which helped build a deep, savory, toasted chili flavor. Sichuan chili powder is similar to red pepper flakes but milder and more finely ground. If you can't find it, gochugaru (Korean red pepper flakes) is a good alternative.

½ cup Sichuan chili powder
2 tablespoons sesame seeds
2 tablespoons Sichuan peppercorns, crushed, divided
½ teaspoon table salt
1 cup vegetable oil
1 (1-inch) piece ginger, sliced into ¼-inch-thick rounds and smashed
2 bay leaves
3 star anise pods
5 green cardamom pods, crushed

Place chili powder, sesame seeds, half of peppercorns, and salt in heatproof bowl. Heat oil, ginger, bay leaves, star anise, cardamom, and remaining peppercorns in small saucepan over low heat. Cook, stirring occasionally, until spices have darkened and mixture is very fragrant, 25 to 30 minutes. Strain oil mixture through fine-mesh strainer into bowl with chili powder mixture (mixture may bubble slightly); discard solids in strainer. Stir well to combine. Let cool completely, transfer mixture to airtight container, and let sit for at least 12 hours before using. (Chili oil can be stored at room temperature for up to 1 week or refrigerated for up to 3 months.)

crispy eggplant salad

why this recipe works Imagine crispy fried eggplant—crunchy on the outside, tender on the inside—soaking up a salty, sweet, spicy dressing. That is what this salad is all about in every satisfying bite. In the test kitchen, we often use our microwave to dehydrate ingredients quickly. So we microwaved the eggplant before shallow-frying it and tossing it with nam prik, a bright Thai condiment made with lime juice, palm sugar, fish sauce, rice vinegar, ginger, garlic, and chiles. Juicy cherry tomatoes, fresh herbs, and crispy fried shallots added color and flavor. Palm sugar yields the best results for this recipe. We prefer Japanese eggplant here, but globe eggplant can be substituted. Italian basil makes a fine substitute for the Thai basil. Chopped dry-roasted peanuts make for a crunchy alternative for fried shallots. Depending on the size of your microwave, you may need to microwave the eggplant in two batches in step 2, if the eggplant is piled up, it will steam rather than dehydrate. Serve this salad with sticky rice, a nice grilled rib eye, or both. Note that this recipe uses unseasoned rice vinegar; we don't recommend using seasoned rice vinegar in its place.

1   Process fish sauce, vinegar, lime juice, palm sugar, ginger, garlic, and chile in blender on high speed until ginger, garlic, and palm sugar are broken down and dressing is mostly smooth, about 1 minute. Transfer to medium serving bowl and stir in tomatoes. Set aside while preparing eggplant.

2   Toss eggplant and salt together in medium bowl. Line entire surface of large microwave-safe dish with double layer of coffee filters and lightly spray with vegetable oil spray. Spread eggplant in even layer over coffee filters. Microwave until eggplant feels dry and pieces shrink to about 1 inch, about 10 minutes, flipping halfway through microwaving to dry sides evenly. Remove plate from microwave and immediately transfer eggplant to paper towel–lined plate.

3   Line rimmed baking sheet or plate with triple layer of paper towels. Add oil to large Dutch oven and heat over medium-high heat to 375 degrees. Fry eggplant, stirring occasionally, until flesh is deep golden brown and edges are crispy, 5 to 7 minutes. Transfer to prepared sheet and blot to remove excess oil. Transfer to bowl with tomatoes and toss to evenly dress.

4   Toss cilantro, mint, and basil together in small bowl. Thoroughly fold half of cilantro mixture into eggplant. Top eggplant mixture with remaining cilantro mixture and sprinkle with shallots. Serve.

SERVES 2 TO 3

- 2   **tablespoons fish sauce**
- 2   **tablespoons unseasoned rice vinegar**
- 2   **tablespoons lime juice**
- 2   **tablespoons palm sugar or packed light brown sugar**
- 1   **(1-inch piece) ginger, peeled and chopped coarse**
- 2   **garlic cloves, chopped coarse**
- ½   **red Thai chile, seeded and sliced thin**
- 6   **ounces cherry tomatoes, halved**
- 2   **large Japanese eggplants (1¼ pounds), halved lengthwise, then cut crosswise into 1½-inch pieces**
- 1   **teaspoon kosher salt**
- 2   **cups vegetable oil for frying**
- 1½ **cups mixed fresh cilantro leaves, mint leaves, and Thai basil leaves**
- ½   **cup Microwave-Fried Shallots (page 48)**

grilled vegetable and halloumi salad

why this recipe works This warm, hearty salad is a flavorful mélange of perfectly charred vegetables and chunks of briny halloumi cheese. Halloumi has a solid consistency and high melting point, making it perfect for grilling. After just 10 minutes on the grill, the radicchio, eggplant, zucchini, and cheese were perfectly browned, tender, and redolent with smoky flavor. We chopped the vegetables and cheese before tossing everything with a honey and thyme vinaigrette and topping the salad with Crispy Chickpeas (page 47).

1   Whisk honey, thyme, garlic, ¼ teaspoon salt, lemon zest and juice, and ⅛ teaspoon pepper together in large bowl; set aside. Brush eggplant, radicchio, zucchini, and halloumi with 2 tablespoons oil and sprinkle with remaining ½ teaspoon salt and remaining ½ teaspoon pepper.

2A   for a charcoal grill Open bottom vent completely. Light large chimney starter half filled with charcoal briquettes (3 quarts). When top coals are partially covered with ash, pour evenly over grill. Set cooking grate in place, cover, and open lid vent completely. Heat grill until hot, about 5 minutes.

2B   for a gas grill Turn all burners to high; cover; and heat grill until hot, about 15 minutes. Turn all burners to medium.

3   Clean and oil cooking grate. Place vegetables and cheese on grill. Cook (covered if using gas), flipping as needed, until radicchio is softened and lightly charred, 3 to 5 minutes, and remaining vegetables and cheese are softened and lightly charred, about 10 minutes. Transfer vegetables and cheese to baking sheet as they finish cooking, let cool slightly, then cut into 1-inch pieces.

4   Whisking constantly, slowly drizzle remaining 2 tablespoons oil into honey mixture until emulsified. Add vegetables and cheese and toss gently to coat. Season with salt and pepper to taste. Sprinkle with chickpeas and serve.

SERVES 4 TO 6

- 3   tablespoons honey
- 1   tablespoon minced fresh thyme or rosemary
- 1   garlic clove, minced
- ¾   teaspoon table salt, divided
- ½   teaspoon grated lemon zest plus 3 tablespoons juice
- ⅛   teaspoon plus ½ teaspoon pepper, divided
- 1   pound eggplant, sliced into ½-inch-thick rounds
- 1   head radicchio (10 ounces), quartered
- 1   zucchini or summer squash, halved lengthwise
- 1   (8-ounce) block halloumi cheese, sliced into ¼-inch-thick slabs
- ¼   cup extra-virgin olive oil, divided
- ½   cup Crispy Chickpeas (page 47)

fiddlehead panzanella

SERVES 6

1 pound fiddleheads, trimmed and cleaned

½ teaspoon table salt, divided, plus salt for blanching fiddleheads

6 ounces ciabatta or sourdough bread, cut into ¾-inch pieces (4 cups)

½ cup extra-virgin olive oil, divided

1 garlic clove, minced to paste

½ teaspoon pepper, divided

¼ cup red wine vinegar

5 ounces grape or cherry tomatoes, halved

2 ounces goat or feta cheese, crumbled (½ cup)

¼ cup chopped fresh basil or mint

why this recipe works Fiddlehead ferns, a foraged delicacy, are often sautéed or pickled. We wanted to create a dish to showcase their showstopping spiral look and unique flavor and texture. We envisioned a bread salad like Italian panzanella but with bright-green fiddleheads. Since fiddleheads should not be eaten raw, blanching before any further preparation ensures that they are edible and fully clean and also keeps their color a vivid green. We tried sautéing them with aromatics after blanching, but that turned our ferns an unappealing shade of brown green, and the aromatics masked their fresh asparagus-like flavor. So we returned to simply blanching them before tossing them with rich, chewy-crispy croutons; grape tomatoes; a simple vinaigrette; fresh basil; and creamy goat cheese. A rasp-style grater makes quick work of turning the garlic into a paste. Be sure to set up the ice bath before cooking the fiddleheads; plunging them into the cold water immediately after blanching retains their bright-green color and ensures that they don't overcook.

1 Bring 4 quarts water to boil in large pot. Fill large bowl halfway with ice and water. Add fiddleheads and 1 tablespoon salt to boiling water and cook until crisp-tender, about 5 minutes. Drain fiddleheads in colander and immediately transfer to ice bath; let sit until cool, about 2 minutes. Transfer fiddleheads to platter lined with triple layer of paper towels and dry well.

2 Toss bread, 3 tablespoons water, and ¼ teaspoon salt together in large bowl, squeezing bread gently until water is absorbed. Add ¼ cup oil and bread mixture to 12-inch nonstick skillet and cook over medium-high heat, stirring often, until browned and crisp, 7 to 10 minutes.

3 Off heat, push bread to sides of skillet. Add 1 tablespoon oil, garlic, and ¼ teaspoon pepper and cook using residual heat of skillet, mashing mixture into skillet, until fragrant, about 10 seconds. Stir bread into garlic mixture, then transfer croutons to bowl to cool slightly, about 5 minutes.

4 Whisk vinegar, remaining ¼ teaspoon salt, remaining 3 tablespoons oil, and remaining ¼ teaspoon pepper together in large bowl. Add fiddleheads, croutons, and tomatoes and toss gently to coat. Season with salt and pepper to taste. Transfer to serving platter and sprinkle with goat cheese and basil. Serve.

caesar green bean salad

why this recipe works This inventive approach to Caesar salad turns to green beans instead of leafy greens for the salad base. To keep the flavors bold and prevent the green beans from becoming waterlogged, we blanched them in boiling salted water and, instead of shocking them in ice water, transferred them to a towel-lined baking sheet to cool down. To make a Caesar dressing that would cling well to the beans, we combined lemon juice, Worcestershire sauce, garlic, anchovies, and extra-virgin olive oil and emulsified the dressing with Dijon mustard. To add texture to the salad and keep with some tradition, we tossed crispy croutons into the dressed beans.

1 Whisk lemon juice, Worcestershire, mustard, garlic, anchovies, pepper, and salt together in bowl. Whisking constantly, slowly drizzle in oil until emulsified; set aside. (Dressing can be refrigerated for up to 24 hours; whisk to recombine before using.)

2 Line baking sheet with clean dish towel. Bring 4 quarts water to boil in large Dutch oven. Add green beans and 1½ teaspoons salt; return to boil; and cook until tender, 5 to 7 minutes. Drain green beans in colander and spread in even layer on prepared sheet. Let green beans cool completely.

3 Transfer dressing, green beans, half of Parmesan, and croutons to large bowl and toss to combine. Season with salt and pepper to taste. Transfer to serving dish. Sprinkle with remaining Parmesan. Serve.

SERVES 4 TO 6

1½ tablespoons lemon juice

1 tablespoon Worcestershire sauce

1 tablespoon Dijon mustard

3 garlic cloves, minced

3 anchovy fillets, rinsed and minced to paste

½ teaspoon pepper

¼ teaspoon table salt, plus salt for blanching beans

3 tablespoons extra-virgin olive oil

1½ pounds green beans, trimmed

2 ounces Parmesan or Pecorino Romano cheese, shaved with vegetable peeler, divided

½ cup Classic Croutons (page 44)

green bean salad with shallot, mustard, and tarragon

why this recipe works Green beans star in this simple, fresh summer salad. To keep the beans tender and bright green while flavoring them throughout, we blanched them in highly concentrated salt water (¼ cup of salt to 2 quarts of water). This quickly softened the pectin in the beans' skins, so they became tender before losing their vibrant color; it also seasoned them inside and out. If you don't own a salad spinner, lay the green beans on a clean dish towel to dry in step 2.

1   Place shallot, vinegar, and salt in large bowl and toss to combine; set aside. Bring 2 quarts water to boil in large saucepan over high heat. Fill large bowl halfway with ice and water. Add green beans and ¼ cup salt to boiling water and cook until green beans are bright green and tender, 5 to 8 minutes.

2   Drain green beans in colander and immediately transfer to ice bath. When green beans are no longer warm to touch, drain in colander and dry thoroughly in salad spinner. (Blanched, shocked, and dried green beans can be refrigerated in zipper-lock bag for up to 2 days.)

3   Add green beans, oil, mustard, capers, tarragon, and pepper to bowl with shallot mixture and toss to combine. Transfer to platter and serve.

SERVES 4 TO 6

- 1   shallot, sliced thin
- 1   tablespoon white wine vinegar
- ¼   teaspoon table salt, plus salt for blanching beans
- 1½ pounds green beans, trimmed and cut into 1- to 2-inch lengths
- 3   tablespoons extra-virgin olive oil
- 1   tablespoon Dijon mustard
- 1   tablespoon capers, rinsed and minced
- 2   teaspoons minced fresh tarragon or chives
- ¼   teaspoon pepper

cape gooseberries

Cape gooseberries resemble their close relative, the tomatillo, and have no connection to American gooseberries (which belong to the currant family) with whom they share a name. Cape gooseberries got their name either because they were grown on the Cape of Good Hope, South Africa, at the turn of the 19th century or because of their cape-like husk. Their scientific name is *Physalis peruviana* (they originated in Peru); they are also known as Inca berry, husk cherry, and golden berry. Today they are cultivated in South America, South Africa, Australia, and New Zealand and make a wonderful salad topper.

cape gooseberry salad with ginger-lime dressing

why this recipe works Lightly sweet Cape gooseberries have a unique taste, with hints of tomato, green grapes, and pineapple, that is enhanced by a bold dressing and creamy, tangy goat cheese in this delicate salad. The simple vinaigrette, made with lime juice, fresh ginger, Dijon mustard, and cayenne pepper, added bright freshness without overpowering the gooseberries' mild flavor. Simply whisking the dressing together in the salad bowl before tossing in the remaining ingredients made the salad easy to prepare. Bibb lettuce added bulk and a delicate buttery bite. Mint gave a refreshing twist to the vinaigrette and complemented the lime juice and ginger. Goat cheese made for a nice creamy counterpoint to the dressing and sweet gooseberries, and a final sprinkle of pistachios added crunch. Adjust the amount of lime juice depending on the sweetness level of your Cape gooseberries.

Whisk lime juice, ginger, mustard, salt, and cayenne together in large bowl. Whisking constantly, slowly drizzle in oil until emulsified. Add lettuce, gooseberries, and mint and toss gently to coat. Season with salt and pepper to taste. Transfer to serving platter and sprinkle with goat cheese and pistachios. Serve.

SERVES 4 TO 6

- 2-3 teaspoons lime juice
- 1 teaspoon grated fresh ginger
- ½ teaspoon Dijon mustard
- ¼ teaspoon table salt
- Pinch cayenne pepper
- ¼ cup extra-virgin olive oil
- 1 head Bibb or Boston lettuce (8 ounces), leaves separated and torn into 2-inch pieces
- 8 ounces Cape gooseberries, husks and stems removed, rinsed well and dried, halved
- ¼ cup chopped fresh mint or parsley
- 1½ ounces goat cheese, crumbled (⅓ cup)
- 2 tablespoons chopped toasted pistachios or almonds

honeydew salad with peanuts and lime

SERVES 4 TO 6

⅓ cup lime juice (3 limes)

1 shallot, sliced thin

2 Thai chiles, stemmed, seeded, and minced

1 garlic clove, minced

½ teaspoon table salt

1-2 tablespoons sugar (optional)

1 tablespoon fish sauce

1 honeydew melon, peeled, halved, seeded, and cut into 1½-inch pieces (6 cups)

5 tablespoons chopped fresh cilantro or mint, divided

5 tablespoons chopped fresh mint or basil, divided

5 tablespoons salted dry-roasted peanuts, chopped fine, divided

why this recipe works Melon salads are ideal hot-weather fare, but they're prone to some common pitfalls: namely, watered-down dressings and garnishes that slide to the bottom of the salad bowl. Because honeydew melons vary in sweetness, we started by tasting our melon to determine how much sugar to incorporate into our dressing. To counter the abundant water contributed by the melon, we made an assertive dressing with lime juice, fish sauce, shallot, and Thai chiles, but we skipped the oil, which would only be repelled by the water on the surface of the melon. Instead we added richness with dry-roasted peanuts, which—when chopped fine—adhered to the surface of the melon pieces and held on to the dressing. To further avoid watering down the dressing, we cut the melon in large chunks, which released less juice and accentuated the contrast between the well-seasoned exterior and the sweet, juicy interior. Taste your melon as you cut it up: If it's very sweet, omit the sugar; if it's less sweet, add sugar to the dressing. This salad makes a light and refreshing accompaniment to grilled meat or fish and steamed white rice.

1   Combine lime juice and shallot in large bowl. Using mortar and pestle (or on cutting board using flat side of chef's knife), mash Thai chiles, garlic, and salt to fine paste. Add chile paste; sugar, if using; and fish sauce to lime juice mixture and stir to combine.

2   Add honeydew, ¼ cup cilantro, ¼ cup mint, and ¼ cup peanuts and toss to combine. Transfer to shallow serving bowl. Sprinkle with remaining 1 tablespoon cilantro, remaining 1 tablespoon mint, and remaining 1 tablespoon peanuts and serve.

crispy and creamy kale salad

SERVES 4

crispy kale topping

3½	ounces kale, stemmed and cut into 2-inch pieces
2	tablespoons vegetable oil
4	teaspoons sesame seeds, toasted
½	teaspoon kosher salt
¼	teaspoon sugar
¼	teaspoon cayenne pepper

salad

5	ounces kale, stemmed and cut into 2-inch pieces
1	cup sliced almonds or chopped pecans, toasted, divided
1½	cups fresh parsley leaves or dill fronds
6	tablespoons water
¼	cup grated Pecorino Romano or Parmesan cheese
3	tablespoons lemon juice
2	teaspoons fresh thyme or rosemary leaves
½	teaspoon kosher salt
¼	teaspoon sugar
¼	cup vegetable oil

why this recipe works Kale, packed with nutrients, has been hailed as a "superfood." But what we love is its versatility. Kale is delicious in pasta, sautéed, crisped into chips, or served wilted or raw in salads. Here we topped dressed kale with crunchy, salty kale chips. We also used almonds in two ways; we blended some into a bright herb and lemon pesto-like dressing for creamy richness, and added more sliced almonds to the salad. The result was simple and texturally interesting. We prefer Tuscan kale (also known as dinosaur or lacinato kale) to curly kale in this recipe, but both will work. Do not use baby kale.

1 for the crispy kale topping Adjust oven rack to middle position and heat oven to 275 degrees. Line rimmed baking sheet with parchment paper. Place kale in large bowl, cover with warm water, and swish to remove grit. Let kale sit in warm water bath for 10 minutes. Remove kale from water and spin dry in salad spinner in multiple batches. Pat kale dry with paper towels if still wet. Toss kale and oil in medium bowl until kale is well coated, about 30 seconds. Spread kale evenly on prepared sheet. Wipe bowl clean with paper towels. Bake kale until dry, crispy, and translucent, 30 to 40 minutes, turning leaves halfway through baking. Carefully remove kale and return it to bowl, leaving excess oil on sheet. (Crispy kale can be stored in paper towel–lined airtight container for up to 24 hours.)

2 Thoroughly combine sesame seeds, salt, sugar, and cayenne in small bowl. Toss crispy kale and sesame seed mixture gently until evenly coated and kale is broken into ½- to 1-inch pieces.

3 for the salad Place kale in large bowl, cover with warm water, and swish to remove grit. Let kale sit in warm water bath for 10 minutes. Remove kale from water and spin dry in salad spinner in multiple batches. Pat kale dry with paper towels if still wet. Combine kale and ¾ cup almonds in large bowl.

4   Process parsley, water, Pecorino, lemon juice, thyme, salt, sugar, and remaining ¼ cup almonds in blender on high speed until finely ground, about 30 seconds. With blender running, slowly add oil and process until incorporated and smooth and creamy, about 1 minute 30 seconds, scraping down sides of blender jar halfway through processing. Transfer ¾ cup dressing to bowl with kale mixture; toss until kale is well coated. Season with salt and pepper to taste. Divide salad among individual plates. Serve, sprinkling individual portions with crispy kale topping and drizzling with remaining dressing.

shaved mushroom and celery salad

SERVES 6

8 ounces cremini or white button mushrooms, trimmed and sliced thin

¼ cup extra-virgin olive oil

1 shallot, halved and sliced thin

1½ tablespoons lemon juice

¼ teaspoon table salt

4 celery ribs, sliced thin, plus ½ cup celery leaves

2 ounces Parmesan or Pecorino Romano cheese, shaved

½ cup fresh parsley leaves or chives

2 tablespoons chopped fresh tarragon

why this recipe works The softness of mushrooms contrasts with the crispness of celery in this salad. To start, we chose earthy, full-flavored cremini mushrooms. We use a mandoline or peeler to shave ingredients such as zucchini and jicama (page 245) for some recipes, or even Parmesan for this dish. But slicing mushrooms with a knife was easier and safer. We marinated the slices in a bright lemon dressing for 10 minutes to soften and season them. Celery and parsley gave freshness; tarragon added pleasant, anise-like bittersweetness; and Parmesan tossed in just before serving brought nutty, salty richness. If your celery came without its leaves, you can substitute an extra 1 to 2 tablespoons chopped fresh parsley. Slice the mushrooms and celery as thinly as possible; this keeps the texture cohesive and allows the dressing to be absorbed more easily. Make sure not to marinate the mushrooms for longer than 10 minutes, or the salad will be watery.

1 Combine mushrooms, oil, shallot, lemon juice, and salt in large bowl. Toss to coat, then let sit until flavors meld, about 10 minutes.

2 Add celery ribs and leaves, Parmesan, parsley, and tarragon to mushroom-shallot mixture and toss to combine. Season with salt and pepper to taste. Serve.

grilled octopus salad with orange and smoked paprika

SERVES 4

- 1 (4-pound) octopus, rinsed
- 2 cups dry white wine
- 6 garlic cloves (4 peeled and smashed, 2 minced)
- 2 bay leaves
- 7 tablespoons extra-virgin olive oil, divided
- ⅓ cup juice plus 1 teaspoon grated lemon zest (2 lemons)
- 3 tablespoons sherry vinegar
- 2 teaspoons smoked paprika
- 1 teaspoon sugar
- ¼ teaspoon table salt
- ¼ teaspoon pepper
- 1 large orange
- 2 celery ribs, sliced thin on bias
- 1 red, orange, or yellow bell pepper, stemmed, seeded, and cut into 2-inch-long matchsticks
- ½ cup pitted brine-cured olives, halved
- 2 tablespoons chopped fresh parsley or chives

why this recipe works Octopus is visually stunning and. when cooked well, it tastes a lot like lobster. It also takes on the flavors of what it is cooked with. Octopus collagen and connective tissue break down with gentle, low-heat cooking, so we slowly simmered it in an aromatic mix of water, wine, garlic, and bay leaves. We quickly grilled the octopus; sliced it thin; and marinated it in lemon juice, olive oil, sherry vinegar, smoked paprika, and garlic. The marinade became a salad dressing when mixed with vegetables, green olives, and parsley. Octopus can be found cleaned and frozen in the seafood section of specialty grocery stores and Asian markets. Be sure to rinse the defrosted octopus well, as sand can collect in the suckers. The octopus's membrane-like skin is easiest to peel while still warm, so be sure to do so as soon as it's cool enough to handle. You can thaw frozen octopus in a large container under cold running water; it will be ready in about 2 hours.

1 Using sharp knife, separate octopus mantle (large sac) and body (lower section with tentacles) from head (midsection containing eyes); discard head. Place octopus, wine, smashed garlic, and bay leaves in large pot; add water to cover octopus by 2 inches; and bring to simmer over high heat. Reduce heat to low; cover; and simmer gently, flipping octopus occasionally, until skin between tentacle joints tears easily when pulled, 45 minutes to 1¼ hours.

2 Transfer octopus to cutting board and let cool slightly; discard cooking liquid. Using paring knife, cut mantle in half, then trim and scrape away skin and interior fibers; transfer to bowl. Using your fingers, remove skin from body, being careful not to remove suction cups from tentacles. Cut tentacles from around core of body in three sections; discard core. Separate tentacles and transfer to bowl.

3 Whisk 6 tablespoons oil, lemon juice and zest, vinegar, paprika, sugar, salt, pepper, and minced garlic together in bowl; transfer to 1-gallon zipper-lock bag and set aside.

4A for a charcoal grill Open bottom vent completely. Light large chimney starter filled with charcoal briquettes (6 quarts). When top coals are partially covered with ash, pour evenly over half of grill. Set grate in place, cover, and open lid vent completely. Heat grill until hot, about 5 minutes.

4B   for a gas grill Turn all burners to high; cover; and heat grill until hot, about 15 minutes. Leave all burners on high.

5   Toss octopus with remaining 1 tablespoon oil. Clean cooking grate, then repeatedly brush grate with well-oiled paper towels until black and glossy, 5 to 10 times. Place octopus on grill (directly over coals if using charcoal). Cook (covered if using gas) until octopus is streaked with dark grill marks and lightly charred at tips of tentacles, 8 to 10 minutes, flipping halfway through; transfer to cutting board.

6   While octopus is still warm, slice on bias ¼ inch thick, then transfer to zipper-lock bag with oil-lemon mixture and toss to coat. Press out as much air from bag as possible and seal bag. Refrigerate for at least 2 hours or up to 24 hours, flipping bag occasionally.

7   Transfer octopus and marinade to large bowl and let come to room temperature, about 2 hours. Cut away peel and pith from orange. Holding fruit over bowl with octopus, use paring knife to slice between membranes to release segments. Add celery, bell pepper, olives, and parsley and toss gently to coat. Season with salt and pepper to taste. Serve.

jicama

A root vegetable with a brown skin and
crisp, juicy white flesh that is often eaten
raw, jicama has a slightly nutty sweet flavor
that falls between a pear and an apple.
A native of Mexico, jicama (also known
as the yam bean, the Mexican potato,
and the Chinese turnip) is packed with
antioxidants. Widely available in grocery
stores across the United States, jicama
makes a great snack, like carrots or bell
pepper, to be eaten on its own or with a
dip. We love jicama's crunch in salads and
it has the distinct advantage of not getting
discolored after peeling or cutting.

orange-jicama salad with sweet and spicy peppers

why this recipe works Fresh oranges in salad are tantalizing, if their juice doesn't dilute the flavor of the dish too much. To prevent that, drain oranges well before tossing them with other ingredients; toss fruit gently; and don't use greens, which bruise easily. If you do want greens, use a small amount and place them, tossed separately, on top of the fruit as in Citrus Salad with Watercress, Dried Cranberries, and Pecans (page 180). In this recipe jicama adds crunch and chiles give heat, balanced by the sweet oranges. Toast the cumin in a dry skillet over medium heat until fragrant (about 30 seconds), then remove the pan from the heat so that the cumin doesn't scorch. For more spice, reserve, mince, and add the ribs and seeds from the jalapeños.

1 Cut away peel and pith from oranges. Halve oranges from end to end. Cut each half lengthwise into 3 wedges, then cut crosswise into ¼-inch pieces. Place orange pieces in fine-mesh strainer set over bowl; let drain to remove excess juice.

2 Whisk lime juice, cumin, ½ teaspoon salt, and mustard together in large bowl. Whisking constantly, slowly drizzle in oil until emulsified.

3 Toss jicama and bell peppers with remaining ¼ teaspoon salt in large bowl until combined. Add jicama mixture, jalapeños, cilantro, scallions, and oranges to bowl with dressing and toss well to combine. Divide salad among individual plates, drizzle with any remaining dressing in bowl, and serve immediately.

SERVES 8

- 6 oranges
- 6 tablespoons lime juice (3 limes)
- 1 teaspoon ground cumin, toasted
- ¾ teaspoon table salt, divided
- ½ teaspoon Dijon mustard
- ½ cup vegetable oil
- 2 pounds jicama, peeled and cut into 2-inch-long matchsticks
- 2 red, orange, or yellow bell peppers, stemmed, seeded, and cut into ⅛-inch-wide strips
- 4 jalapeño or serrano chiles, stemmed, seeded, quartered lengthwise, and quarters sliced crosswise ⅛ inch thick
- 1 cup fresh cilantro or parsley, chopped
- 6 scallions, green parts only, sliced thin on bias

green papaya

The papaya fruit (known as pawpaw in the Caribbean) originated in southern Mexico but is now a part of life worldwide and is frequently used in Southeast Asian cuisines, especially in salads. Antioxidant-rich, the papaya is also said to aid digestion through an enzyme called papain. Although green and orange papaya are very different in taste, texture, and appearance, they are the same fruit picked at different stages of development. The tender, creamy, sweet, orange-fleshed papaya is fully mature (though the exterior may still be green) and unctuously sweet and fragrant. The crisp white flesh of immature green papaya has very little inherent flavor but takes on other flavors easily, such as in som tam. It is also refreshingly crisp and crunchy. Naturally, it is also delicious pickled because it adopts the flavor of spices it is preserved with.

som tam

why this recipe works Som tam (som—sour, tam—pounding), a northeastern Thai classic, is a crunchy, tart-spicy dish made with green papaya. In Thailand, papaya is often held in the hand and shredded with a machete-size knife but grating the fruit with a box grater worked. Its firm flesh can be hard to chew, so traditionally, a mortar and pestle are used to pound the shredded papaya to soften it, which allows the dressing to penetrate easily. We tested pounding, blanching, and salting. We liked salting, but to save a step and prevent the papaya from getting oversalted, we simply macerated it in our garlic, lime juice, fish sauce, palm sugar, and Thai chile dressing for 30 minutes to an hour. Dried shrimp added a savory, fishy flavor. We added green beans and tomatoes for crunch, finishing the dish with crunchy peanuts. Do not use ripe, orange papaya; it will not work here. You can swap in 1½ pounds jicama (peeled, quartered, and shredded) for the papaya, if desired. You can substitute 1–2 serranos or ½–1 jalapeño for the Thai chiles. For a spicier dish, use the larger number of chiles.

1   Using mortar and pestle (or on cutting board using flat side of chef's knife), mash 1 tablespoon sugar; Thai chiles; shrimp, if using; and garlic to fine paste. Transfer to large bowl. Whisk in lime juice, fish sauce, and remaining 1 tablespoon sugar until sugar has dissolved. Quarter each papaya half. Using large holes of box grater or shredding disk of food processor, shred papaya. Transfer papaya to bowl with dressing and toss to coat. Let sit until flavors meld, at least 30 minutes or up to 1 hour, tossing occasionally.

2   Microwave green beans and 1 tablespoon water in covered bowl, stirring occasionally, until tender, about 4 minutes. Drain green beans and immediately rinse with cold water. Once cool, drain again and dry thoroughly with paper towels. Add green beans and tomatoes to papaya mixture and toss to combine. Season with extra lime juice and fish sauce to taste. Transfer salad to serving platter and sprinkle with peanuts. Serve.

SERVES 4 TO 6

- 2 tablespoons palm sugar or packed brown sugar, divided
- 2-4 Thai chiles, stemmed and sliced thin
- 2 tablespoons minced dried shrimp (optional)
- 1 garlic clove, minced
- 3 tablespoons lime juice (2 limes), plus extra for seasoning
- 2 tablespoons fish sauce, plus extra for seasoning
- 1 green papaya (2 pounds), peeled, halved lengthwise, and seeded
- 4 ounces green beans, trimmed and cut on bias into 1-inch lengths
- 3 ounces cherry or grape tomatoes, quartered
- 3 tablespoons chopped dry-roasted peanuts

roasted pattypan squash and corn salad

SERVES 4 TO 6

dressing

1 ounce dandelion greens, trimmed and torn into bite-size pieces (1 cup)

3 tablespoons roasted sunflower seeds

3 tablespoons water

1 tablespoon maple syrup

1 tablespoon cider vinegar

1 garlic clove, minced

¼ teaspoon table salt

⅛ teaspoon red pepper flakes

¼ cup sunflower oil or extra-virgin olive oil

salad

2 tablespoons sunflower oil or extra-virgin olive oil

2 teaspoons maple syrup

½ teaspoon table salt

⅛ teaspoon pepper

1½ pounds baby pattypan squash, halved horizontally

4 ears corn, kernels cut from cob

1 pound ripe tomatoes, cored, cut into ½-inch thick wedges, and wedges halved crosswise

1 ounce dandelion greens, trimmed and torn into bite-size pieces (1 cup)

2 tablespoons roasted sunflower seeds

why this recipe works To make a salad showcasing a vegetable native to the Americas—pattypan squash—we paired it with other native foods: sweet corn and fresh tomatoes in a vibrant dressing of pureed sunflower seeds and peppery dandelion greens. Pattypans come in different sizes; we chose baby green and yellow ones for their tender skin and vibrant flavor (some say the squash loses flavor as it matures). Roasting the squash on a sheet pan was the fastest and easiest way to cook it all in one batch. Cutting it in half horizontally before roasting allowed us to keep its lovely shape intact, and adding corn to the sheet pan reduced our overall cooking time. First we tossed the squash and corn in oil and maple syrup to complement the squash's sweet, creamy profile and promote browning. We didn't even have to turn the squash during roasting—it retained its bright color and was fully cooked through. You can use baby arugula or watercress instead of dandelion greens. Preheat your oven while you make the dressing. Use baby pattypan squash that measure between 1½ and 2 inches in diameter. If you can't find baby pattypan squash, you can use zucchini or summer squash cut crosswise into 1-inch-thick rounds.

1 for the dressing Adjust oven rack to lowest position, place rimmed baking sheet on rack, and heat oven to 500 degrees. Process dandelion greens, sunflower seeds, water, maple syrup, vinegar, garlic, salt, and pepper flakes in food processor until finely ground, about 1 minute, scraping down sides of bowl as needed. With processor running, slowly drizzle in oil until incorporated. (Dressing can be refrigerated for up to 2 days.)

2 for the salad Whisk oil, maple syrup, salt, and pepper together in large bowl. Add squash and corn and toss to coat. Working quickly, spread vegetables in single layer on hot sheet, arranging squash cut side down. Roast until cut side of squash is browned and tender, 15 to 18 minutes. Transfer pan to wire rack and let cool slightly, about 15 minutes.

3 Combine roasted squash and corn, half of dressing, tomatoes, and dandelion greens in large bowl and toss gently to combine. Drizzle with remaining dressing and sprinkle with sunflower seeds. Serve.

pattypan

If you've seen this vegetable, with the cute name and cute look, at the grocery store and wondered how to cook it, here's your answer. Technically a summer squash, pattypans are available year-round, so they are perfect both for summer grilling and winter roasting. Delicious stuffed, they make great individual servings because of their size. Small; round; and yellow, green, or white, with scalloped edges, pattypans are delicious, with a rich buttery flavor and creamy texture. Not often used in salads, we find that they are an unexpectedly delicious and hearty addition that makes for a satisfying vegetarian meal or a rich and colorful first course. The squash keep for 4–5 days in your refrigerator, stored in a zipper-lock bag. Simply rinse, pat dry, and use. No peeling required.

peach caprese salad

why this recipe works A traditional caprese shows off ripe tomatoes and fresh mozzarella simply, using good-quality extra-virgin olive oil and slightly sweet balsamic vinegar. We wanted to preserve this salad's purity but swap in another juicy summer gem: ripe fresh peaches. Balsamic vinegar simply muddied our fruit's brightness but we found that fresh lemon juice enhanced and complemented the sweet peaches. To make the salad cohesive, we tossed peach slices with a lemon-and-oil dressing before assembling the salad, ensuring that each bite was fully coated and seasoned. For the best results, use high-quality, ripe, in-season peaches with a fragrant aroma and flesh that yields slightly when gently pressed. We like using 4-ounce balls of fresh mozzarella in this recipe.

1 Whisk oil, lemon juice, salt, and pepper together in large bowl. Add peaches and toss gently to coat.

2 Shingle peaches and mozzarella on serving platter. Drizzle any remaining dressing from bowl over top. Sprinkle with basil. Season with salt and pepper to taste. Serve.

SERVES 4 TO 6

3 tablespoons extra-virgin olive oil

1½ tablespoons lemon juice

¼ teaspoon table salt

⅛ teaspoon pepper

1 pound ripe but slightly firm peaches, quartered and pitted, each quarter cut into 4 slices

12 ounces fresh mozzarella cheese, balls halved and sliced ¼ inch thick

6 large fresh basil or mint leaves, torn into small pieces

grilled peach and tomato salad with burrata and basil

SERVES 4 TO 6

peaches

1½ pounds ripe but slightly firm peaches (4 peaches), halved and pitted

2 tablespoons unsalted butter, melted

salad

12 ounces ripe tomatoes, cored and cut into ½-inch pieces

¾ teaspoon table salt, divided

5 tablespoons extra-virgin olive oil, divided

1 tablespoon white wine vinegar

8 ounces burrata cheese, room temperature

⅓ cup chopped fresh basil or parsley

why this recipe works For this salad, we chose to grill our peaches to enhance their aroma and sweetness. To prevent the peaches from sticking to the grill and to add welcome Maillard browning, we first halved them and brushed their cut faces with melted butter. We grilled them over high heat to give the fruit a custardy-soft texture and subtle grill flavor. When grill marks formed, we moved them to a covered baking pan over indirect heat until they were fully softened. Once the peaches were cool enough to handle, we discarded their skins and cut them into wedges. We then tossed the peaches with tomato chunks in a simple vinaigrette of white wine vinegar and extra-virgin olive oil. Creamy burrata cheese added texture and richness to this stunning dish, which is also fabulous made with nectarines or plums. For the best results, use high-quality, ripe, in-season tomatoes and peaches with a fragrant aroma and flesh that yields slightly when gently pressed. Using a metal baking pan on the cooler side of the grill won't harm the pan, but you can use a disposable aluminum pan if preferred; do not use a glass dish. If burrata is unavailable, sliced fresh mozzarella makes a suitable substitute.

1 **for the peaches** Brush cut side of peaches with melted butter.

2A **for a charcoal grill** Open bottom vent completely. Light large chimney starter three-quarters filled with charcoal briquettes (4½ quarts). When top coals are partially covered with ash, pour evenly over half of grill. Set cooking grate in place, cover, and open lid vent completely. Heat grill until hot, about 5 minutes.

2B **for a gas grill** Turn all burners to high; cover; and heat grill until hot, about 15 minutes. Leave primary burner on high and turn off other burner(s).

3 Clean and oil cooking grate. Arrange peaches cut side down on hotter side of grill and cook (covered if using gas) until grill marks have formed, 5 to 7 minutes, moving peaches as needed to ensure even cooking.

4   Transfer peaches cut side up to 13 by 9-inch baking pan and cover loosely with aluminum foil. Place pan on cooler side of grill. If using gas, turn primary burner to medium. Cover and cook until peaches are very tender and paring knife slips in and out with little resistance, 10 to 15 minutes. When peaches are cool enough to handle, discard skins, then let cool completely.

5   **for the salad** While peaches cool, toss tomatoes with ¼ teaspoon salt and let drain in colander for 30 minutes. Cut each peach half into 4 wedges and cut each wedge in half crosswise.

6   Whisk ¼ cup oil, vinegar, and remaining ½ teaspoon salt together in large bowl. Add peaches and tomatoes and toss gently to combine; transfer to shallow serving bowl. Place burrata on top of salad and drizzle with remaining 1 tablespoon oil. Season with pepper to taste, and sprinkle with basil. Serve, breaking up burrata with spoon and allowing creamy liquid to meld with dressing.

salade niçoise

SERVES 6

dressing

- ½ cup lemon juice (3 lemons)
- 1 shallot, minced
- 2 tablespoons finely chopped fresh basil, parsley, or dill
- 1 tablespoon minced fresh thyme or rosemary
- 2 teaspoons minced fresh oregano
- 1 teaspoon Dijon mustard
- ¾ cup extra-virgin olive oil

salad

- 1¼ pounds small red potatoes, quartered
- Table salt for cooking vegetables
- 2 tablespoons dry vermouth
- 2 heads Boston or Bibb lettuce (1 pound), torn into bite-size pieces
- 12 ounces olive oil–packed tuna, drained
- 3 small tomatoes, cored and cut into eighths
- 1 small red onion, sliced very thin
- 8 ounces green beans, trimmed and halved crosswise
- 6 Easy-Peel Hard-Cooked Eggs (page 42), quartered
- ¼ cup pitted Niçoise olives
- 10–12 anchovy fillets, rinsed (optional)
- 2 tablespoons capers, rinsed (optional)

why this recipe works Salade niçoise originated as a working man's dish in the city of Nice in France. It was often served to fishermen when they returned home after a hard day's work. Traditional recipes include one fish—tuna or anchovies—and tomatoes, hard-cooked eggs, spring onions, and local olives on greens. Some local versions include small fava beans, mesclun, cucumber, and radishes too. For our salade niçoise, we wanted to combine well-dressed, well-seasoned components that would complement, not crowd, one another. We paired fruity extra-virgin olive oil with lemon juice for the dressing, then added fresh herbs, shallot, and Dijon mustard. Apart from the tuna, we used ingredients such as vine-ripened tomatoes, Boston lettuce, and low-starch Red Bliss potatoes, which held their shape perfectly. We seasoned and dressed each component of the salad individually. Prepare all the vegetables before you begin cooking the potatoes. For even cooking, use small red potatoes measuring 1 to 2 inches in diameter. Compose the salad on your largest serving platter and leave some space between the mounds of potatoes, tomatoes and onion, and green beans so that leaves of lettuce peek through.

1 for the dressing Whisk lemon juice, shallot, basil, thyme, oregano, and mustard together in medium bowl. Whisking constantly, slowly drizzle in oil until emulsified. Season with salt and pepper to taste. Set aside. (Dressing can be refrigerated up to 24 hours; whisk to recombine before using.)

2 for the salad Bring potatoes and 4 quarts cold water to boil in Dutch oven or stockpot over high heat. Add 1 tablespoon salt and cook until potatoes are tender when poked with paring knife, 5 to 8 minutes. Using slotted spoon, gently transfer potatoes to medium bowl (do not discard boiling water). Toss warm potatoes with vermouth and season with salt and pepper to taste; let sit for 1 minute. Toss in ¼ cup dressing; set aside.

3 While potatoes cook, toss lettuce with ¼ cup dressing in large bowl until coated. Arrange bed of lettuce on very large, flat platter. Place tuna in now-empty bowl and break up with fork. Add ½ cup dressing and stir to combine; mound tuna in center of lettuce. Toss tomatoes and onion with 3 tablespoons dressing in now-empty bowl and season with salt and pepper to taste. Arrange tomato mixture in mound at edge of lettuce bed. Arrange potatoes in separate mound at opposite edge of lettuce bed.

4 Return water to boil; add green beans and 1 table-spoon salt. Cook until crisp-tender, 3 to 5 minutes. Meanwhile, fill large bowl halfway with ice and water. Drain green beans; transfer to ice bath; and let sit until just cool, about 30 seconds. Dry green beans well on triple layer of paper towels. Toss green beans with 3 tablespoons dressing in now-empty bowl and season with salt and pepper to taste. Arrange in separate mound at edge of lettuce bed.

5 Arrange eggs; olives; and anchovies, if using, in separate mounds at edge of lettuce bed. Drizzle eggs with remaining 2 tablespoons dressing; sprinkle salad with capers, if using. Serve immediately.

classic potato salad

why this recipe works Potato salads are arguably the ultimate make-ahead salads. They need time to chill, and doing the prep work ahead of time means that you don't have to scramble at the last minute before a picnic. But this make-ahead recipe abbreviates the waiting time too and offers flavorful, tender potatoes and crunchy bits of onion and celery, accented by a creamy dressing. We found that seasoning the potatoes while they were hot maximized flavor, so we tossed hot russet potatoes with white vinegar. One celery rib added just enough crunch. Choosing between scallions, shallots, and onions, we picked red onion because we liked it best for its bright color and taste. For a pickled flavor, we decided to use relish, which required no preparation and gave the potato salad a subtle sweetness. Note that this recipe calls for celery seeds (which add complexity of flavor), not celery salt; if only celery salt is available, use the same amount but omit the salt in step 3. When testing the potatoes for doneness, simply taste a piece; do not overcook the potatoes or they will become mealy and break apart. The potatoes must be just warm, or even fully cooled, when you add the dressing. If the potato salad seems a little dry, add up to 2 tablespoons more mayonnaise.

1   Place potatoes and 1 tablespoon salt in large saucepan and add water to cover by 1 inch. Bring to boil over medium-high heat. Reduce heat to medium and simmer, stirring occasionally, until potatoes are tender and paring knife can be slipped in and out of potatoes with little resistance, about 8 minutes.

2   Drain potatoes and transfer to large bowl. Add vinegar and use rubber spatula to toss gently to combine. Let sit until potatoes are just warm, about 20 minutes.

3   While potatoes sit, combine mayonnaise, celery, relish, onion, parsley, mustard, celery seeds, pepper, and salt in small bowl. Using rubber spatula, gently fold mayonnaise mixture and eggs, if using, into potatoes. Refrigerate until chilled, about 1 hour. Serve.

SERVES 4 TO 6

- 2 pounds russet potatoes, peeled and cut into ¾-inch pieces
- ½ teaspoon table salt, plus salt for cooking potatoes
- 2 tablespoons distilled white vinegar
- ½ cup mayonnaise
- 1 celery rib, chopped fine
- 3 tablespoons sweet pickle relish
- 2 tablespoons finely chopped red onion
- 2 tablespoons minced fresh parsley or chives
- ¾ teaspoon dry mustard
- ¾ teaspoon celery seeds
- ¼ teaspoon pepper
- 2 Easy-Peel Hard-Cooked Eggs (page 42), peeled and cut into ¼-inch pieces (optional)

german potato salad

SERVES 6 TO 8

2 pounds small red potatoes,
unpeeled, halved if small or
quartered if large

Table salt for cooking potatoes

8 slices bacon, cut into ½-inch pieces

1 red onion, chopped fine

½ teaspoon sugar

½ cup distilled white vinegar

1 tablespoon whole-grain mustard

¼ teaspoon pepper

¼ cup chopped fresh parsley or chives

why this recipe works Unlike other potato salads, German potato salad is best served warm and offers big flavors from bacon and vinegar. To avoid the common problems of disintegrating potatoes and a flavorless vinaigrette, we used low-starch small red potatoes, cut in half and cooked in heavily salted water. For flavor, we fried up plenty of bacon, then used part of the rendered fat in the vinaigrette, along with white vinegar, whole-grain mustard, sugar, and some of the potato cooking water, which added body to the dressing. Use small red potatoes measuring 1 to 2 inches in diameter. A traditional skillet (as opposed to a nonstick skillet) will allow the bacon to form caramelized bits on the skillet bottom. This will result in a richer-tasting dressing and a more flavorful salad.

1   Place potatoes and 1 tablespoon salt in large saucepan or Dutch oven and add water to cover by 1 inch. Bring to boil over high heat; reduce heat to medium; and simmer until potatoes are tender and paring knife can be slipped in and out of potatoes with little resistance, about 10 minutes. Reserve ½ cup potato cooking water, then drain potatoes; return potatoes to pot and cover to keep warm.

2   While potatoes are simmering, cook bacon in 12-inch skillet over medium heat, stirring occasionally, until brown and crispy, 5 to 7 minutes. Using slotted spoon, transfer bacon to paper towel–lined plate; pour off all but ¼ cup fat. Add onion to skillet and cook over medium heat, stirring occasionally until softened and beginning to brown, about 4 minutes. Stir in sugar until dissolved, about 30 seconds. Add vinegar and reserved potato cooking water; bring to simmer and cook until mixture is reduced to about 1 cup, about 3 minutes. Off heat, whisk in mustard and pepper. Add potatoes, parsley, and bacon to skillet and toss to combine; season with salt to taste. Transfer to serving bowl and serve.

gado gado

dressing

- 2 tablespoons red curry paste
- 1 tablespoon vegetable oil
- 3 garlic cloves, minced
- ½ cup coconut milk
- ⅓ cup water
- ¼ cup chunky peanut butter
- 2 tablespoons fish sauce
- 4 teaspoons packed dark brown sugar
- 1 tablespoon tamarind paste
- 2 teaspoons sriracha, plus extra for seasoning
- ¼ cup dry-roasted peanuts, chopped

salad

- 12 ounces small red potatoes, unpeeled

  Table salt for cooking vegetables
- 8 ounces green beans, trimmed
- 8 ounces cauliflower florets, cut into 1-inch pieces
- ½ head green cabbage, cored and sliced thin (6 cups)
- 1 cucumber, peeled and sliced ½ inch thick
- 4 Easy-Peel Hard-Cooked Eggs (page 42), halved lengthwise

why this recipe works Literally translated as "mix mix," gado gado is a classic Indonesian salad that pairs a variety of steamed seasonal vegetables, cabbage, and hard-cooked eggs with a creamy coconut milk–based peanut sauce. To make the peanut sauce, we combined coconut milk with sautéed minced garlic and red curry paste, which packs the flavors of lemongrass, shallots, makrut lime, and chile into a convenient package. Fish sauce and brown sugar approximated the flavors of two more traditional ingredients, fermented shrimp paste and sweetened soy sauce. A little sriracha provided the requisite heat and chile flavor, and tamarind paste provided a tart fruitiness. To give the sauce plenty of peanut flavor, we used chunky peanut butter and added a garnish of freshly chopped peanuts for texture. Finally, for the vegetables, we kept things simple by simmering low-starch, small red potatoes in a saucepan until tender and then blanching green beans and cauliflower in the same water. Shredded cabbage and sliced cucumber, plus the traditional hard-cooked eggs, rounded out the salad, which makes a filling snack or hearty dinner.

1 for the dressing Cook curry paste, oil, and garlic in small saucepan over medium-high heat, stirring often, until mixture begins to stick to pan bottom, 2 to 3 minutes. Whisk in coconut milk, water, peanut butter, fish sauce, sugar, tamarind, and sriracha. Bring to simmer, then reduce heat to low and cook until slightly thickened, 5 to 8 minutes. Transfer to bowl and let cool completely, about 30 minutes, then stir in peanuts. (Dressing can be refrigerated for up to 3 days; whisk to recombine before using.)

2 for the salad Place potatoes and 1 tablespoon salt in large saucepan and add water to cover by 1 inch. Bring to boil over high heat; reduce heat to medium-low; and simmer until potatoes are just tender and paring knife can be slipped in and out of potatoes with little resistance, 10 to 15 minutes. Using slotted spoon, transfer potatoes to baking sheet lined with several layers of paper towels and let drain.

3 Return cooking water to boil over high heat; add green beans; and cook until just tender, 4 to 8 minutes. Using slotted spoon, transfer green beans to colander and rinse under cold running water to cool; transfer to sheet with potatoes.

4 Return cooking water to boil over high heat; add cauliflower; and cook until just tender, 6 to 8 minutes. Using slotted spoon, transfer cauliflower to colander and rinse under cold running water to cool; transfer to sheet with potatoes and green beans.

5 Divide cabbage among individual plates. Cut potatoes into ½-inch wedges. Arrange potatoes, green beans, cauliflower, cucumber, and eggs over cabbage. Drizzle with remaining dressing and season with extra sriracha to taste. Serve.

rhubarb, celery, and radish salad

SERVES 4

- 3 rhubarb stalks, 1 cut into ½-inch pieces, 2 sliced on bias ¼ inch thick
- 1 jalapeño or serrano chile, stemmed, seeded, and cut into ½-inch pieces
- 2 tablespoons lime juice plus 1 tablespoon grated lime zest
- 1 small shallot, sliced thin
- ½ teaspoon pepper
- ¼ teaspoon plus ⅛ teaspoon table salt, divided
- ¼ cup plus 1 teaspoon extra-virgin olive oil, divided
- 8 ounces smoked trout or mackerel (optional)
- 1 celery rib, sliced thin on bias, plus ½ cup celery leaves
- 5 radishes, trimmed and cut into ¼-inch wedges
- ⅛ teaspoon chipotle chile powder
- 2 ounces feta or goat cheese, crumbled (½ cup)
- ½ cup fresh cilantro or mint leaves

why this recipe works Ever wonder what to do with all that rhubarb in your garden if you've had enough pie or jam? Then try this refreshing salad that packs crunch with mouthwatering flavor. The acidity of rhubarb, celery's herbaceousness, and peppery radishes play off each other beautifully. Adding rich and buttery smoked trout makes the salad a meal. We use rhubarb two ways here: thinly sliced and in the dressing. Letting the rhubarb dressing sit briefly allows salt to draw liquid from the rhubarb which becomes part of the dressing. And suddenly you've expanded your rhubarb repertoire. You can substitute ½ cup fresh parsley leaves for the celery leaves. Some smoked trout comes with pin bones in it and some does not. Make sure to check your fish for pin bones before flaking it into pieces. For more spice, reserve, mince, and add the ribs and seeds from the jalapeño.

1 Pulse rhubarb pieces, jalapeño, lime zest and juice, shallot, pepper, and ¼ teaspoon salt in food processor until finely chopped, about 10 pulses. Transfer to bowl and let sit until rhubarb releases its juice, 20 to 25 minutes. Whisk in ¼ cup oil and set aside.

2 Remove skin (and pin bones, if necessary) from trout, if using. Using 2 forks, flake into bite-size pieces. Toss sliced rhubarb, celery, radishes, chile powder, remaining 1 teaspoon oil, and remaining ⅛ teaspoon salt together in bowl. Transfer to serving bowl and sprinkle with feta and smoked trout. Spoon ½ cup dressing over salad and sprinkle with celery leaves and cilantro leaves. Serve, passing remaining dressing separately.

rhubarb

Since it is often paired with strawberries and made into pie, rhubarb is sometimes taken for a fruit. It is actually a sour, astringent vegetable that is transformed into dessert by the power of sugar. But rhubarb can be used in savory dishes such as salads too, adding unexpected fresh, crisp tartness to food. We use it both as dressing and as salad ingredient. Rhubarb leaves contain oxalic acid and anthrone glyacides, making them poisonous, but the stalk has historically been used for medicinal purposes, as a vegetable, and in sweets. The plant was grown in England and Europe long before the 18th century and the story goes that it was introduced into America in 1770 when Benjamin Franklin had a case shipped here from London as a medicine. Rhubarb is available in the summertime, in shades of red and green. Buy either color; the color doesn't indicate ripeness or affect the taste. Separate the stalks from the leaves. Before cooking with rhubarb, wash the stalks well and run a paring knife from top to bottom of each stalk to pull off fibrous threads.

sea vegetables

Sea vegetables include the dozens of edible plants formerly known as seaweed, such as hijiki, kombu, nori, sea beans, and wakame. These are integral to East and Southeast Asian cuisines and add an umami flavor that we like in some of our salads and soups. It doesn't hurt that apart from tasting great, sea vegetables are packed with antioxidants and minerals. They are also pantry-friendly and easy to prepare, often needing just a little rehydration to soften up (see page 227 for more about prepping sea vegetables).

seaweed salad

why this recipe works This refreshing salad is a delicious accompaniment to East and Southeast Asian foods but its combination of three briny sea vegetables makes it a great pairing for seafood dishes from other cuisines too. There's sweet-salty, delicate wakame, the green seaweed in miso soup that you just want to bite into; kombu, a kelp, which adds mushroomy, not fishy, umami (kombu appears in traditional Japanese dashi or broth); and hijiki, with the same umami and a mineral quality. Note that this recipe uses unseasoned rice vinegar; we don't recommend using seasoned rice vinegar in its place.

1   Place wakame and hijiki in medium bowl and add warm water to cover completely. Place kombu in separate medium bowl and add warm water to cover completely. Let seaweed sit until softened (wakame should double in size and kombu should be pliable), about 15 minutes, stirring occasionally.

2   Drain wakame and hijiki in fine-mesh strainer, pressing firmly on seaweed to extract as much water as possible. Transfer wakame and hijiki to paper towel–lined plate and pat dry; set aside.

3   Drain kombu, rinse well, and pat dry with paper towels. Place kombu on cutting board with long side facing you. Roll kombu away from you into tight cylinder, then slice thin crosswise.

4   Whisk vegetable oil, vinegar, sugar, soy sauce, sesame oil, and ginger together in large bowl. Add sesame seeds, reserved wakame and hijiki, and kombu, and toss to combine. Sprinkle with scallions and serve.

MAKES ABOUT 2 CUPS

6 tablespoons (½ ounce) wakame

1½ tablespoons (⅛ ounce) hijiki

¼ ounce kombu

¼ cup vegetable oil

3 tablespoons unseasoned
  rice vinegar

2 tablespoons packed brown sugar

1½ tablespoons soy sauce

1½ teaspoons toasted sesame oil

¾ teaspoon grated fresh ginger

1 tablespoon sesame seeds, toasted

2 scallions, sliced thin on bias

shrimp salad with corn and chipotle

SERVES 4

1 pound extra-large shrimp (21 to 25 per pound), peeled, deveined, and tails removed

5 tablespoons lime juice (4 limes), divided, spent halves reserved

5 sprigs fresh parsley

1 teaspoon whole black peppercorns

1 tablespoon sugar

1 teaspoon table salt

½ cup cooked corn kernels

¼ cup mayonnaise

1 small shallot, minced

2 tablespoons minced canned chipotle chile in adobo sauce

1 tablespoon minced fresh cilantro or parsley

10 cups (10 ounces) mesclun

why this recipe works This shrimp salad heads to the Southwest, adding corn, chipotle chiles, and cilantro to the mix. To keep the shrimp tender, we cooked it in court bouillon, a stock made for poaching fish. To avoid overcooked shrimp, we started with cold cooking liquid, then heated both shrimp and liquid to a near simmer. We paired the shrimp with crunchy shallot, celery, cooked sweet corn, and smoky chipotles. This recipe can also be prepared with large shrimp (31 to 40 per pound); the cooking time will be 1 to 2 minutes less. The recipe can be easily doubled; cook the shrimp in a 7-quart Dutch oven and increase the cooking time to 12 to 14 minutes.

1   Combine shrimp, ¼ cup lime juice, reserved lime halves, parsley sprigs, whole peppercorns, sugar, and salt with 2 cups cold water in medium saucepan. Place saucepan over medium heat and cook shrimp, stirring several times, until pink, firm to touch, and centers are no longer translucent, 8 to 10 minutes (water should be just bubbling around edge of pan and register 165 degrees). Remove pan from heat, cover, and let shrimp sit in broth for 2 minutes.

2   Meanwhile, fill medium bowl with ice water. Drain shrimp into colander; discard lime halves, parsley sprigs, and spices. Immediately transfer shrimp to ice water to stop cooking and let chill thoroughly, about 3 minutes. Remove shrimp from ice water and pat dry with paper towels. (Shrimp can be refrigerated for up to 24 hours.)

3   Whisk corn, mayonnaise, shallot, chipotle, cilantro, and remaining 1 tablespoon lime juice together in medium bowl. Cut shrimp in half lengthwise and then cut each half into thirds; add shrimp to corn mixture and toss to combine. Season with salt and pepper to taste. Serve on mesclun.

smoked salmon
niçoise salad

why this recipe works To vary the classic French Salade Niçoise (page 216), we swap out traditional tuna for flavor-packed smoked salmon and turn this into a beautiful dinner or brunch plate. We also gave the dressing a twist by adding sour cream and dill, ingredients traditionally paired with smoked salmon. These give the salad a certain richness but we also kept customary salade niçoise ingredients such as hard cooked eggs, green beans, potatoes, and olives. Here we cooked the vegetables together, starting the potatoes first and adding the green beans later, ensuring that both finish cooking at the same time. For even cooking, use small red potatoes measuring 1 to 2 inches in diameter.

1 for the dressing Combine sour cream, lemon juice, water, dill, salt, and pepper in small bowl. (Dressing can be refrigerated for up to 4 days.)

2 for the salad Bring 2 quarts water to boil in large saucepan over medium-high heat. Add potatoes and 1½ tablespoons salt; return to boil and cook for 10 minutes. Add green beans and continue to cook until both vegetables are tender, about 4 minutes. Drain.

3 Toss mesclun and ¼ cup sour cream mixture together in large bowl. Divide mesclun, potatoes, green beans, and eggs evenly among individual plates. Top each portion with salmon and olives. Drizzle salads with remaining dressing. Serve.

SERVES 4

dressing

- ⅔ cup sour cream or Greek yogurt
- 2 tablespoons lemon juice
- 2 tablespoons water
- 1 tablespoon chopped fresh dill or parsley
- ¼ teaspoon table salt
- ⅛ teaspoon pepper

salad

- 1 pound small red potatoes, unpeeled, halved

  Table salt for cooking vegetables
- 8 ounces green beans, trimmed
- 10 ounces (10 cups) mesclun greens
- 4 Easy-Peel Hard-Cooked Eggs (page 42), halved
- 8 ounces sliced smoked salmon
- ½ cup pitted olives, halved

steak fajita salad

SERVES 4

1 pound flank steak, trimmed

1 teaspoon chipotle chile powder, divided

1 teaspoon table salt, divided

½ teaspoon pepper

2 tablespoons vegetable oil, divided

2 green bell peppers, stemmed, seeded, and sliced thin

1 small red onion, sliced thin

2 ears corn, kernels cut from cob

2 tablespoons water

2 romaine lettuce hearts (12 ounces), cut into 1-inch pieces

1 cup Chipotle-Yogurt Sauce (page 247), divided

½ cup Crispy Tortilla Strips (recipe follows)

why this recipe works We think the best part of fajitas is mixing and matching toppings to create layers of spicy, smoky, fresh flavor that work together in one delicious bite. Would that work in a salad? It did, allowing each element of the dish to shine. We cooked the flank steak in a 12-inch nonstick skillet instead of grilling it, first searing the chile-spiced meat, then flipping it every minute to ensure even cooking. Then we quickly charred bell pepper and red onion and added fresh corn for sweet pops of crunch. A spicy chipotle–yogurt sauce gave smoky richness to the salad, and as a nod to the tortillas of traditional fajitas, crispy tortilla strips added a welcome crunch.

1   Pat steak dry with paper towels and sprinkle with ½ teaspoon chile powder, ½ teaspoon salt, and pepper. Heat 2 teaspoons oil in 12-inch nonstick skillet over medium-high heat until just smoking. Add steak and cook, turning every minute, until well browned on both sides and meat registers 130 degrees (for medium), 10 to 14 minutes. Transfer to cutting board, tent with aluminum foil, and let rest for 5 minutes.

2   While steak rests, heat remaining 4 teaspoons oil in now-empty skillet over medium-high heat until shimmering. Add bell pepper, onion, corn, water, remaining ½ teaspoon chile powder, and remaining ½ teaspoon salt. Cook, scraping up any browned bits, until peppers and onions are softened and browned, about 8 minutes.

3   Slice steak against grain ¼ inch thick. Toss lettuce with half of sauce to coat, then season with salt and pepper to taste. Divide among individual serving plates. Top with steak and cooked vegetables. Drizzle with remaining sauce and sprinkle with tortilla strips. Serve.

crispy tortilla strips
makes 2 cups
For crunchy tortilla strips that add texture to our salad, we turned to the oven instead of frying.

- 8 (6-inch) corn tortillas, cut into ½-inch-wide strips
- 1 tablespoon vegetable oil

Adjust oven rack to middle position and heat oven to 425 degrees. Toss tortilla strips with oil; spread on rimmed baking sheet; and bake, stirring frequently, until deep golden brown and crispy, 8 to 12 minutes. Transfer to paper towel–lined plate and season with salt to taste. (Tortilla strips can be stored in airtight container at room temperature for up to 1 week.)

grilled sweet potato salad

SERVES 4 TO 6

1 small red onion, sliced into ½-inch-thick rounds

3 tablespoons lime juice (2 limes), plus lime wedges for serving

2 tablespoons honey

1 teaspoon minced canned chipotle chile in adobo sauce

1 teaspoon table salt, divided

¾ teaspoon pepper, divided

½ teaspoon ground cumin

⅓ cup vegetable oil

2½ pounds sweet potatoes, peeled and cut into ½-inch-thick rounds

1 (13 by 9-inch) disposable aluminum pan

2 ounces (2 cups) baby arugula

2 ounces feta or goat cheese, crumbled (½ cup)

3 scallions, sliced thin on bias

¼ cup chopped fresh cilantro or parsley

why this recipe works To bring together two favorite summer traditions—potato salad and grilling—with a twist, we used a winter ingredient, sweet potatoes. We steamed and charred sweet potatoes on the grill, after first tossing them with a spiced dressing in a disposable aluminum pan. The dressing generated steam and helped cook the sweet potatoes through while also seasoning them. Once the sweet potatoes were steamed, we transferred them from the pan to the hot cooking grate to give them some flavorful char. Threading toothpicks through onion rounds kept them intact and prevented them from falling through the grate during cooking. To finish, we sprinkled feta, scallions, and cilantro over the grilled salad. We recommend using medium potatoes, 2 to 3 inches in diameter, because they'll fit neatly in the disposable aluminum pan.

1 Thread 1 toothpick horizontally through each onion round. Whisk lime juice, honey, chipotle, ½ teaspoon salt, ¼ teaspoon pepper, and cumin together in large bowl. Whisking constantly, slowly drizzle in oil until emulsified; set aside.

2 Toss potatoes, onion rounds, ¼ cup dressing, remaining ½ teaspoon salt, and remaining ½ teaspoon pepper together in separate bowl. Place onion rounds in bottom of disposable pan, layer potatoes over top, then pour in any remaining liquid from bowl. Cover disposable pan tightly with aluminum foil.

3A **for a charcoal grill** Open bottom vent completely. Light large chimney starter filled with charcoal briquettes (6 quarts). When top coals are partially covered with ash, pour evenly over grill. Set cooking grate in place, cover, and open lid vent completely. Heat grill until hot, about 5 minutes.

3B **for a gas grill** Turn all burners to high; cover; and heat grill until hot, about 15 minutes. Turn all burners to medium. Adjust burners as needed to maintain grill temperature around 400 degrees.

4 Clean and oil cooking grate. Place disposable pan on grill. Cover grill and cook until vegetables are tender, 20 to 25 minutes, shaking disposable pan halfway through cooking to redistribute potatoes. Remove disposable pan from grill.

5 Place vegetables on cooking grate. Cook (covered if using gas) until lightly charred and tender, 2 to 4 minutes per side. Transfer vegetables and arugula to bowl with remaining dressing, discarding toothpicks from onion rounds and separating rings. Toss vegetables to coat, then transfer to serving platter. Sprinkle feta, scallions, and cilantro over top. Serve with lime wedges.

simplest tomato salad

SERVES 4 TO 6

1½ pounds mixed ripe tomatoes,
    cored and sliced ¼ inch thick

3 tablespoons extra-virgin olive oil

1 tablespoon minced shallot

1 teaspoon lemon juice

½ teaspoon table salt

¼ teaspoon pepper

2 tablespoons pine nuts, toasted

1 tablespoon torn fresh basil leaves
    or chopped chives

why this recipe works A simple, made-in-minutes tomato salad is one of the elemental joys of summer. This recipe starts with the ripest tomatoes you can find, at the farmers' market; grocery store; or best of all, in your garden. Our three variations tweak the ingredients paired with the tomato—pine nuts, capers, or Pecorino Romano—to create subtly different flavor profiles. Because tomatoes are already fairly acidic, we found that a dressing made with the typical 3:1 ratio of oil to acid was too sharp here. Adjusting the amount of lemon juice to minimize the acidity perfectly balanced the salad. A minced shallot gave just a bit of sweetness. In each of the three variations, different herbs—basil, parsley, and fresh oregano—added freshness. The success of this recipe depends on using ripe, in-season tomatoes. Serve with crusty bread to sop up the dressing.

Arrange tomatoes on large, shallow platter. Whisk oil, shallot, lemon juice, salt, and pepper together in bowl. Spoon dressing over tomatoes. Sprinkle with pine nuts and basil. Serve immediately.

variations

simplest tomato salad with capers and parsley
Omit pine nuts. Add 1 tablespoon rinsed capers, 1 rinsed and minced anchovy fillet, and ⅛ teaspoon red pepper flakes to dressing. Substitute chopped fresh parsley for basil.

simplest tomato salad with pecorino romano and oregano
Add ½ teaspoon grated lemon zest and ⅛ teaspoon red pepper flakes to dressing. Substitute 1 ounce shaved Pecorino Romano or Parmesan cheese for pine nuts and 2 teaspoons chopped fresh oregano for basil.

cherry tomato salad with mango and lime-curry vinaigrette

why this recipe works There are many ways to spin a tomato. Literally. Cherry tomatoes make a lovely salad but they can exude too much juice. To remove some liquid without draining away flavor, we salted them and used a salad spinner to separate the liquid from the flesh. This juice was reduced to a flavorful concentrate with shallot, olive oil, and lime juice, and reunited with the tomatoes as a dressing. Tomatoes don't need enhancing but mangos, almonds, and curry powder added sweetness and crunch to supplement the tomatoes. If you don't have a salad spinner, wrap the bowl tightly with plastic wrap after the salted tomatoes have sat for 30 minutes and gently shake to remove excess liquid. Strain the liquid and proceed with the recipe as directed. If you have less than ½ cup of juice after spinning, proceed with the recipe using the entire amount of juice you do have and reduce it to 3 tablespoons as directed (the cooking time will be shorter).

1   Toss tomatoes with sugar and salt in bowl and let sit for 30 minutes. Transfer tomatoes to salad spinner and spin until seeds and excess liquid have been removed, 45 to 60 seconds, stopping to redistribute tomatoes several times during spinning; reserve liquid left in spinner. Add tomatoes, mango, almonds, and cilantro to large bowl; set aside.

2   Strain ½ cup tomato liquid through fine-mesh strainer into liquid measuring cup; discard remaining liquid. Bring tomato liquid, shallot, lime juice, and curry powder to simmer in small saucepan over medium heat and cook until reduced to 3 tablespoons, 6 to 8 minutes. Transfer to small bowl and let cool completely, about 5 minutes. Whisking constantly, slowly drizzle in oil. Drizzle dressing over salad and toss gently to coat. Season with salt and pepper to taste. Serve.

SERVES 4 TO 6

1½	pounds cherry or grape tomatoes, quartered
½	teaspoon sugar
¼	teaspoon table salt
1	mango, cut into ½-inch pieces
½	cup toasted slivered almonds or chopped pistachios
3	tablespoons chopped fresh cilantro or mint
1	shallot, minced
4	teaspoons lime juice
¼	teaspoon curry powder
2	tablespoons extra-virgin olive oil

tomato salad
with steak tips

why this recipe works This salad speaks for itself. Meaty sirloin steak tips cooked medium-rare are served with ripe tomatoes, gem lettuce, and feta. All you need now is a nice glass of fruity red wine. Pea greens or microgreens make a nice addition to the herb mixture if you've got them. Sirloin steak tips, also known as flap meat, can be sold as whole steaks, cubes, and strips. To ensure uniform pieces, we prefer to purchase whole steaks and cut them ourselves. For optimal tenderness, make sure to slice the cooked steak against the grain (perpendicular to the fibers).

1   Pat steak tips dry with paper towels and sprinkle with ½ teaspoon salt and ¼ teaspoon pepper. Heat 1 tablespoon oil in 12-inch nonstick skillet over medium-high heat until just smoking. Add steak tips and cook until well browned all over and meat registers 120 to 125 degrees (for medium-rare), 8 to 10 minutes. Transfer to cutting board, tent with aluminum foil, and let rest for 5 minutes. Slice steak against grain ¼ inch thick.

2   Arrange tomatoes on large, shallow platter; drizzle with extra oil; and season with salt and pepper to taste. Whisk shallot, lemon juice, remaining 3 tablespoons oil, remaining ½ teaspoon salt, and remaining ¼ teaspoon pepper together in large bowl. Add lettuce and herbs and toss to combine, then arrange over tomatoes on platter. Top with steak, sprinkle with feta and chickpeas, season with salt and pepper to taste, and serve.

SERVES 4 TO 6

1½   pounds sirloin steak tips, trimmed and cut into 3-inch pieces

1   teaspoon table salt, divided

½   teaspoon pepper, divided

¼   cup extra-virgin olive oil, divided, plus extra for serving

1½   pounds mixed ripe tomatoes, cored and sliced ¼ inch thick

1   tablespoon minced shallot

1   teaspoon lemon juice

5   ounces (5 cups) little gem lettuce or mesclun

1   cup torn fresh basil, parsley, and/or oregano

2   ounces feta cheese, crumbled (½ cup)

½   cup Crispy Chickpeas (page 47) or Spiced Pepitas or Sunflower Seeds (page 50)

tofu

Tofu, pressed soy bean curd, is a great source of protein and is available in a variety of textures: extra-firm, firm, medium-firm, soft, and silken. We prefer extra-firm or firm tofu for stir-fries aws they hold their shape in high-heat cooking applications but they're also great marinated or tossed raw into salads. The creamy texture of medium and soft tofu is perfect for pan-frying for a crispy exterior and a silky interior.

marinated tofu and vegetable salad

why this recipe works For an East Asian–inspired, no-cook dinner salad, we marinated tofu with a bright dressing and combined it with crunchy uncooked cabbage, snow peas, and bell pepper. Marinating is a great way to imbue raw tofu with flavor without having to cook it. A sriracha-based salad dressing did double duty as the marinade, bringing in a touch of heat and tons of flavor. Firm tofu is tender and supple when eaten raw, but still sturdy. Do not substitute other varieties in this recipe. Note that this recipe uses unseasoned rice vinegar; we don't recommend using seasoned rice vinegar in its place.

1   Gently press tofu cubes dry with paper towels. Whisk vinegar, sriracha, honey, and salt together in large bowl. Whisking constantly, slowly drizzle in oil until emulsified.

2   Gently toss tofu in dressing until evenly coated, then cover and refrigerate for 20 minutes.

3   Add cabbage, snow peas, and bell pepper to bowl with tofu and toss gently to combine. Season with salt and pepper to taste, sprinkle with scallions and sesame seeds, and serve.

SERVES 4

- 28 ounces firm tofu, cut into ¾-inch cubes
- ¼ cup unseasoned rice vinegar
- 2 tablespoons sriracha
- 2 teaspoons honey
- ¼ teaspoon table salt
- 3 tablespoons toasted sesame oil
- ½ small head napa cabbage, cored and sliced thin (4 cups)
- 6 ounces snow peas or snap peas, strings removed, cut in half crosswise
- 1 red, orange, or yellow bell pepper, stemmed, seeded, and cut into ½-inch pieces
- 2 scallions, sliced thin on bias
- 2 tablespoons toasted sesame seeds

shaved salad with pan-seared scallops

why this recipe works Mexican salads inspired this combination of sweet mango, crisp cucumber, jicama, peppery radish, and spicy jalapeño. We shaved or sliced all of them thin; the tossed vegetable ribbons made a bed for sweetly meaty scallops. Lime dressing, cilantro, and toasted pepitas pulled the elegant main course together. We recommend buying "dry" scallops, which don't have chemical additives and taste better than "wet." Dry scallops will look ivory or pinkish; wet scallops are bright white. Persian cucumbers (also called "mini cucumbers") are similar to seedless cucumbers in flavor and texture. Use a sharp "Y-shaped" vegetable peeler or mandolin to shave the jicama and cucumbers. For more spice, reserve, mince, and add the ribs and seeds from the jalapeño.

1 Place scallops on clean dish towel, then top with second clean dish towel and gently press to dry. Let scallops sit between towels at room temperature for 10 minutes.

2 Meanwhile, gently toss jicama, mango, cucumbers, mesclun, radishes, shallot, and jalapeño in large bowl, then arrange attractively on individual plates.

3 Line large plate with double layer of paper towels. Sprinkle scallops with ½ teaspoon salt and pepper. Heat 1 tablespoon oil in 12-inch nonstick skillet over medium-high heat until just smoking. Add half of scallops in single layer, flat side down, and cook, without moving them, until well browned, 1½ to 2 minutes. Using tongs, flip scallops and continue to cook until sides of scallops are firm and centers are opaque, 30 to 90 seconds longer. Transfer scallops to prepared plate. Wipe out skillet with paper towels and repeat with 1 tablespoon oil and remaining scallops.

4 Divide scallops evenly among salad on prepared plates. Whisk honey, lime zest and juice, and remaining ½ teaspoon salt together in bowl. Whisking constantly, slowly drizzle in remaining ¼ cup oil until emulsified. Drizzle salad and scallops with dressing, then sprinkle with cilantro and pepitas. Serve.

variation
appetizer-sized shaved salad with pan-seared scallops
Decrease scallops to 1 pound and omit mesclun.

SERVES 4

1½ pounds large sea scallops, tendons removed

1 pound jicama, peeled and shaved into ribbons

1 mango, peeled, pitted, and sliced thin

3 Persian cucumbers or 8 ounces English cucumber, shaved lengthwise into ribbons

4 ounces (4 cups) mesclun

2 radishes, trimmed and sliced thin

1 shallot, sliced thin

1 jalapeño or serrano chile, stemmed, halved, seeded, and sliced thin crosswise

1 teaspoon table salt, divided

¼ teaspoon pepper

6 tablespoons extra-virgin olive oil, divided

1 tablespoon honey

2 teaspoons grated lime zest plus ¼ cup juice (2 limes)

¼ cup fresh cilantro or parsley leaves

3 tablespoons roasted pepitas or sunflower seeds

zucchini noodle–chicken salad with ginger and garam masala

SERVES 4

1 mango, peeled and cut into ¼-inch pieces

2 tablespoons chopped fresh cilantro or mint

2 teaspoons lemon juice

8 teaspoons vegetable oil, divided

4 garlic cloves, minced

4 teaspoons garam masala, divided

2 teaspoons grated fresh ginger

½ teaspoon table salt, divided

½ teaspoon pepper, divided

1 pound boneless, skinless chicken breasts, trimmed and cut into ½-inch pieces

1½ pounds zucchini noodles, cut into 6-inch lengths, divided

1 recipe Herb-Yogurt Sauce (recipe follows)

why this recipe works For a fast and flavorful salad, we paired quick-cooking zucchini noodles and chicken. Garam masala (a north Indian spice blend that contains cumin, coriander, cinnamon, bay leaf, and black pepper); garlic; and ginger, traditionally used in north Indian meat dishes, give our chicken deep flavor. A cilantro-mint yogurt sauce evoked a cooling raita, and diced mango added a touch of sweetness to the dish. Cooking the zucchini noodles in two batches ensured that they didn't overcook and turn mushy. If possible, use smaller, in-season zucchini, which have thinner skins and fewer seeds. We prefer to spiralize our zucchini at home but you can use store-bought zucchini noodles here. You will need 2 pounds of zucchini to get 1½ pounds of zucchini noodles. Cook the zucchini to your desired level of doneness but be careful not to overcook.

1 Combine mango, cilantro, and lemon juice in bowl; season with salt and pepper to taste and set aside until ready to serve. Whisk 2 teaspoons oil, garlic, 2 teaspoons garam masala, ginger, ¼ teaspoon salt, and ¼ teaspoon pepper together in medium bowl, then add chicken and toss to coat.

2 Heat 2 teaspoons oil in 12-inch nonstick skillet over medium-high heat until shimmering. Add chicken and cook until browned on all sides, 4 to 6 minutes. Transfer to clean bowl, cover with aluminum foil to keep warm, and set aside until ready to serve.

3 Heat 2 teaspoons oil in now-empty skillet over medium-high heat until shimmering. Add 1 teaspoon garam masala, ⅛ teaspoon salt, ⅛ teaspoon pepper, and half of zucchini noodles and cook, tossing frequently, until crisp-tender, about 1 minute. Transfer to individual plates and repeat with remaining 2 teaspoons oil, remaining 1 teaspoon garam masala, remaining ⅛ teaspoon salt, remaining ⅛ teaspoon pepper, and remaining zucchini noodles. Top zucchini noodles with chicken, mango mixture, and sauce. Serve.

herb-yogurt sauce

makes 1 cup

Creamy yogurt makes for a simple sauce perfect to drizzle over a variety of greens or grains. Do not substitute low-fat or nonfat yogurt here.

- 1 cup plain whole-milk yogurt
- 1 teaspoon grated lemon zest plus 2 tablespoons juice
- 2 tablespoons minced fresh cilantro or mint
- 2 tablespoons minced fresh mint or parsley
- 1 garlic clove, minced

Whisk all ingredients together in bowl. Cover and refrigerate until flavors meld, at least 30 minutes. Season with salt and pepper to taste. (Sauce can be refrigerated for up to 4 days.)

variation
chipotle-yogurt sauce

Omit cilantro and mint. Substitute lime zest and juice for lemon zest and juice. Add 1 tablespoon minced canned chipotle chile in adobo sauce.

zucchini noodle salad with tahini-ginger dressing

SERVES 4 TO 6

tahini-ginger dressing

- ½ cup tahini
- 5 tablespoons soy sauce
- 2 tablespoons unseasoned rice vinegar
- 4 teaspoons grated fresh ginger
- 1 tablespoon honey
- 2 teaspoons hot sauce
- 1 garlic clove, minced
- ½ teaspoon table salt

salad

- 2 tablespoons toasted sesame oil
- 12 ounces broccoli florets, cut into ½-inch pieces
- 2½ pounds zucchini noodles, cut into 12-inch lengths
- 1 red, orange, or yellow bell pepper, stemmed, seeded, and cut into ¼-inch-wide strips
- 1 carrot, peeled and shredded
- 4 scallions, sliced thin on bias
- 1 tablespoon sesame seeds, toasted

why this recipe works There's a reason zucchini noodles are so popular: The squash is easy to work with and produces long, satisfying noodles with a pleasant texture, neutral flavor, and low amount of carbs. We took advantage of that ease and neutrality to create a boldly flavored, East Asian–inspired salad with zucchini noodles as the base. We tested both boiling the noodles and stir-frying them to cook them, but in the end, realized that leaving the zucchini noodles raw gave us the best texture and flavor. We also added other vegetables for color and texture: red bell pepper, shredded carrot, and sautéed broccoli, and we replaced the usual peanut sauce with tahini, a nutty, buttery paste made from ground sesame seeds. Soy sauce, ginger, rice vinegar, and garlic rounded out the dressing. If possible, use smaller, in-season zucchini, which have thinner skins and fewer seeds. We prefer to spiralize our zucchini at home for the best flavor, but you can use store-bought zucchini noodles. You will need 3 pounds of zucchini to get 2½ pounds of zucchini noodles. Note that this recipe uses unseasoned rice vinegar; we don't recommend using seasoned rice vinegar in its place.

1 for the dressing Process all ingredients in blender until smooth, about 30 seconds. Transfer to large serving bowl. (Dressing can be refrigerated up to 24 hours; whisk to recombine before using.)

2 for the salad Heat oil in 12-inch nonstick skillet over medium-high heat until shimmering. Add broccoli and cook until softened and spotty brown, about 5 minutes. Transfer to plate and let cool slightly.

3 Add zucchini, bell pepper, carrot, scallions, and broccoli to bowl with dressing and toss to combine. Sprinkle with sesame seeds. Serve.

shaved zucchini salad with pepitas

why this recipe works One of the great things about zucchini is that it's a blank canvas for flavor. To make the most of it, we decided to shave it into long ribbons with a vegetable peeler. This gave us ample surface area to coat with a flavorful dressing. Tangy queso fresco, crunchy toasted pepitas, and fresh cilantro provided textural contrast. Using in-season zucchini and good olive oil is crucial here. Look for small zucchini, which are younger and have thinner skins. Be ready to serve this dish quickly after it is assembled.

Using vegetable peeler, shave zucchini lengthwise into very thin ribbons. Whisk oil, lime zest and juice, garlic, salt, and pepper together in large bowl. Add zucchini, cilantro, and queso fresco and toss to combine. Season with salt and pepper to taste. Sprinkle with pepitas and serve immediately.

SERVES 4 TO 6

1½ pounds zucchini or summer squash

2 tablespoons extra-virgin olive oil

½ teaspoon grated lime zest plus 1 tablespoon juice

1 garlic clove, minced

¾ teaspoon table salt

¼ teaspoon pepper

½ cup chopped fresh cilantro or parsley

2 ounces queso fresco or feta, crumbled (½ cup)

¼ cup pepitas or sunflower seeds, toasted

shaved zucchini salad
with pepitas, *page 249*

bean
& grain
salads

lentil salad with spinach, walnuts, and parmesan

SERVES 4 TO 6

1 teaspoon table salt for brining

1 cup dried lentilles du Puy, picked over and rinsed

5 garlic cloves, lightly crushed and peeled

1 bay leaf

½ teaspoon table salt

4 ounces (4 cups) baby spinach

5 tablespoons extra-virgin olive oil

3 tablespoons sherry vinegar

1 large shallot, minced

¼ cup grated Parmesan or Pecorino Romano cheese

¼ cup walnuts or pecans, toasted and chopped coarse

why this recipe works For this earthy lentil salad, we first needed to ensure that the lentils would stay intact throughout cooking. Lentilles du Puy were the perfect choice, since they are small and firm and hold their shape better than standard green or brown lentils. A salt-soak softened their skins, leading to fewer blowouts. Cooking the lentils in the oven heated them gently and uniformly, and we easily boosted their flavor by simply adding some crushed cloves of garlic and a bay leaf to the pot. With our lentils perfectly cooked, we turned to flavorings. A simple vinaigrette worked perfectly to balance their flavor. We added in hearty spinach while Parmesan and walnuts brought some textural variety to the salad. Lentilles du Puy, also called French green lentils, are our first choice for this recipe, but brown, black, or regular green lentils are fine, too (note that cooking times will vary depending on the type used). Salt-soaking helps keep the lentils intact, but if you don't have time, they'll still taste good. You need a medium ovensafe saucepan for this recipe.

1 Dissolve 1 teaspoon salt in 1 quart warm water (about 110 degrees) in bowl. Add lentils and soak at room temperature for 1 hour. Drain well.

2 Adjust oven rack to middle position and heat oven to 325 degrees. Combine lentils, 4 cups water, garlic, bay leaf, and salt in medium ovensafe saucepan. Cover; transfer saucepan to oven; and cook until lentils are tender but remain intact, 40 minutes to 1 hour.

3 Meanwhile, place spinach and 2 tablespoons water in bowl. Cover and microwave until spinach is wilted and volume is reduced by half, about 4 minutes. Remove bowl from microwave and keep covered for 1 minute. Transfer spinach to colander and press gently to release liquid. Transfer spinach to cutting board and chop coarse. Return to colander and press again.

4 Drain lentils well, discarding garlic and bay leaf. In large bowl, whisk oil and vinegar together. Add shallot, lentils, and spinach and toss to combine. Season with salt and pepper to taste. Transfer to serving dish and sprinkle with Parmesan and walnuts. Serve warm or at room temperature.

crispy lentil and herb salad

why this recipe works Many lentil salads use boiled lentils, but we decided to fry ours in this salad inspired by lentil preparations in countries such as India, Lebanon, Syria, and Turkey. Salt-soaking the lentils before frying was crucial to ensure that they turned tender and lightly crispy and didn't burn. We tested various lentils and found that the firm texture of lentilles du Puy held up well to quickly frying in a saucepan. Instead of tossing the components together with a dressing, we used yogurt as an anchor for the other ingredients, spreading it on a platter and topping it with a lightly dressed blend of fresh herbs tossed with the crunchy lentils and sweet bits of dried cherries. Pita was a must for scooping everything up in one perfect bite. You can use brown lentils instead of the lentilles du Puy. Be sure to use a large saucepan to fry the lentils, as the oil mixture will bubble and steam.

1 Dissolve 1 teaspoon salt in 1 quart water in bowl. Add lentils and let sit at room temperature for at least 1 hour or up to 24 hours. Drain well and pat dry with paper towels.

2 Heat vegetable oil in large saucepan over medium heat until shimmering. Add lentils and cook, stirring constantly, until crispy and golden in spots, 8 to 12 minutes (oil should bubble vigorously throughout; adjust heat as needed). Carefully drain lentils in fine-mesh strainer set over bowl, then transfer lentils to paper towel-lined plate. Discard oil. Sprinkle with cumin and ¼ teaspoon salt and toss to combine; set aside. (Cooled lentils can be stored in airtight container at room temperature for up to 24 hours.)

3 Whisk yogurt, 2 tablespoons olive oil, lemon zest and juice, and garlic together in bowl and season with salt and pepper to taste. Spread yogurt mixture over serving platter. Toss parsley, dill, cilantro, remaining pinch salt, and remaining 1 tablespoon olive oil together in bowl, then gently stir in lentils and cherries and arrange on top of yogurt mixture, leaving 1-inch border. Drizzle with pomegranate molasses. Serve with pita.

SERVES 4

- 1 teaspoon table salt for brining
- ½ cup dried lentilles du Puy, picked over and rinsed
- ⅓ cup vegetable oil for frying
- ½ teaspoon ground cumin
- ¼ teaspoon plus pinch table salt, divided
- 1 cup plain Greek yogurt
- 3 tablespoons extra-virgin olive oil, divided
- 1 teaspoon grated lemon zest plus 1 teaspoon juice
- 1 garlic clove, minced
- ½ cup fresh parsley leaves
- ½ cup torn fresh dill
- ½ cup fresh cilantro leaves
- ¼ cup dried cherries, chopped
- Pomegranate molasses
- Pita, warmed

crispy lentil and
herb salad, *page 255*

spiced lentil salad with butternut squash

why this recipe works Lentil salads are highly adaptable: You can use your favorite variety, keep the lentils simple or stir in other ingredients, and serve them warm or cold. For a unique and balanced lentil salad to add to our repertoire, we paired sophisticated, bold-tasting black lentils with butternut squash; the squash's sweetness was a nice foil for this earthy legume. To accentuate the delicate squash flavor, we tossed small pieces with balsamic vinegar and extra-virgin olive oil and roasted them in a hot oven. Putting the rack in the lowest position encouraged deep, even browning. We soaked the lentils in a saltwater solution to season them throughout and ensure fewer blowouts. To infuse the lentils with more flavor as they cooked, we chose a mix of warm, floral spices. For even cooking, we used the oven rather than the stovetop. More balsamic vinegar in the dressing echoed the sweetness of the roasted squash. Parsley and chopped red onion gave the dish some color and freshness, and toasted pepitas provided just the right amount of textural contrast. You can also use lentilles du Puy (also called French green lentils), brown lentils, or green lentils in this recipe, though cooking times will vary. Salt-soaking helps keep the lentils intact, but if you don't have time, they'll still taste good. You need a medium ovensafe saucepan for this recipe.

1 Dissolve 1 teaspoon salt in 1 quart warm water (about 110 degrees) in bowl. Add lentils and soak at room temperature for 1 hour. Drain well.

2 Meanwhile, adjust oven racks to middle and lowest positions and heat oven to 450 degrees. Toss squash, 1 tablespoon oil, 1½ teaspoons vinegar, salt, and pepper together in bowl. Spread squash on rimmed baking sheet and roast on lower rack until well browned and tender, 20 to 25 minutes, stirring halfway through roasting. Let cool slightly, about 5 minutes. Reduce oven temperature to 325 degrees.

3 Heat 1 tablespoon oil, garlic, coriander, cumin, ginger, and cinnamon in medium ovensafe saucepan over medium heat until fragrant, about 1 minute. Stir in 4 cups water and lentils. Cover; transfer saucepan to upper oven rack; and cook until lentils are tender but remain intact, 40 minutes to 1 hour.

4 Drain lentils well. Whisk mustard and remaining 1½ tablespoons vinegar together in large bowl. Whisking constantly, slowly drizzle in remaining 3 tablespoons oil until emulsified. Add lentils, squash, parsley, and onion and toss to combine. Season with salt and pepper to taste, sprinkle with pepitas, and serve warm or at room temperature.

SERVES 4 TO 6

- 1 teaspoon table salt for brining
- 1 cup dried black lentils, picked over and rinsed
- 1 pound butternut squash, peeled, seeded, and cut into ½-inch pieces (3 cups)
- 5 tablespoons extra-virgin olive oil, divided
- 2 tablespoons balsamic vinegar, divided
- ¼ teaspoon table salt
- ¼ teaspoon pepper
- 1 garlic clove, minced
- ½ teaspoon ground coriander
- ¼ teaspoon ground cumin
- ¼ teaspoon ground ginger
- ⅛ teaspoon ground cinnamon
- 1 teaspoon Dijon mustard
- ½ cup fresh parsley or mint leaves
- ¼ cup finely chopped red onion
- 1 tablespoon toasted pepitas or sunflower seeds

southwestern black bean salad

why this recipe works For a black bean salad with bold but balanced flavors that evoked the Southwest, we used a judicious mixture of black beans, corn, avocado, tomato, and cilantro. Sautéing the corn (both fresh and frozen worked well) in a skillet until it was toasty and just starting to brown added a pleasant nuttiness to the kernels. For a dressing that could stand up to the hearty beans, we used lots of lime juice and spicy chipotle chile, with a little honey to balance the bright citrus. Raw onion was too harsh in the dressing, but thinly sliced scallions provided a pleasant onion flavor. You will need three to four ears of corn in order to yield 2 cups of fresh kernels.

1   Heat 2 tablespoons oil in 12-inch skillet over medium-high heat until shimmering. Add corn and cook until spotty brown, about 5 minutes; let cool slightly.

2   Whisk scallions, lime juice, chipotle, honey, salt, and pepper together in large bowl. Whisking constantly, slowly drizzle in remaining 2 tablespoons oil until emulsified. Add beans, avocados, tomatoes, cilantro, and corn and toss to combine. Season with salt and pepper to taste, and serve.

SERVES 6 TO 8

- ¼ cup extra-virgin olive oil, divided
- 2 cups fresh or thawed frozen corn
- 4 scallions, sliced thin
- ⅓ cup lime juice (3 limes)
- 1 tablespoon minced canned chipotle chile in adobo sauce
- 1 teaspoon honey
- ½ teaspoon table salt
- ½ teaspoon pepper
- 2 (15-ounce) cans black beans, rinsed
- 2 ripe avocados, halved, pitted, and chopped
- 2 tomatoes, cored and chopped
- ¼ cup chopped fresh cilantro or parsley

layered tex-mex salad

¼ cup mayonnaise

¼ cup sour cream or Greek yogurt

¼ cup jarred salsa

2 tablespoons chopped fresh cilantro or parsley

2 teaspoons lime juice

1 romaine lettuce heart (6 ounces), torn into bite-size pieces

½ small red onion, sliced thin

12 ounces cherry or 10 ounces grape tomatoes, halved if small or quartered if large

1 cup fresh or thawed frozen corn

1 (15-ounce) can black beans, rinsed

2 ripe avocados, halved, pitted, and chopped

6 ounces sharp cheddar or Monterey Jack cheese, shredded (1½ cups)

2 ounces tortilla chips, crushed (2 cups)

why this recipe works This salad packs a flavor and texture punch and looks great doing it. Cherry tomatoes; ripe avocados; black beans; and crisp, cool romaine lettuce are layered in a striking and nostalgic presentation in a glass bowl. The layering makes the salad last longer and be easy to transport, so it's a great option to bring to a party or a picnic. A creamy dressing forms two of the layers: one over the lettuce, the next on the other ingredients. The salad can be tossed just before serving. Add the tortilla chips just before serving so they don't get soggy.

1   Whisk mayonnaise, sour cream, salsa, cilantro, and lime juice together in medium bowl. (Dressing can be refrigerated for up to 24 hours.)

2   Place lettuce in large, straight-sided glass serving bowl. Spread half of dressing over lettuce, then layer with onion, tomatoes, corn, beans, avocados, and cheddar. Spread remaining dressing over salad. Sprinkle with tortilla chips. Serve. (Salad can be refrigerated for up to 24 hours; reserve tortilla chips until just before serving.)

marinated cauliflower and chickpea salad

why this recipe works For this deeply vibrant bean salad, we marinated earthy cauliflower. We paired the vegetable with creamy chickpeas robust enough to absorb the marinade without turning mushy. First, we blanched the cauliflower for a few minutes, softening its exterior so that the marinade could be absorbed more readlly. Heating the marinade before tossing it with the salad also helped absorption. For the marinade, we bloomed saffron in hot water to coax out its distinct, complex flavor and aroma. Then we heated smashed garlic cloves in olive oil to infuse the oil with more flavor and tame the garlic's harsh edge. Smoked paprika and rosemary enhanced the marinade's vibrant brick-red hue and earthy flavor. Thin slices of lemon provided bright citrus flavor. Marinating the chickpeas and cauliflower for at least 4 hours allowed the flavors to meld and deepen. Use a small sprig of rosemary or its flavor will be overpowering. This dish can be served cold or at room temperature.

1   Bring 2 quarts water to boil in large saucepan. Add cauliflower florets and 1 tablespoon salt and cook until florets begin to soften, about 3 minutes. Drain florets and transfer to paper towel-lined baking sheet.

2   Combine ½ cup hot water and saffron in bowl; set aside. Heat oil and garlic in small saucepan over medium-low heat until fragrant and beginning to sizzle but not browned, 4 to 6 minutes. Stir in sugar, paprika, and rosemary sprig and cook until fragrant, about 30 seconds. Off heat, stir in vinegar, pepper, salt, and saffron mixture.

3   In large bowl, combine florets, vinegar mixture, chickpeas, and lemon. Transfer mixture to 1-gallon zipper-lock bag and refrigerate for at least 4 hours or up to 3 days, flipping bag occasionally. Transfer mixture to serving bowl with slotted spoon and sprinkle with parsley. Serve.

SERVES 6 TO 8

- 1   head cauliflower (2 pounds), cored and cut into 1-inch florets
- 2   teaspoons table salt, plus salt for cooking cauliflower
- ¼   teaspoon saffron threads, crumbled
- ¾   cup extra-virgin olive oil
- 10 garlic cloves, smashed and peeled
- 3   tablespoons sugar
- 1   tablespoon smoked paprika
- 1   small sprig fresh rosemary or thyme
- ¼   cup sherry vinegar
- ¼   teaspoon pepper
- 1   (15-ounce) can chickpeas, rinsed
- 1   lemon, sliced thin
- 2   tablespoons minced fresh parsley or cilantro

chickpea salad with carrots, arugula, and olives

SERVES 6

2 (15-ounce) cans chickpeas, rinsed

¼ cup extra-virgin olive oil

2 tablespoons lemon juice

¾ teaspoon table salt

½ teaspoon pepper

Pinch cayenne pepper

3 carrots, peeled and shredded

1 cup baby arugula or baby spinach, chopped

½ cup pitted olives, chopped

why this recipe works For a flavorful, easy, and good-looking side salad or light lunch, we combined nutty chickpeas and carrots with arugula and olives. But simply tossing the ingredients with a lemon dressing resulted in a lackluster salad with a pool of dressing at the bottom of the bowl. We wanted the seasoning to go beyond the surface of the chickpeas and fully infuse each one with big, bold flavor. The key was to warm the chickpeas before mixing them with the dressing: The seed coats that cover the chickpeas are rich in pectin, which breaks down when exposed to heat and moisture, creating a more porous surface that our dressing could easily penetrate. Letting the dressed chickpeas rest for 30 minutes put the flavor over the top and also allowed the chickpeas to cool. Use the large holes of a box grater to shred the carrots.

1 Microwave chickpeas in medium bowl until hot, about 2 minutes. Stir in oil, lemon juice, salt, pepper, and cayenne and let sit until flavors meld, about 30 minutes. (Chickpea mixture can be refrigerated for up to 2 days.)

2 Add carrots, arugula, and olives to chickpea mixture and toss to combine. Season with salt and pepper to taste. Serve. (Salad can be refrigerated for up to 2 hours.)

variations

chickpea salad with carrots, raisins, and almonds

Substitute lime juice for lemon juice and ½ cup golden raisins, ¼ cup chopped fresh mint or parsley, and ¼ cup toasted sliced almonds or chopped hazelnuts for arugula and olives.

chickpea salad with oranges, red onion, and chipotle

Substitute 3 oranges, segmented; ½ cup thinly sliced red onion; ½ cup fresh cilantro or parsley leaves; and 2 teaspoons minced canned chipotle chile in adobo sauce for carrots, arugula, and olives.

chickpea salad with roasted red peppers and feta

SERVES 4 TO 6

2 (15-ounce) cans chickpeas, rinsed

¼ cup extra-virgin olive oil

2 tablespoons lemon juice

¾ teaspoon table salt

½ teaspoon pepper

Pinch cayenne pepper

½ cup chopped jarred roasted red peppers

2 ounces feta or goat cheese, crumbled (½ cup)

¼ cup chopped fresh parsley or cilantro

why this recipe works Canned chickpeas are an ideal ingredient for a salad because, apart from being convenient, they take on flavors easily and provide texture. After we heated them in the microwave, the chickpeas became soft and tender, which helped them quickly absorb the tangy dressing. Sweet roasted red peppers and briny feta cheese transformed the chickpeas into a bright and savory salad.

1 Microwave chickpeas in medium bowl until hot, about 1½ minutes. Stir in oil, lemon juice, salt, pepper, and cayenne and let sit until flavors meld, about 30 minutes.

2 Add red peppers, feta, and parsley and toss to combine. Season with salt and pepper to taste. Serve.

fattoush with chickpeas

why this recipe works This Levantine salad combines fresh, flavorful produce with crisp pita chips and bright herbs. We also added chickpeas, another ingredient favored in the Levant, to make the salad even heartier. Many recipes eliminate excess moisture from the salad by seeding and salting the cucumbers and tomatoes. We skipped this step in order to preserve the crisp texture of the cucumber and the flavorful seeds and jelly of the tomatoes. Instead, we made the pita moisture repellent by brushing its craggy sides with plenty of olive oil before baking. The oil prevented the pita chips from absorbing so much moisture from the salad that they became soggy while still allowing the chips to pick up flavor from the lemony dressing. Serve this salad as soon as you've made it so that the pita doesn't sit too long. Despite the oil, it will get soggy over time. The success of fattoush depends on ripe, in-season tomatoes.

1 Adjust oven rack to middle position and heat oven to 375 degrees. Using kitchen shears, cut around perimeter of each pita and separate into 2 thin rounds. Cut each round in half. Place pitas, smooth side down, on wire rack set in rimmed baking sheet. Brush ¼ cup oil over surface of pitas. (Pitas do not need to be uniformly coated. Oil will spread during baking.) Season with salt and pepper to taste. Bake until pitas are crisp and pale golden brown, 10 to 14 minutes. Set aside to cool. (Cooled pitas can be stored in zipper-lock bag for up to 24 hours.)

2 While pitas bake, whisk lemon zest and juice, garlic, salt, and remaining ¼ cup oil together in large bowl. Add chickpeas to dressing. Let sit until flavors meld, about 10 minutes.

3 Add tomatoes, cucumber, arugula, mint, and scallions to bowl with dressing and chickpeas. Break pitas into ½-inch pieces and add to bowl with vegetables. Toss to combine. Season with salt and pepper to taste. Serve immediately.

SERVES 4 TO 6

- 2 (8-inch) pitas
- ½ cup extra-virgin olive oil, divided
- ½ teaspoon grated lemon zest plus ¼ cup juice (2 lemons)
- 1 garlic clove, minced
- ¼ teaspoon table salt
- 1 (15-ounce) can chickpeas, rinsed
- 1 pound tomatoes, cored and cut into ¾-inch pieces
- 1 English cucumber, peeled and sliced ⅛ inch thick
- 1 cup baby arugula, chopped coarse
- ½ cup chopped fresh mint or cilantro
- 4 scallions, sliced thin

fattoush with chickpeas, *page 269*

edamame and shrimp salad

SERVES 4

2 tablespoons unseasoned
rice vinegar

1 tablespoon honey

1 small garlic clove, minced

1 teaspoon table salt

3 tablespoons extra-virgin olive oil

18 ounces shelled edamame beans
(3 cups)

2 ounces (2 cups) baby arugula

1½ cups Sautéed Shrimp (page 43)

½ cup shredded fresh basil or parsley

½ cup chopped fresh mint or cilantro

2 radishes, trimmed, halved,
and sliced thin

1 shallot, halved and sliced thin

¼ cup roasted sunflower seeds
or pepitas

why this recipe works Immature soy beans—edamame—are great in salads because their bright, fresh flavor and satisfying texture pair perfectly with leafy greens. Tart vinaigrettes and bold-flavored vegetables can easily overpower the beans' mildness, though. So we chose to use rice vinegar for its mild acidity, incorporating a little honey for sweetness and to help emulsify the dressing. The subtle peppery flavor and delicate, tender leaves of baby arugula worked well as a flavor and texture complement, and sweet sautéed shrimp added heft. Mint and basil helped bring a light, summery flavor to the salad; thinly sliced shallot gave mild onion flavor; and just a couple radishes provided crunch and color. One small clove of garlic contributed its flavor without taking over the dish. A sprinkling of roasted sunflower seeds added nuttiness and depth to this bright salad. You can substitute frozen edamame beans that have been thawed and patted dry for the fresh edamame in this recipe. Note that this recipe uses unseasoned rice vinegar; we don't recommend using seasoned rice vinegar in its place.

Whisk vinegar, honey, garlic, and salt together in large bowl. Whisking constantly, slowly drizzle in oil until emulsified. Add edamame, arugula, shrimp, basil, mint, radishes, and shallot and toss to combine. Sprinkle with sunflower seeds and season with salt and pepper to taste. Serve.

fava beans

The leguminous fava bean plant has been cultivated since ancient times in the eastern Mediterranean region. We use the fava bean (also called broad bean) in salads to add heartiness, chew, and color. Favas are in season from mid to late spring. Smaller pods have tender, sweet beans. Avoid overly large beans bulging in the pods (those favas will be tough and woody) or any with brown spots. Store fresh favas in an open plastic produce bag in the refrigerator for up to a week. Frozen favas make a good substitute for fresh. We don't suggest the bottled beans that are available in supermarkets—they have tough skins and are high in sodium.

fava bean and radish salad

why this recipe works This vibrant, flavorful salad featuring fava beans, radishes, and pea shoots celebrates springtime in every bite. Since it takes time to prepare fresh favas, we wanted to make sure that this salad was interesting enough to be worth the effort. The fresh pea shoots supplied a layer of texture and a bit of natural sweetness. We added thin half-moons of peppery radishes to provide a nice crunchy, spicy bite and flecks of contrasting red and white to our otherwise green salad. Basil and a lemony dressing were the final additions. This recipe works best with fresh fava beans, but if you can't find them, you can substitute 1 pound (3 cups) of frozen shucked fava beans, thawed. Skip step 1 if using frozen favas. Be sure to set up the ice bath before cooking the fava beans, as plunging them immediately in the cold water after blanching retains their bright-green color and ensures that they don't overcook.

1   Bring 4 quarts water to boil in large pot over high heat. Fill large bowl halfway with ice and water. Add fava beans to boiling water and cook for 1 minute. Using slotted spoon, transfer fava beans to ice bath and let cool, about 2 minutes. Transfer fava beans to triple layer of paper towels and dry well. Using paring knife, make small cut along edge of each bean through waxy sheath, then gently squeeze sheath to release bean; discard sheath.

2   Whisk oil, lemon juice, garlic, salt, pepper, and coriander together in large bowl. Add radishes, pea shoots, basil, and fava beans and toss gently to coat. Serve immediately.

SERVES 4 TO 6

- 3 **pounds fava beans, shucked (3 cups)**
- ¼ **cup extra-virgin olive oil**
- 3 **tablespoons lemon juice**
- 2 **garlic cloves, minced**
- ½ **teaspoon table salt**
- ¼ **teaspoon pepper**
- ¼ **teaspoon ground coriander**
- 10 **radishes, trimmed, halved, and sliced thin**
- 1½ **ounces (1½ cups) pea shoots or microgreens**
- ¼ **cup chopped fresh basil or mint**

fava bean salad with artichokes, asparagus, and peas

SERVES 6

- 2 teaspoons grated lemon zest, plus 1 lemon
- 4 baby artichokes (3 ounces each)
- 1 teaspoon baking soda
- 1 pound fava beans, shucked (1 cup)
- 1 tablespoon extra-virgin olive oil, plus extra for drizzling
- 1 leek, white and light green parts only, halved lengthwise, sliced thin, and washed thoroughly
- 1 teaspoon table salt
- 3 garlic cloves, minced
- 1 cup chicken or vegetable broth
- 1 pound asparagus, trimmed and cut on bias into 2-inch lengths
- 1 pound fresh peas, shelled (1¼ cups)
- 2 tablespoons shredded fresh basil
- 1 tablespoon chopped fresh mint

why this recipe works This warm vegetable salad is comforting on a cool spring evening. Inspired by vignole, a vibrant Roman braise, we lightly cooked fresh fava beans, artichokes, leek, asparagus, and peas and served them with torn lettuce leaves dressed with olive oil, red wine vinegar, and salt. We braised the artichokes until they were almost cooked through, and then we added in the asparagus, peas, and finally the favas, finishing the salad with fresh herbs and lemon zest. This recipe is best with in-season vegetables; if you can't find fresh fava beans and peas, substitute 1 cup of frozen, thawed fava beans and 1¼ cups of frozen peas; add the peas to the skillet with the beans in step 4. Be sure to set up the ice bath before cooking the fava beans, as plunging them immediately in the cold water after blanching retains their bright-green color and ensures that they don't overcook.

1   Cut lemon in half, squeeze halves into container filled with 2 quarts water, then add spent halves. Working with 1 artichoke at a time, trim stem to about ¾ inch and cut off top quarter of artichoke. Break off bottom 3 or 4 rows of tough outer leaves by pulling them downward. Using paring knife, trim outer layer of stem and base, removing any dark green parts. Cut artichoke into quarters and submerge in lemon water.

2   Bring 2 cups water and baking soda to boil in small saucepan. Fill large bowl halfway with ice and water. Add fava beans to boiling water and cook for 1 minute. Using slotted spoon, transfer fava beans to ice bath and let cool, about 2 minutes. Transfer fava beans to triple layer of paper towels and dry well.

3   Heat oil in 12-inch skillet over medium heat until shimmering. Add leek, 1 tablespoon water, and salt and cook until softened, about 3 minutes. Stir in garlic and cook until fragrant, about 30 seconds.

4   Remove artichokes from lemon water, shaking off excess water, and add to skillet. Stir in broth and bring to simmer. Reduce heat to medium-low; cover; and cook until artichokes are almost tender, 6 to 8 minutes. Stir in asparagus and peas; cover; and cook until crisp-tender, 5 to 7 minutes. Stir in fava beans and cook until heated through and artichokes are fully tender, about 2 minutes. Off heat, stir in basil, mint, and lemon zest. Season with salt and pepper to taste and drizzle with extra oil. Serve immediately.

pinto bean, ancho, and beef salad with pickled poblanos

why this recipe works This salad pays homage to the Mexican ingredients that inspired its creation. Ancho chiles, frequently used in Mexican cuisine, are dried poblanos; we employed both fresh and dried forms, using ancho chile powder as a rub for our steak and quick-pickling poblanos for sweet-sour spiciness. Grated jicama brought crunch to our salad of pinto beans, red onion, cilantro, and lime juice. The dressed salad made a refreshing counterpoint to the rich, chile spice-rubbed skirt steak, which we seared in a skillet. Crumbled cotija gave the dish an umami, salty bite. Finally, we sprinkled the salad with finely chopped unsweetened chocolate. Its complex bitterness and aroma rounded out the dish. Be sure to slice the steak thin against the grain or it will be very chewy. It is important to chop the chocolate fine, as bigger pieces of chocolate will be overpoweringly bitter.

1   Microwave vinegar, sugar, and ¼ teaspoon salt in medium bowl until simmering, 3 to 4 minutes. Whisk to dissolve any residual sugar and salt, then stir in poblanos. Let sit, stirring occasionally, for 30 minutes. Drain and set aside.

2   Meanwhile, pat steak dry with paper towels, then sprinkle with chile powder, ¼ teaspoon pepper, and ½ teaspoon salt. Heat 1 tablespoon oil in 12-inch skillet over medium-high heat until just smoking. Add steak and cook until well browned and meat registers 120 to 125 degrees (for medium-rare), about 2 minutes per side. Transfer steak to cutting board, tent with aluminum foil, and let rest for 5 minutes.

3   Gently toss beans, jicama, onion, cilantro, lime juice, remaining ½ teaspoon salt, remaining ½ teaspoon pepper, and remaining 1 tablespoon oil to combine, then transfer to serving platter. Slice steak thin against grain and arrange over top of salad. Sprinkle with cotija; chocolate, if using; poblanos; and extra cilantro. Serve.

SERVES 4

- 1 cup red wine vinegar
- ⅓ cup sugar
- 1¼ teaspoons table salt, divided
- 4 ounces poblano chiles, stemmed, seeded, and sliced ⅛ inch thick
- 1 (1-pound) skirt steak, trimmed and cut into thirds
- 2 teaspoons ancho chile powder
- ¾ teaspoon pepper, divided
- 2 tablespoons vegetable oil, divided
- 2 (15-ounce) cans pinto beans, rinsed
- 12 ounces jicama, peeled and grated (1½ cups)
- ½ cup finely chopped red onion
- ¼ cup chopped fresh cilantro leaves and stems, plus extra for sprinkling
- 3 tablespoons lime juice (2 limes)
- 1½ ounces cotija cheese, crumbled (⅓ cup)
- ½ ounce unsweetened chocolate, chopped fine (optional)

pinto bean, ancho, and
beef salad with pickled
poblanos, *page 277*

black-eyed pea salad with peaches and pecans

SERVES 4 TO 6

1 teaspoon grated lime zest plus
2½ tablespoons juice (2 limes)

1 teaspoon honey

1 small garlic clove, minced

¾ teaspoon table salt

2 tablespoons extra-virgin olive oil

2 (15-ounce) cans black-eyed
peas, rinsed

2 peaches or nectarines, halved,
pitted, and chopped coarse

3 ounces frisée or escarole, trimmed
and cut into 2-inch pieces

¼ cup finely chopped red onion

¼ cup pecans or whole almonds,
toasted and chopped

¼ cup fresh basil or parsley leaves,
torn into ½-inch pieces

1 jalapeño or serrano chile, stemmed,
seeded, and chopped fine

why this recipe works With their delicate skins and creamy interiors, black-eyed peas are great when paired with a tart dressing and crunchy ingredients in a salad. They're popular in the South, so we looked to Southern cuisine for inspiration and decided on using a combination of peaches and pecans. Peaches added sweet juiciness while pecans provided crunch and richness. For a little spice, we seeded a jalapeño so that its heat wouldn't overwhelm its sharp, fruity flavor and then chopped it fine. For greens we turned to frisée, a delicate but slightly bitter-tasting kind of chicory that's milder in flavor than other chicory varieties but has similar feathery leaves. Finely chopped red onion added a sharp bite, and basil contributed fresh flavor, nicely complementing the sweetness of the peaches. To tame the bitter flavor of the greens and any lingering heat from the jalapeño, we added a little honey to the dressing and finished it with some lime juice for bright acidity. If you can't find peaches or nectarines, substitute one orange, peeled and cut into ½-inch pieces. Toast the pecans until they begin to darken slightly in color, 3 to 5 minutes. For more spice, reserve, mince, and add the ribs and seeds from the jalapeño.

Whisk lime zest and juice, honey, garlic, and salt together in large bowl. Whisking constantly, slowly drizzle in oil until emulsified. Add black-eyed peas, peaches, frisée, onion, pecans, basil, and jalapeño and toss to combine. Season with salt and pepper to taste, and serve.

shrimp and white bean salad

SERVES 4

¼ cup extra-virgin olive oil

1 red, orange, or yellow bell pepper, stemmed, seeded, and chopped fine

1 small red onion, chopped fine

½ teaspoon table salt

2 garlic cloves, minced

¼ teaspoon red pepper flakes

2 (15-ounce) cans cannellini or small white beans, rinsed

2 ounces (2 cups) baby arugula or baby spinach

2 cups Sautéed Shrimp (page 43)

2 tablespoons lemon juice

why this recipe works Northern Italians combine their beloved cannellini beans with all sorts of ingredients. We riffed on this love of white beans and added tender shrimp to turn it into a salad reminiscent of Italy. The dish consists of beans lightly cooked with shrimp, vegetables, and garlic until the flavors blend, a combination that works to great effect; the sweetness of the mild, creamy beans is the perfect foil for the briny, tender shrimp. Canned beans passed muster and are the heart of this dish, but the shrimp play the starring role. We looked for a cooking method that would boost the flavor of the shrimp and found that searing on the stovetop worked best. We also briefly cooked red onion and red bell pepper, which kept their flavors fresh and their textures appealingly crunchy. The gentle peppery bite of arugula successfully married all the other flavors to make a delectable salad.

1 Heat oil in 12-inch nonstick skillet over medium heat until shimmering. Add bell pepper, onion, and salt and cook until softened, about 5 minutes. Stir in garlic and pepper flakes and cook until fragrant, about 30 seconds. Stir in beans and cook until heated through, about 5 minutes.

2 Add arugula and shrimp along with any accumulated juices and toss gently until arugula is wilted, about 1 minute. Stir in lemon juice and season with salt and pepper to taste. Serve.

squid and white bean salad

why this recipe works Savory white beans and lean, mild squid are a great pairing. The delicate flavor of the beans complements but doesn't overpower the subtle seafood flavor of the squid. We started by preparing the squid. To achieve some flavorful browning, we immediately ruled out steaming and boiling. We also decided that grilling was too fussy for just a pound of squid, so we settled on sautéing. We used a baking soda brine to tenderize the squid and make it less likely to overcook. Cooking the squid in two batches also encouraged more-even browning. Using canned beans kept the overall cooking time short, and simmering them in an aromatic liquid infused them with flavor. Nutty sherry vinegar and tangy pepperoncini were winning additions, and to bring out more of the pepperoncini flavor, we also added some of the brine. Scallions and whole parsley leaves provided a finishing touch of freshness. Be sure to use small squid (with bodies that are 3 to 4 inches in length) because they cook more quickly and are more tender than larger squid.

1 Dissolve baking soda and 1 tablespoon salt in 3 cups water in medium container. Add squid, cover, and refrigerate for 15 minutes. Dry squid thoroughly with paper towels and toss with 1 tablespoon oil.

2 Heat 1 tablespoon oil in medium saucepan over medium heat until shimmering. Add onion and salt and cook, stirring occasionally, until softened and lightly browned, 5 to 7 minutes. Stir in garlic and cook until fragrant, about 30 seconds. Stir in beans and ¼ cup water and bring to simmer. Reduce heat to low; cover; and continue to simmer, stirring occasionally, for 2 to 3 minutes. Set aside.

3 Heat 1 tablespoon oil in 12-inch nonstick skillet over high heat until just smoking. Add half of squid in single layer and cook, without moving it, until well browned, about 3 minutes. Flip squid and continue to cook, without moving it, until well browned on second side, about 2 minutes; transfer to bowl. Wipe skillet clean with paper towels and repeat with 1 tablespoon oil and remaining squid.

4 Whisk pepperoncini brine, vinegar, and remaining 2 tablespoons oil together in large bowl. Add squid, beans and any remaining cooking liquid, pepperoncini, parsley, and scallions and toss to combine. Season with salt and pepper to taste. Serve.

SERVES 4

- 1 tablespoon baking soda
- 1 tablespoon table salt for brining
- 1 pound small squid, bodies sliced crosswise into ½-inch-thick rings, tentacles halved
- 6 tablespoons extra-virgin olive oil, divided
- 1 red onion, chopped fine
- ¼ teaspoon table salt
- 3 garlic cloves, minced
- 2 (15-ounce) cans cannellini or small white beans, rinsed
- ⅓ cup pepperoncini, stemmed and sliced into ¼-inch-thick rings, plus 2 tablespoons brine
- 2 tablespoons sherry vinegar
- ½ cup fresh parsley or cilantro leaves
- 3 scallions, green parts only, sliced thin

classic three-bean salad

1 cup red wine vinegar

¾ cup sugar

½ cup vegetable oil

2 garlic cloves, minced

1 teaspoon table salt, plus salt for beans

Pinch pepper

8 ounces green beans, trimmed and cut into 1-inch lengths

8 ounces yellow wax beans, trimmed and cut into 1-inch lengths

1 (15-ounce) can red kidney beans or pinto beans, rinsed

½ red onion, sliced thin

¼ cup minced fresh parsley or cilantro

why this recipe works Recipes for that familiar picnic standby of canned green, yellow, and kidney beans tossed in a sweet, vinegary dressing have changed little since the salad's heyday in the 1950s. We wanted an updated, fresher-tasting three-bean salad, so we used a combination of canned kidney beans and fresh yellow and green beans. For the dressing, we relied on vegetable oil for mildness and red wine vinegar for tang. Heating the oil and vinegar with sugar, garlic, salt, and pepper intensified the vinaigrette's flavor and sweetness. Plan ahead: The salad must be refrigerated overnight to allow the flavors to meld.

1 Heat vinegar, sugar, oil, garlic, salt, and pepper in small saucepan over medium heat until sugar dissolves, about 5 minutes. Transfer to serving bowl and let cool completely.

2 Meanwhile, bring 3 quarts water to boil in large saucepan over high heat and fill medium bowl halfway with ice and water. Add 1 tablespoon salt, green beans, and yellow beans to boiling water and cook until beans are crisp-tender, about 5 minutes. Drain beans and plunge immediately into ice bath to stop cooking; let sit until chilled, about 2 minutes. Drain well.

3 Toss green beans, yellow beans, kidney beans, onion, and parsley with cooled vinegar mixture. Refrigerate, covered, overnight to let flavors meld. Let sit at room temperature for 30 minutes before serving. (Salad can be refrigerated for up to 4 days.)

variation
three-bean salad with cumin, cilantro, and oranges
Cut away peel and pith from oranges. Holding fruit over bowl, use paring knife to slice between membranes to release segments. Halve segments lengthwise.Set aside. Substitute ¼ cup lime juice (2 limes) for ¼ cup vinegar and heat 1 teaspoon ground cumin with vinegar mixture. Substitute minced fresh cilantro for parsley and add halved orange segments to vinegar mixture along with beans.

arugula, roasted red pepper, and white bean salad

SERVES 4 TO 6

⅓ cup red wine vinegar

¼ cup extra-virgin olive oil

¼ cup chopped fresh parsley or cilantro

2 tablespoons minced shallot

¾ teaspoon table salt

½ teaspoon pepper

1 recipe roasted bell peppers, cut into 2 by ½-inch strips (recipe follows)

1 (15-ounce) can small white or cannellini beans, rinsed

⅓ cup pitted olives, chopped coarse

5 ounces (5 cups) arugula or baby spinach

why this recipe works Velvety strips of roasted bell peppers (recipe follows) added meaty substance to a simple white bean and arugula salad, making it dinner-worthy. Briny olives and a tart vinaigrette balanced the bell peppers' sweetness. This salad is most attractive when made with red and yellow bell peppers. We like to use small white beans here. Pair with crusty bread for a light meal.

1 Whisk vinegar, oil, parsley, shallot, salt, and pepper together in large bowl. Add bell peppers, beans, and olives and stir gently until well coated. Let sit until flavors meld, about 15 minutes.

2 Set aside 1½ cups bell pepper mixture. Add arugula to remaining bell pepper mixture and toss to combine. Transfer to serving platter and top with reserved bell pepper mixture. Serve.

roasted bell peppers

makes 1½ cups

Cooking times will vary depending on your broiler and the thickness of the bell pepper walls, so watch the bell peppers carefully as they cook. We prefer to use a combination of red and yellow bell peppers for our Arugula, Roasted Red Pepper, and White Bean Salad.

3 **large bell peppers
   (about 1½ pounds)**

1   Line rimmed baking sheet with aluminum foil and spray with vegetable oil spray. Slice ½ inch from tops and bottoms of bell peppers. Gently remove stems from tops. Twist and pull out each core, using knife to loosen at edges if necessary. Cut slit down 1 side of each bell pepper.

2   Turn each bell pepper skin side down and gently press so it opens to create long strip. Slide knife along insides of bell peppers to remove remaining ribs and seeds.

3   Arrange bell pepper strips, tops, and bottoms skin side up on prepared sheet and flatten all pieces with your hand. Adjust oven rack 3 to 4 inches from broiler element and heat broiler. Broil until skin is puffed and most of surface is well charred, 10 to 13 minutes, rotating sheet halfway through broiling.

4   Using tongs, pile bell peppers in center of foil. Gather foil over bell peppers and crimp to form pouch. Let steam for 10 minutes. Open foil packet and spread out bell peppers. When cool enough to handle, peel bell peppers and discard skins. (Bell peppers can be refrigerated for up to 3 days.)

white bean salad with valencia oranges and celery

why this recipe works We took ordinary canned beans and turned them into the rightful stars of this salad. The key was steeping the beans in a garlicky broth first. This afforded us time to tame the bite of a raw shallot in vinegar and pull together the other ingredients. Once the beans were steeped and the shallot soaked, this salad came together in a minute. Canned beans are a convenient shortcut, but we hoped to fool eaters into thinking we'd spent hours in the kitchen. This recipe will also work with other types of canned beans. It's important to let the salad sit for 20 minutes before serving so that the beans absorb the flavors of the other ingredients.

1   Heat 1 tablespoon oil and garlic in medium saucepan over medium-high heat until just beginning to brown, about 2 minutes. Add 2 cups water and 1 teaspoon salt and bring to simmer. Off heat, add beans, cover, and let sit for 20 minutes. Combine vinegar and shallot in large bowl and let sit for 20 minutes.

2   Cut away peel and pith from oranges. Holding fruit over bowl, use paring knife to slice between membranes to release segments. Drain beans and discard garlic. Add beans, oranges, celery, parsley, and remaining oil to shallot mixture and toss until thoroughly combined. Season with salt and pepper to taste. Let sit until flavors meld, about 20 minutes. Serve.

SERVES 6

⅓ cup extra-virgin olive oil, divided

4 garlic cloves, smashed and peeled

   Table salt for steeping beans

3 (15-ounce) cans cannellini or small white beans, rinsed

¼ cup sherry vinegar

1 shallot, minced

2 Valencia or navel oranges

¾ cup thinly sliced celery

½ cup chopped fresh parsley or cilantro

barley salad with pomegranate, pistachios, and feta

SERVES 6 TO 8

1½ cups pearl barley

½ teaspoon table salt, plus salt for cooking barley

2 tablespoons pomegranate molasses

½ teaspoon ground cinnamon

¼ teaspoon ground cumin

3 tablespoons extra-virgin olive oil, plus extra for drizzling

½ cup coarsely chopped fresh cilantro or mint

⅓ cup golden raisins or chopped dried apricots

¼ cup shelled pistachios or whole almonds, toasted and chopped coarse

3 ounces feta or goat cheese, cubed or crumbled (¾ cup)

6 scallions, green parts only, sliced thin

½ cup pomegranate seeds

why this recipe works Barley, said to be the first domesticated wild grass, has been widely used in Egypt since ancient times. Cumin is the nation's most used spice and pomegranates hold a sacred place in the culture. Inspired by these Egyptian flavors, we created a salad with barley as the base. First we had to choose a cooking method for our barley that allowed the grains to remain distinct. We turned to the trusty pasta method, in which we simply boil the grains in plenty of salted water until they're tender and then spread them on a baking sheet to dry rather than allowing them to clump in the pot. For flavor, we incorporated toasty pistachios, beloved in the Middle East; tangy pomegranate molasses; and cilantro, all balanced by warm, earthy spices and sweet golden raisins. Salty feta cheese, scallions, and pomegranate seeds adorned the top of our colorful composed salad. If you can't find pomegranate molasses, make your own (recipe follows). Do not substitute hulled barley or hull-less barley in this recipe. If using quick-cooking or presteamed barley (read the package carefully to determine this), you will need to decrease the barley cooking time in step 1.

1 Bring 4 quarts water to boil in Dutch oven. Add barley and 1 tablespoon salt; return to boil; and cook until tender, 20 to 40 minutes. Drain barley; spread onto rimmed baking sheet; and let cool completely, about 15 minutes. (Barley can be refrigerated for up to 3 days.)

2 Whisk molasses, cinnamon, cumin, salt, and oil together in large bowl. Add barley, cilantro, raisins, and pistachios and toss gently to combine. Season with salt and pepper to taste. Spread barley salad evenly on serving platter and top with feta, scallions, and pomegranate seeds in separate diagonal rows. Drizzle with extra oil and serve.

pomegranate molasses

makes ⅓ cup

Whisk this molasses into vinaigrettes, drizzle it on vegetables, brush it on roasted meats, or stir it into dips. Reducing the juice at a simmer instead of a boil drives off fewer flavor compounds, giving you fresher flavor. To speed up evaporation, we use a 12-inch skillet, which has more surface area than a saucepan.

- 2 cups unsweetened pomegranate juice
- ½ teaspoon sugar
  Pinch table salt

Bring pomegranate juice, sugar, and salt to simmer in 12-inch skillet over high heat. Reduce heat to low and simmer, stirring and scraping thickened juice from sides of skillet occasionally, until mixture is thick and syrupy and measures ⅓ cup, 12 to 15 minutes. Let cool slightly before transferring to container. (Cooled molasses can be refrigerated for up to 1 month.)

farro salad with asparagus, snap peas, and tomatoes

SERVES 4 TO 6

6 ounces asparagus, trimmed and cut into 1-inch lengths

6 ounces sugar snap peas or snow peas, strings removed, cut into 1-inch lengths

¼ teaspoon table salt, plus salt for cooking vegetables and farro

1½ cups whole farro

2 tablespoons lemon juice

2 tablespoons minced shallot

1 teaspoon Dijon mustard

¼ teaspoon pepper

3 tablespoons extra-virgin olive oil

6 ounces cherry or grape tomatoes, halved

3 tablespoons chopped fresh dill or mint

2 ounces feta or goat cheese, crumbled (½ cup), divided

why this recipe works An ancient grain, farro has been cultivated in Italy for centuries. It's easy to see why. Nutty, hearty, and chewy, it fills you up nicely and works in salads as well as vegetable dishes, soups, and stews. For this salad we used whole farro, which is traditionally soaked overnight before being cooked gradually for more than an hour to soften. We learned that boiling the farro in plenty of salted water and then draining it yielded nicely firm but tender grains simply and quickly, allowing us to skip the soak. We paired the grain with asparagus and snap peas, briefly boiled to bring out their vibrant color and crisp bite. A lemon-dill dressing, cherry tomatoes, and feta cheese finished this fresh, colorful, and filling spring salad. We prefer the flavor and texture of whole farro; pearl farro can be used, but the texture may be softer. Do not use quick-cooking or presteamed farro (read the package carefully to determine this) in this recipe.

1 Bring 4 quarts water to boil in Dutch oven. Add asparagus, snap peas, and 1 tablespoon salt and cook until crisp-tender, about 3 minutes. Using slotted spoon, transfer vegetables to large plate and let cool completely, about 15 minutes.

2 Add farro to water; return to boil; and cook until grains are tender with slight chew, 15 to 30 minutes. Drain farro; spread onto rimmed baking sheet; and let cool completely, about 15 minutes. (Farro can be refrigerated for up to 3 days.)

3 Whisk lemon juice, shallot, mustard, pepper, and salt together in large bowl. Whisking constantly, slowly drizzle in oil until emulsified. Add asparagus, snap peas, farro, tomatoes, dill, and ¼ cup feta and toss gently to combine. Season with salt and pepper to taste. Transfer to serving platter and sprinkle with remaining ¼ cup feta. Serve.

millet salad with corn and queso fresco

why this recipe works The mellow corn flavor and fine texture of tiny millet seeds make them versatile in savory dishes. We set out to feature the small seeds in a grain-style salad that would enhance the sweet flavor of the millet. The seeds release starch as they cook, which can create large clumps. We found that boiling the millet in a lot of water, as we would cook pasta, resulted in distinct, individual cooked seeds because the seed couldn't clump together. This made them perfect for tossing with dressing. Spreading out the millet on a baking sheet allowed it to cool and further prevented clumping. Then we proceeded to build the flavors of our salad. We used corn to complement the millet's natural flavor and to add texture, and cherry tomatoes, queso fresco, and a minced jalapeño gave the salad some southwestern flavor. To dress our salad we whipped up a quick, bright vinaigrette using lime zest and juice. A small amount of mayonnaise helped emulsify the dressing so that it would evenly coat the millet. Chopped cilantro added freshness and color. For more spice, reserve, mince, and add the ribs and seeds from the jalapeño.

1   Bring 3 quarts water to boil in large pot. Add millet and 1 teaspoon salt and cook until grains are tender, about 20 minutes. Drain millet, spread onto rimmed baking sheet, and drizzle with 1½ teaspoons lime juice. Let cool completely, about 15 minutes.

2   Whisk honey, mayonnaise, salt, lime zest, and remaining 2 tablespoons lime juice together in large bowl. Whisking constantly, slowly drizzle in oil until emulsified. Add millet and toss to combine. Fold in tomatoes, corn, queso fresco, cilantro, and jalapeño. Season with salt and pepper to taste, and serve.

SERVES 4 TO 6

- 1   cup millet
- ¼   teaspoon table salt, plus salt for cooking millet
- 1   teaspoon grated lime zest, plus 2½ tablespoons juice (2 limes), divided
- 2   teaspoons honey
- ½   teaspoon mayonnaise
- 3   tablespoons extra-virgin olive oil
- 8   ounces cherry or grape tomatoes, quartered
- ½   cup frozen corn, thawed
- 1½ ounces queso fresco or feta cheese, crumbled (⅓ cup)
- ¼   cup chopped fresh cilantro or parsley
- 1   jalapeño or serrano chile, stemmed, seeded, and minced

oat berry, chickpea, and arugula salad

why this recipe works Oats are not just for breakfast anymore. Chewy, nutty oat berries (whole oats that have been hulled) make a wonderful base for a substantial grain salad. To ensure that the oat berries retained the perfect chewy, tender texture when served cold, we cooked them in a large amount of water, pasta-style, and then drained and rinsed them under cold water to stop the cooking so that the grains wouldn't end up mushy. Assertive, peppery arugula paired well with the oat berries, and we added chickpeas for a little more heft and complementary buttery flavor and creamy texture. Roasted red peppers added sweetness, and feta brought creaminess and salty bite. A simple lemon and cilantro dressing spiked with cumin, paprika, and cayenne provided the perfect amount of spice and brightness.

1 Bring 2 quarts water to boil in large saucepan. Add oat berries and ½ teaspoon salt; partially cover; and cook, stirring often, until tender but still chewy, 45 to 50 minutes. Drain oat berries and rinse under cold running water until cool. Drain well, then transfer to large bowl. (Oat berries can be refrigerated for up to 3 days.)

2 Whisk lemon juice, cilantro, honey, garlic, cumin, paprika, cayenne, and salt together in small bowl. Whisking constantly, slowly drizzle in oil until emulsified, then drizzle over oat berries. Stir in chickpeas, arugula, red peppers, and feta. Season with salt and pepper to taste, and serve.

SERVES 4 TO 6

1 cup oat berries (groats), rinsed

¼ teaspoon table salt, plus salt for cooking oat berries

2 tablespoons lemon juice

2 tablespoons minced fresh cilantro or parsley

1 teaspoon honey

1 garlic clove, minced

¼ teaspoon ground cumin

⅛ teaspoon paprika

   Pinch cayenne pepper

3 tablespoons extra-virgin olive oil

1 (15-ounce) can chickpeas or white beans, rinsed

6 ounces (6 cups) baby arugula or baby spinach

½ cup jarred roasted red peppers, patted dry and chopped

2 ounces feta or goat cheese, crumbled (½ cup)

quinoa, black bean, and mango salad with lime dressing

SERVES 4 TO 6

dressing

5 tablespoons lime juice (3 limes)

½ jalapeño or serrano chile, seeded and chopped

1 teaspoon table salt

¾ teaspoon ground cumin

½ cup extra-virgin olive oil

⅓ cup fresh cilantro or parsley leaves

salad

1½ cups prewashed white quinoa

2¼ cups water

½ teaspoon table salt

1 red, orange, or yellow bell pepper, stemmed, seeded, and chopped

1 mango, peeled, pitted, and cut into ¼-inch pieces

1 (15-ounce) can black beans, rinsed

2 scallions, sliced thin

1 avocado, halved, pitted, and sliced thin

why this recipe works The quinoa seed is often called a "supergrain" because it's a nutritionally complete protein. We wanted to feature quinoa's delicate texture and nutty flavor in a salad good enough for a main course. We toasted the quinoa to bring out its flavor before adding liquid to the pan and simmering the grains until they were nearly tender. Then, as we do with other grains, we spread the quinoa on a rimmed baking sheet to cool without clumping. The residual heat finished cooking it, giving us fluffy grains. Black beans, mango, and bell pepper added heartiness, flavor, and color to the salad. Scallions brought bite, and avocado provided creaminess. We like the convenience of prewashed quinoa; rinsing removes the quinoa's bitter protective coating (called saponin). If you buy unwashed quinoa, rinse it and then spread it out on a clean dish towel to dry for 15 minutes. For more spice, reserve, mince, and add the ribs and seeds from the jalapeño.

1   for the dressing Process lime juice, jalapeño, salt, and cumin in blender until jalapeño is finely chopped, about 15 seconds. With blender running, add oil and cilantro; continue to process until smooth and emulsified, about 20 seconds. (Dressing can be refrigerated for up to 3 days; whisk to recombine before using.)

2   for the salad Toast quinoa in large saucepan over medium-high heat, stirring often, until very fragrant and quinoa makes continuous popping sound, 5 to 7 minutes. Stir in water and salt and bring to simmer. Cover; reduce heat to low; and simmer gently until most of water has been absorbed and quinoa is nearly tender, about 15 minutes. Spread quinoa onto rimmed baking sheet and let cool for 20 minutes; transfer to large bowl. (Quinoa can be refrigerated for up to 3 days.)

3   Add bell pepper, mango, beans, scallions, and dressing to quinoa and toss to combine. Season with salt and pepper to taste. (Salad can be held at room temperature for up to 2 hours before serving.) Divide among individual plates. Serve, topping individual portions with avocado.

quinoa lettuce wraps with feta and olives

why this recipe works Whatever the filling, lettuce wraps make a perfect light lunch. We filled these with an easy and flavorful vegetarian quinoa salad. To complement the quinoa's nuttiness, we paired it with salty feta, briny olives, and fresh mint and oregano. Rather than crumbling the feta into the salad, we blended it with some yogurt and vinegar to make a flavorful vinaigrette. Once the quinoa cooled, we tossed it with cucumber, tomatoes, olives, shallot, and some of the vinaigrette, reserving the rest for drizzling once we portioned our salad into the lettuce leaves. The large, crisp leaves of Boston or Bibb lettuce made perfectly sized cups. We like the convenience of prewashed quinoa; rinsing removes the quinoa's bitter protective coating (called saponin). If you buy unwashed quinoa, rinse it and then spread it out on a clean dish towel to dry for 15 minutes.

1 for the vinaigrette Process feta, yogurt, mint, vinegar, oregano, salt, and pepper in blender until smooth, about 15 seconds. With blender running, slowly add oil until emulsified, about 30 seconds. (Vinaigrette can be refrigerated for up to 24 hours.)

2 for the salad Toast quinoa in large saucepan over medium-high heat, stirring often, until very fragrant and quinoa makes continuous popping sound, 5 to 7 minutes. Stir in water and salt and bring to simmer. Cover; reduce heat to low; and simmer gently until most of water has been absorbed and quinoa is nearly tender, about 15 minutes. Spread quinoa onto rimmed baking sheet and let cool for 20 minutes; transfer to large bowl. (Quinoa can be refrigerated for up to 3 days.)

3 Add tomatoes, cucumber, shallot, olives, and ⅔ cup vinaigrette to quinoa and toss to combine. Season with salt and pepper to taste. Serve with lettuce leaves, spooning ⅓ cup quinoa mixture into each leaf and drizzling with remaining vinaigrette.

SERVES 4

vinaigrette

- 4 ounces feta cheese, crumbled (1 cup)
- ½ cup plain yogurt
- ¼ cup minced fresh mint
- 3 tablespoons red wine vinegar
- 2 tablespoons minced fresh oregano or 1½ teaspoons dried
- ½ teaspoon table salt
- ¼ teaspoon pepper
- ½ cup extra-virgin olive oil

salad

- 1½ cups prewashed white quinoa
- 2¼ cups water
- ½ teaspoon table salt
- 2 tomatoes, cored, seeded, and cut into ¼-inch pieces
- 1 cucumber, halved lengthwise, seeded, and cut into ¼-inch pieces
- 1 shallot, minced
- ¼ cup pitted olives, chopped
- 2 heads Boston or Bibb lettuce (1 pound), leaves separated

quinoa lettuce wraps with feta and olives, *page 301*

quinoa taco salad

SERVES 4 TO 6

¾ cup prewashed white quinoa

3 tablespoons extra-virgin olive oil, divided

1 small onion, chopped fine

½ teaspoon table salt, divided

2 teaspoons minced canned chipotle chile in adobo sauce

2 teaspoons tomato paste

1 teaspoon anchovy paste (optional)

½ teaspoon ground cumin

1 cup chicken or vegetable broth

2 tablespoons lime juice

¼ teaspoon pepper

1 head escarole (1 pound) or frisée, trimmed and sliced thin

2 scallions, sliced thin

½ cup chopped fresh cilantro or parsley, divided

1 (15-ounce) can black beans, rinsed

8 ounces cherry or grape tomatoes, quartered

1 ripe avocado, halved, pitted, and chopped

2 ounces queso fresco or feta cheese, crumbled (½ cup)

why this recipe works We reworked taco salad with quinoa and made it hearty, full of flavor, and nutritious. Nutty quinoa made a surprisingly good replacement for ground beef; toasted and simmered in broth with chipotles in adobo, tomato paste, anchovy paste, and cumin, the quinoa acquired a rich, spiced, meaty flavor. We also substituted escarole for lettuce to add a welcome hint of bitter crunch; cut back on cheese, opting for queso fresco; and added lots of fragrant cilantro. Black beans, avocado, cherry tomatoes, and scallions completed the picture. This salad is so hearty that it doesn't even need tortilla chips, but if you like, you can certainly serve it with tortilla chips or multigrain chips. We like the convenience of prewashed quinoa; rinsing removes the quinoa's bitter protective coating (called saponin). If you buy unwashed quinoa, rinse it and then spread it out on a clean dish towel to dry for 15 minutes.

1   Toast quinoa in large saucepan over medium-high heat, stirring often, until very fragrant and quinoa makes continuous popping sound, 5 to 7 minutes; transfer to bowl.

2   Heat 1 tablespoon oil in now-empty saucepan over medium heat until shimmering. Add onion and ¼ teaspoon salt and cook until onion is softened and lightly browned, 5 to 7 minutes.

3   Stir in chipotle; tomato paste; anchovy paste, if using; and cumin and cook until fragrant, about 30 seconds. Stir in broth and quinoa, increase heat to medium-high, and bring to simmer. Cover; reduce heat to low; and simmer until quinoa is tender and liquid has been absorbed, 18 to 22 minutes, stirring halfway through cooking. Let sit off heat, covered, for 10 minutes. Spread quinoa onto rimmed baking sheet and let cool completely, about 20 minutes.

4   Whisk lime juice, pepper, remaining 2 tablespoons oil, and remaining ¼ teaspoon salt together in large bowl. Add escarole, scallions, and ¼ cup cilantro and toss to combine. Gently fold in beans, tomatoes, and avocado. Transfer to serving platter and top with quinoa, queso fresco, and remaining ¼ cup cilantro. Serve.

wheat berry and endive salad with blueberries and goat cheese

why this recipe works Wheat berries are whole kernels of wheat without the husk. We pair this chewy, nutty grain with crisp endive, creamy goat cheese, and sweet fresh blueberries for this substantial and pretty salad. We cooked the wheat berries like pasta until they were tender but still had some nice chew. We used less salt than we do for other grains; too much and the grains didn't absorb enough water and remained hard. A bright vinaigrette made with champagne vinegar, shallot, chives, and mustard brought all the ingredients together harmoniously. If using quick-cooking or presteamed wheat berries (read the package carefully to determine this), you will need to decrease the wheat berry cooking time in step 1.

1 Bring 4 quarts water to boil in large pot. Add wheat berries and ¼ teaspoon salt; partially cover; and cook, stirring often, until wheat berries are tender but still chewy, 50 minutes to 1 hour 10 minutes. Drain wheat berries and rinse under cold running water until cool. Drain well. (Wheat berries can be refrigerated for up to 3 days.)

2 Whisk vinegar, shallot, chives, mustard, pepper, and salt together in large bowl. Whisking constantly, slowly drizzle in oil until emulsified. Add wheat berries, endive, blueberries, and pecans and toss to combine. Season with salt and pepper to taste, transfer to a serving platter, sprinkle with goat cheese, and serve.

SERVES 4 TO 6

- 1½ cups wheat berries
- ½ teaspoon table salt, plus salt for cooking wheat berries
- 2 tablespoons champagne vinegar
- 1 tablespoon minced shallot
- 1 tablespoon minced fresh chives or parsley
- 1 teaspoon Dijon mustard
- ¼ teaspoon pepper
- 6 tablespoons extra-virgin olive oil
- 2 heads Belgian endive (4 ounces each), halved, cored, and sliced crosswise ¼ inch thick
- 7½ ounces (1½ cups) blueberries, blackberries, or raspberries
- ¾ cup pecans, walnuts, or whole almonds, toasted and chopped
- 4 ounces goat or feta cheese, crumbled (1 cup)

black rice salad with snap peas and ginger-sesame vinaigrette

SERVES 4 TO 6

1½ cups black rice

¼ teaspoon table salt, plus salt for cooking rice

1 teaspoon plus 3 tablespoons unseasoned rice vinegar, divided

2 teaspoons minced shallot

2 teaspoons honey

2 teaspoons Asian chili-garlic sauce

1 teaspoon grated fresh ginger

⅛ teaspoon pepper

¼ cup extra-virgin olive oil

1 tablespoon toasted sesame oil

6 ounces sugar snap peas or snow peas, strings removed, halved crosswise on bias

5 radishes, trimmed, halved, and sliced thin

1 red, orange, or yellow bell pepper, stemmed, seeded, and chopped fine

¼ cup minced fresh cilantro or chives

why this recipe works Also known as purple rice or forbidden rice, black rice is an ancient grain that was once reserved for the emperors of China. Now we can all enjoy its roasted, nutty taste, delicious in everything from salads to puddings. Here we make a striking dish where emerald-green snap peas, red-and-white radishes, and red bell peppers sit like jewels against the black rice. Black rice is easy to overcook, so our major obstacle was finding the right cooking method. Cooking it like pasta, in lots of boiling water, gave it space to move around. Once it was done, we drained it, drizzled it with a little vinegar for a flavor boost, and let it cool completely on a baking sheet. This ensured perfectly cooked grains that were chewy and not mushy. We mixed up a vinaigrette with sesame oil, ginger, chili-garlic sauce, and honey; stirred in some cilantro; and our salad was complete. Note that this recipe uses unseasoned rice vinegar; we don't recommend using seasoned rice vinegar in its place.

1 Bring 4 quarts water to boil in Dutch oven over medium-high heat. Add rice and 1 teaspoon salt and cook until rice is tender, 20 to 25 minutes. Drain rice, spread onto rimmed baking sheet, and drizzle with 1 teaspoon vinegar. Let rice cool completely, about 15 minutes. (Rice can be refrigerated for up to 3 days.)

2 Whisk shallot, honey, chili-garlic sauce, ginger, pepper, salt, and remaining 3 tablespoons vinegar together in large bowl. Whisking constantly, slowly drizzle in olive oil and sesame oil until emulsified. Add rice, snap peas, radishes, bell pepper, and cilantro and toss to combine. Season with salt and pepper to taste. Serve.

black rice and sea bean salad

SERVES 4 TO 6

5   ounces sea beans, trimmed and cut into 2-inch lengths

1½ cups black rice

1   grapefruit

¼   cup white wine vinegar

1   shallot, chopped fine

1   garlic clove, minced

1   teaspoon honey

6   tablespoons extra-virgin olive oil

2   tablespoons chopped fresh mint or cilantro

why this recipe works A salad succeeds when it contrasts tastes, colors, and textures in a visually appealing and flavorful way. Here, the firmness of black rice, also called purple rice or forbidden rice, plays off salty, crunchy sea beans, or halophytes; sweet-tart grapefruit; fresh, floral mint; and honey in the dressing. Sea beans develop their strong, briny flavor from the salty water and air in the marshes where they typically grow upright. One hurdle was tempering their saltiness. Blanching them first helped, and it also gave them a vibrant green color, which looked stunning when tossed with the black rice. Since it's easy to overcook black rice, the best way to get it evenly done was to cook it like pasta (in the water we used for blanching the sea beans), with space to move around. After draining the rice, we let it cool completely on a baking sheet. This ensured perfectly cooked grains with chew but no mushiness. Sea beans are usually available at farmers' markets, well-stocked supermarkets, natural foods stores, or online.

1   Bring 4 quarts water to boil in large pot. Fill large bowl halfway with ice and water. Add sea beans to boiling water and cook until crisp-tender, about 1 minute. Using slotted spoon, transfer sea beans to ice bath and let sit until cool, about 5 minutes.

2   Transfer sea beans to triple layer of paper towels and dry well. Return water in pot to boil; add rice; and cook until rice is tender, 20 to 25 minutes. Drain rice; spread onto rimmed baking sheet; and let cool completely, about 15 minutes.

3   Cut away peel and pith from grapefruit. Quarter grapefruit, then slice crosswise into ¼-inch-thick pieces. Whisk vinegar, shallot, garlic, and honey together in large serving bowl. Whisking constantly, slowly drizzle in oil until emulsified. Add sea beans, rice, grapefruit, and mint to vinaigrette in bowl and toss to coat. Serve.

brown rice salad with fennel, mushrooms, and walnuts

why this recipe works Often eaten as a substitute for white rice, brown rice has a delicious earthiness that sets it apart. This works well in our salad, enhanced by chewy mushrooms and crunchy walnuts. Brown rice can become gummy or tough when cooked; we found that the pasta method ensured evenly cooked grains. To season the rice, we dressed it with vinegar while it was still warm.

1 Bring 3 quarts water to boil in large pot. Add rice and 2 teaspoons salt and cook, stirring occasionally, until rice is tender, 22 to 25 minutes. Drain rice, spread onto rimmed baking sheet, and drizzle with 1 tablespoon vinegar. Let rice cool completely, about 15 minutes; transfer to large bowl. (Rice can be refrigerated for up to 3 days.)

2 Heat 1 tablespoon oil in 12-inch skillet over medium-high heat until shimmering. Add mushrooms and ½ teaspoon salt and cook, stirring occasionally, until skillet is dry and mushrooms are browned, 6 to 8 minutes; transfer to plate and let cool.

3 Heat 1 tablespoon oil in now-empty skillet over medium-high heat until shimmering. Add fennel and ¼ teaspoon salt and cook, stirring occasionally, until just browned and crisp-tender, 3 to 4 minutes; transfer to plate with mushrooms and let cool.

4 Whisk shallot, pepper, remaining ½ teaspoon salt, remaining 2 tablespoons vinegar, and remaining 2 tablespoons oil together in small bowl, then drizzle over rice. Add mushroom-fennel mixture and toss to combine. Let sit until flavors meld, about 10 minutes.

5 Add ½ cup walnuts, tarragon, and 1 tablespoon parsley and toss to combine. Season with salt and pepper to taste. Sprinkle with remaining walnuts and remaining 1 tablespoon parsley and serve.

SERVES 4 TO 6

1½ cups long-grain brown rice

1¾ teaspoons table salt, divided, plus salt for cooking rice

3 tablespoons white wine vinegar, divided

¼ cup extra-virgin olive oil, divided

1 pound white or cremini mushrooms, trimmed and quartered

1 large fennel bulb, stalks discarded, bulb halved, cored, and sliced thin

1 shallot, minced

½ teaspoon pepper

⅔ cup walnuts or whole almonds, toasted and chopped coarse, divided

2 tablespoons minced fresh tarragon or chives

2 tablespoons minced fresh parsley or dill, divided

harvest salad

vinaigrette

- 2 tablespoons plus 2 teaspoons cider vinegar
- 2 tablespoons water
- 4 teaspoons Dijon mustard
- 2 teaspoons caraway seeds, toasted and cracked
- ¼ teaspoon table salt
- ¼ teaspoon pepper
- ¼ cup extra-virgin olive oil

salad

- 1 pound sweet potatoes, unpeeled, halved lengthwise and sliced crosswise ¼ inch thick
- 3 teaspoons extra-virgin olive oil
- ¼ teaspoon table salt
- 8 ounces (8 cups) baby kale or baby spinach
- 1 cup Cooked Wild Rice (recipe follows)
- 1 Granny Smith apple, cored and cut into ½-inch pieces
- 4 ounces feta or goat cheese, crumbled (1 cup)
- ¼ cup dried cranberries or dried cherries

why this recipe works When autumn is in the air, fall food is on our minds. Caramelized roasted sweet potatoes and crunchy, tart apples make for a perfect seasonal salad that fills you up and stores well. Wild rice is a chewy counterpoint, and to continue the harvest theme, we whisked up a cider and caraway vinaigrette, toasting and cracking the seeds but leaving them whole for appealing texture. For toppings, feta cheese added briny contrast and dried cranberries contributed color and more tartness, helping turn mealtime into an autumnal affair. To crack the caraway seeds, rock the bottom edge of a skillet over the toasted seeds on a cutting board until they crack. Serve with Savory Seed Brittle (page 51).

1 for the vinaigrette Whisk vinegar, water, mustard, caraway seeds, salt, and pepper together in bowl. Whisking constantly, slowly drizzle in oil until emulsified. (Vinaigrette can be refrigerated for up to 2 days; whisk to recombine before using.)

2 for the salad Adjust oven rack to middle position and heat oven to 400 degrees. Toss potatoes, oil, and salt together in bowl, then spread in even layer on aluminum foil–lined rimmed baking sheet. Roast until potatoes are beginning to brown, 15 to 20 minutes, flipping slices halfway through roasting. Let potatoes cool for 5 minutes, then season with salt and pepper to taste. (Sweet potatoes can be refrigerated for up to 2 days.)

3 Toss kale with half of vinaigrette in large bowl to coat, then season with salt and pepper to taste. Transfer to serving platter and top with rice, sweet potatoes, apple, feta, and cranberries. Drizzle with remaining vinaigrette and serve.

cooked wild rice
makes 2 cups

Make a half portion of this recipe, if you wish, by halving the amount of rice but using 2 quarts water and ½ teaspoon salt.

> ¾ **cup wild rice, picked over**
> **and rinsed**
> **Table salt for cooking rice**

Bring 2 quarts water to boil in Dutch oven over medium-high heat. Add rice and ½ teaspoon salt and cook until rice is tender, 35 to 40 minutes. Drain rice; spread onto rimmed baking sheet; and let cool completely, about 15 minutes. (Rice can be refrigerated for up to 3 days.)

turmeric rice and chicken salad with herbs

why this recipe works We drew inspiration for this salad from chicken shawarma, a street-food favorite throughout the eastern Mediterranean and the Middle East. We used traditional shawarma seasonings—garlic, turmeric, paprika, cumin, and just a touch of cinnamon—to create a fragrant, flavorful dressing for rice and chicken. For fluffy, well-seasoned rice that didn't clump or get hard as it cooled, we boiled the grains in an abundance of salted water, as we do for pasta. Then we spread them on a baking sheet to cool without clumping. We mixed in crunchy sliced cucumbers and radishes and juicy tomatoes. Instead of lettuce, we added herbs—cilantro, parsley, mint, and dill all worked, the torn leaves adding intense bursts of freshness and flavor in every bite. A lemony-tart herbed yogurt drizzled over the finished salad added richness and pulled everything together. We like using Perfect Poached Chicken (page 43) here, but any cooked chicken would work. Persian cucumbers (sometimes called "mini cucumbers") are small, slim cucumbers similar to seedless cucumbers in flavor and texture; you can use 6 ounces of English cucumber if Persian cucumbers are not available.

1   Bring 4 quarts water to boil in large pot. Add rice and 1½ teaspoons salt and cook, stirring occasionally, until rice is tender but not soft, about 15 minutes. Drain rice; spread onto rimmed baking sheet; and let cool completely, about 15 minutes.

2   Microwave oil, garlic, cumin, paprika, turmeric, cayenne, and cinnamon in medium bowl until simmering and fragrant, 30 to 60 seconds. Let cool slightly, then whisk in lemon juice and salt.

3   Combine rice, dressing, chicken, tomatoes, cucumbers, radishes, and cilantro in large bowl and toss gently to combine. Season with salt and pepper to taste. Serve with yogurt sauce.

SERVES 4

- 1   cup long-grain white or jasmine rice
- ½   teaspoon table salt, plus salt for cooking rice
- 3   tablespoons extra-virgin olive oil
- 2   garlic cloves, minced
- 1   teaspoon ground cumin
- 1   teaspoon paprika
- 1   teaspoon ground turmeric
- ⅛   teaspoon cayenne pepper
-     Pinch ground cinnamon
- 3   tablespoons lemon juice
- 2   cups cooked chicken, chopped
- 6   ounces cherry or grape tomatoes, halved
- 2   Persian cucumbers, quartered lengthwise and sliced crosswise ¼ inch thick
- 3   radishes, trimmed, quartered, and sliced thin
- 1   cup torn fresh cilantro, dill, parsley, or mint
- ½   cup Herb Yogurt Sauce (page 247)

nam khao

SERVES 4 TO 6

2¼ cups water

1½ cups jasmine or long-grain white rice, rinsed

3 tablespoons lime juice (2 limes)

2 tablespoons fish sauce

1½ tablespoons palm sugar or packed brown sugar

1 tablespoon Thai red curry paste

1 teaspoon grated fresh ginger

2 shallots, sliced thin

1 teaspoon vegetable oil

2 ounces Chinese sausage or ham steak, cut into ½-inch pieces

1½ quarts peanut or vegetable oil for frying

½ cup fresh cilantro or Thai basil leaves

½ cup fresh mint leaves, torn

4 scallions, sliced thin on bias

¼ cup dry-roasted peanuts, chopped coarse

why this recipe works Nam khao, a rice salad found at restaurants and street stalls throughout Laos, is originally from Tha Deua, a Laotian port village. A blend of crunchy, soft, tangy, salty, sweet, and nutty flavors, nam khao features tightly packed deep-fried rice balls with a crunchy crust and soft, chewy interior. The balls are broken into bite-size pieces and tossed with fermented pork sausage, fresh herbs, peanuts, and a citrusy dressing. Its flavors inspired us to make our own version. Rather than form balls, we fried half the cooked rice in loose clusters and tossed it with plain cooked rice for a blend of crunchy and chewy. We substituted sweet and salty Chinese sausage for traditional fermented pork sausage; ham steak makes a great substitution, too. Do not substitute basmati rice for the jasmine rice. We use store-bought red curry paste for this salad. Use a Dutch oven that holds 6 quarts or more for this recipe.

1 Bring water and rice to simmer in large saucepan over high heat. Reduce heat to low; cover; and simmer gently until rice is tender and water has been fully absorbed, about 10 minutes. Off heat, lay clean dish towel underneath lid and let sit for 10 minutes. Spread rice onto greased large plate and let cool for 10 minutes.

2 Meanwhile, whisk lime juice, fish sauce, sugar, curry paste, and ginger in large bowl until sugar has dissolved. Stir in shallots and set aside.

3 Heat vegetable oil in large Dutch oven over medium heat until shimmering. Add sausage and cook until spotty brown, about 3 minutes; transfer to separate bowl. Wipe pot clean with paper towels.

4 Line rimmed baking sheet with triple layer of paper towels. Add peanut oil to now-empty pot until it measures about 1 inch deep and heat over medium-high heat to 400 degrees. Shape half of rice into rough 2-inch clusters. Carefully add half of rice clusters to hot oil and cook, without stirring them, until light golden brown, about 5 minutes. Adjust burner, if necessary, to maintain oil temperature between 375 and 400 degrees. Using slotted spoon or spider skimmer, transfer fried rice to prepared sheet. Return oil to 400 degrees and repeat with remaining rice clusters; transfer to sheet and let drain for 10 minutes.

5 Using your fingers, break up fried rice into bite-size pieces. Add fried rice, sausage, cilantro, mint, scallions, and remaining cooked rice to dressing and toss gently to combine. Transfer salad to serving platter and top with peanuts. Serve.

palm sugar

Made from the sap of a variety of palm trees, such as palmyra, toddy, date, and coconut, palm sugar has been traditionally used in South and Southeast Asian countries for millennia. Usually molded into bricks or cones, palm sugar is now also available in a convenient granulated form. It gave sweetness to the region's foods and desserts long before white granulated sugar was brought by Europeans to Asia. The minimally processed sugar is made using a method similar to that used for maple syrup. Less sweet than white sugar, palm sugar has a distinct slightly salty, caramel taste and its color ranges from golden to brown. We like it in salads inspired by Southeast Asian dishes, such as Nam Khao, and salads such as Som Tam (page 209), but we substitute white or brown sugar depending on the recipe.

rice salad with dates and pistachios

SERVES 8

2½ cups long-grain white or
    basmati rice

    Table salt for cooking rice

 6 scallions, chopped

 1 cup shelled pistachios or whole
    almonds, toasted and chopped

½ cup pitted dates, chopped, or
    dried cranberries (½ cup)

½ cup minced fresh parsley,
    cilantro, or mint

⅔ cup extra-virgin olive oil

¼ cup lemon juice (2 lemons)

⅛ teaspoon ground cinnamon

why this recipe works Reminiscent of pilaf, this rice salad with sweet dates and crunchy pistachios makes a great pairing with rich barbecued meats or kebabs. Scallions added crunch, color, and a hint of onion flavor. To rid the rice of excess starch, we cooked the grains as we would pasta, boiling them in a large volume of water.

1   Bring 4 quarts water to boil in large pot. Add rice and 1 tablespoon salt. Return to boil and cook uncovered, stirring occasionally, until rice is tender but not soft, 10 to 12 minutes. Drain rice; spread onto rimmed baking sheet; and let cool completely, about 15 minutes.

2   Toss rice, scallions, pistachios, dates, and parsley together in large bowl. Whisk oil, lemon juice, and cinnamon together in medium bowl. Pour dressing over salad and toss to combine. Season with salt and pepper to taste, and serve. (Rice salad can be refrigerated for up to 2 days; let come to room temperature before serving.)

rice salad with oranges, olives, and almonds

why this recipe works There are countless ways to spin a rice salad. For this version, we pair tender, fluffy grains of rice with briny olives and sweet oranges. We wanted to preserve the rice's tender texture once it cooled so that it could stand up to a vinaigrette and plenty of mix-ins. Toasting the rice brought out its nutty flavor and helped keep the grains distinct and separate. We also cooked the rice like pasta and boiled it in plenty of water, which washed away its excess starch and staved off stickiness. Spreading the cooked rice on a baking sheet allowed it to cool quickly and with less clumping. To flavor the salad, we tossed the cooled rice with a simple orange vinaigrette and fresh orange segments, chopped olives, and crunchy toasted almonds. We let the salad sit before serving to give the flavors time to meld.

1 Bring 4 quarts water to boil in Dutch oven. Meanwhile, toast rice in 12-inch skillet over medium heat until faintly fragrant and some grains turn opaque, 5 to 8 minutes. Add rice and 1½ teaspoons salt to boiling water and cook, stirring occasionally, until rice is tender but not soft, about 15 minutes. Drain rice; spread onto rimmed baking sheet; and let cool completely, about 15 minutes.

2 Cut away peel and pith from oranges. Holding fruit over bowl, use paring knife to slice between membranes to release segments. Whisk oil, vinegar, garlic, pepper, salt, and orange zest and juice together in large bowl. Add rice, orange segments, olives, almonds, and oregano; toss gently to combine; and let sit until flavors meld, about 20 minutes. Serve.

SERVES 4 TO 6

- 1½ cups basmati rice
- 1 teaspoon table salt, plus salt for cooking rice
- 2 oranges, plus ¼ teaspoon grated orange zest plus 1 tablespoon juice
- 2 tablespoons extra-virgin olive oil
- 2 teaspoons sherry vinegar
- 1 small garlic clove, minced
- ½ teaspoon pepper
- ⅓ cup large pitted brine-cured olives, chopped
- ⅓ cup slivered almonds or chopped pecans or walnuts, toasted
- 2 tablespoons minced fresh oregano or chives

red rice and quinoa salad

SERVES 4 TO 6

¾ cup red rice

Table salt for cooking rice and quinoa

¾ cup prewashed white quinoa

3 tablespoons lime juice (2 limes), divided

2 oranges

¼ cup extra-virgin olive oil

1 small shallot, minced

1 tablespoon minced fresh cilantro or parsley plus 1 cup leaves

¼ teaspoon red pepper flakes

6 ounces pitted dates or dried cherries, chopped (1 cup)

why this recipe works Red rice is a variety of rice with a red husk. Both red rice and quinoa have a nutty flavor and are highly nutritious; we wanted to combine these two satisfying and nourishing ingredients in one powerhouse salad. To make our work easier, we cooked the red rice and the quinoa in the same pot using the pasta method. Red rice has a longer cooking time than quinoa, so we gave it a 15-minute head start and then added the quinoa to ensure that the grains were both done at the same time. Then we drained them, drizzled them with lime juice to add bright flavor, and let them cool completely. Next, we added oranges, cut into segments, and reserved some of their juice to brighten up our refreshing dressing. We also used dates for more sweetness and some pleasant chew. Cilantro added a fresh bite, and red pepper flakes contributed a bit of spiciness to round out the salad. We like the convenience of prewashed quinoa; rinsing removes the quinoa's bitter protective coating (called saponin). If you buy unwashed quinoa, rinse it and then spread it out on a clean dish towel to dry for 15 minutes.

1 Bring 4 quarts water to boil in large pot over high heat. Add rice and 1 tablespoon salt and cook, stirring occasionally, for 15 minutes. Add quinoa to pot and continue to cook until grains are tender, 12 to 14 minutes. Drain rice-quinoa mixture, spread onto rimmed baking sheet, and drizzle with 2 tablespoons lime juice. Let mixture cool completely, about 15 minutes.

2   Meanwhile, cut away peel and pith from oranges. Holding fruit over bowl, use paring knife to slice between membranes to release segments. Cut segments in half crosswise. If needed, squeeze orange membranes to equal 2 tablespoons juice in bowl.

3   Whisk oil, shallot, minced cilantro, pepper flakes, 2 tablespoons orange juice, and remaining 1 tablespoon lime juice together in large bowl. Season with salt and pepper to taste. Add rice-quinoa mixture, orange segments, cilantro leaves, and dates and toss to combine. Season with salt and pepper to taste. Serve.

pasta
& noodle
salads

one-pot pasta salad with chicken

why this recipe works This great summer salad is colorful, hearty, and can be served at room temperature. We added fresh green beans to the pasta water for the last 5 minutes of cooking. Once the pasta bean mixture had cooled, we added peppery arugula, juicy tomatoes, olives, feta, diced chicken, and a punchy dressing with red wine vinegar and pepperoncini (pickled hot Italian peppers). The pasta firms as it cools, so overcooking it actually ensures the proper texture. If the salad is not being eaten right away, don't add the arugula until right before serving. We like using Perfect Poached Chicken (page 43) here but any cooked chicken would work. We like fusilli for this salad but you can substitute another small, curly pasta, if desired.

1   Bring 4 quarts water to boil in large pot. Whisk oil, vinegar, anchovies, garlic, and pepper flakes together in large bowl. Add tomatoes, olives, and pepperoncini to dressing and toss to combine; set aside.

2   Add pasta and 1 tablespoon salt to boiling water and cook, stirring occasionally, until pasta is tender, about 12 minutes (do not drain). Add green beans to boiling water with pasta and continue to cook until pasta is very soft and green beans are bright green and just tender, about 5 minutes. Drain pasta and green beans in colander and rinse under cold water until chilled. Drain well and transfer to bowl with dressing mixture.

3   Add chicken, arugula, and feta to pasta mixture and toss to combine. Season with salt and pepper to taste. Serve. (Salad can be made without arugula and refrigerated for up to 2 days; toss with arugula before serving.)

SERVES 4 TO 6

5 tablespoons extra-virgin olive oil

¼ cup red wine vinegar

2 anchovy fillets, rinsed and minced

1 garlic clove, minced

¾ teaspoon red pepper flakes

10 ounces grape or cherry tomatoes, halved

½ cup pitted olives, halved

½ cup finely chopped pepperoncini

6 ounces (2 cups) fusilli or other short, curly pasta

Table salt for cooking pasta and green beans

8 ounces green beans, trimmed and cut into 2-inch lengths

3 cups cooked chicken, cut into 1-inch pieces

2 ounces (2 cups) baby arugula or baby spinach

4 ounces feta or goat cheese, crumbled (1 cup)

fusilli salad with salami and sun-dried tomato vinaigrette

why this recipe works Deli pasta salad might seem like a convenient, quick lunch but it often ends up being disappointing, with mushy pasta; too much mayo; and dull, overcooked vegetables. So we took lunch into our own hands. Inspired by traditional antipasto flavors, we used thick-cut salami and provolone for a rich, salty bite while briny sliced kalamata olives added tart, meaty chew. But what really sets this salad apart is its bright olive oil–based vinaigrette accented by tangy sun-dried tomatoes and their packing oil. If you want to make it ahead, we found that the salad took on even more tomato flavor after marinating for a day or two. If making ahead, stirring in some boiling water before serving loosens the dressing and quickly takes the chill off the pasta. Chopped baby spinach added just before serving provided extra color and freshness. We like fusilli here, but you can substitute another small, curly pasta, if desired.

1 Bring 4 quarts water to boil in large pot. Add pasta and 1 tablespoon salt and cook, stirring often, until tender. Drain pasta, rinse with cold water, and drain again, leaving pasta slightly wet.

2 Whisk tomatoes, vinegar, basil, garlic, pepper, and salt together in large bowl. Whisking constantly, drizzle in olive oil and tomato oil. Add salami, provolone, olives, and pasta and toss to combine. (To make ahead, toss pasta, salami, cheese, and olives with half of vinaigrette; refrigerate pasta mixture and remaining vinaigrette separately for up to 2 days. To serve, bring to room temperature, then stir vinaigrette and ¼ cup boiling water into pasta mixture and add remaining vinaigrette to salad.)

3 Add spinach and toss gently to combine. Season with salt, pepper, and extra vinegar to taste. Serve.

SERVES 4 TO 6

- 8 ounces fusilli or other short, curly pasta
- ¾ teaspoon table salt, plus salt for cooking pasta
- ¾ cup oil-packed sun-dried tomatoes, rinsed, patted dry, and minced, plus 2 tablespoons packing oil
- ¼ cup red wine vinegar, plus extra for seasoning
- 2 tablespoons chopped fresh basil or parsley
- 1 garlic clove, minced
- ¾ teaspoon pepper
- ¼ cup extra-virgin olive oil
- 4 (¼-inch-thick) slices deli salami or pepperoni (8 ounces), cut into 1-inch-long matchsticks
- 4 (¼-inch-thick) slices deli provolone cheese (8 ounces), cut into 1-inch-long matchsticks
- ½ cup pitted olives, sliced crosswise
- 2 ounces (2 cups) baby spinach or baby arugula, chopped

zesty shrimp pesto pasta salad

SERVES 4 TO 6

pesto

¼ cup walnuts or pecans, toasted

2 garlic cloves, peeled

2 cups packed fresh cilantro or parsley

1 cup packed fresh basil leaves

7 tablespoons extra-virgin olive oil

1 tablespoon grated lime zest plus 3 tablespoons juice (2 limes)

½ jalapeño or serrano chile, seeds and ribs removed

3 anchovy fillets, rinsed and patted dry

salad

1 pound fusilli or other short, curly pasta

Table salt for cooking pasta

1 tablespoon extra-virgin olive oil

1½ cups Sautéed Shrimp (page 43), halved

12 ounces grape or cherry tomatoes, halved

why this recipe works Instead of the traditional basil and pine nut pesto used for pasta, we turned up the heat by adding jalapeños and making a spicy dressing for our pasta salad with shrimp. We processed basil, cilantro, toasted walnuts, lime, jalapeño, and anchovies into a bold, sharp paste that we tossed with cooked, room temperature fusilli. Even if you don't like anchovies, we recommend using them here for their rich flavor, their fishy bite disappeared when combined with the other ingredients. For more spice, reserve, mince, and add the ribs and seeds from the jalapeño. Toast the walnuts in a skillet to maximize their flavor. We like fusilli here, but you can substitute another small, curly pasta, if desired.

1 for the pesto Process walnuts, garlic, cilantro, basil, oil, lime zest and juice, jalapeño, and anchovies in food processor or blender until smooth, stopping to scrape down sides of bowl as necessary. Transfer to small bowl and season with salt to taste. Cover with plastic wrap. (The pesto can be prepared a day in advance and refrigerated until needed.)

2 for the salad Bring 4 quarts water to boil in large pot. Add pasta and 1 tablespoon salt to boiling water. Cook until al dente. Reserve ¼ cup cooking water, drain pasta, and transfer to large serving bowl. Stir in reserved cooking water and oil and let cool completely. When cooled, toss with shrimp, tomatoes, and pesto. Serve. (Salad can be refrigerated for up to 24 hours; to serve, add warm water and additional olive oil as needed to refresh its texture and toss with shrimp before serving.)

pea and pistachio pesto pasta salad

why this recipe works For a fresh springtime pasta salad, we made a fragrant pale green pesto with mint, creamy ricotta cheese, and sweet frozen peas. Delicately flavored pistachios took the role of the usual pine nuts, and lemon zest contributed bright, clean-tasting notes. Adding a bit of the pasta cooking water to the pesto helped thin it out so that it would coat each piece of pasta. For textural interest, we kept a portion of the pistachios and peas whole and stirred them in at the end. Cooking the pasta until it is completely tender and leaving it slightly wet after rinsing helps create tender chew in the finished salad.

1 Bring 4 quarts water to boil in large pot. Add pasta and 1 tablespoon salt and cook, stirring often, until tender. Reserve ¾ cup cooking water. Drain pasta; rinse with cold water; and drain again, leaving pasta slightly wet.

2 Process ricotta and 2 tablespoons reserved cooking water in food processor until smooth, about 1 minute. Add ¾ cup peas, ¼ cup pistachios, Pecorino, oil, mint, garlic, lemon zest, pepper, and salt and process until smooth, about 1 minute, scraping down sides of bowl as needed.

3 Toss pasta, pesto, remaining ½ cup peas, and remaining ¼ cup pistachios in large bowl, adding remaining reserved cooking water as needed to adjust consistency. Cover and let sit for 15 minutes. Season with salt and pepper to taste and serve. (Salad can be refrigerated in airtight container for up to 24 hours; to serve, add warm water and additional oil as needed to refresh its texture.)

SERVES 4 TO 6

- 1 pound penne, fusilli, or campanelle
- ½ teaspoon table salt, plus salt for cooking pasta
- 2 ounces (¼ cup) whole-milk or part-skim ricotta cheese
- 1¼ cups frozen peas, thawed, divided
- ½ cup pistachios, toasted and chopped, divided
- ¾ cup grated Pecorino Romano or Parmesan cheese
- ¾ cup extra-virgin olive oil
- 2 tablespoons chopped fresh mint or chives
- 1 garlic clove, minced
- 1 teaspoon grated lemon zest
- ¼ teaspoon pepper

pasta salad with eggplant, tomatoes, and basil

SERVES 6 TO 8

1   pound eggplant, cut into ½-inch-thick rounds

½   cup extra-virgin olive oil, plus extra for brushing eggplant

1   teaspoon table salt, divided, plus salt for cooking pasta

⅛   teaspoon pepper

1   garlic clove, minced

½   teaspoon grated lemon zest plus ¼ cup juice (2 lemons)

½   teaspoon red pepper flakes

1   pound farfalle, fusilli, orecchiette, or other bite-size pasta

2   large tomatoes, cored, seeded, and cut into ½-inch pieces

½   cup chopped fresh basil or parsley

why this recipe works We wanted a colorful summer pasta salad that wasn't overdressed with mayonnaise and featured plenty of vegetables, so we made a lemony dressing to bind eggplant, pasta, and tomatoes together. Getting the right balance of acidity was essential; too little and the salad tasted bland, too much caused the pasta to turn mushy and dulled the flavor and appearance of the vegetables. Here ¼ cup of lemon juice was all that was needed to brighten our salad. Tossing the pasta with the dressing while it was still hot allowed it to absorb the dressing's flavors better. For the vegetables, we grilled eggplant until it was charred and then stirred raw summer tomatoes and fresh basil into the pasta at the end. The eggplants can be broiled until golden brown if you prefer not to grill them.

1A for a charcoal grill Open bottom vent completely. Light large chimney starter filled with charcoal briquettes (6 quarts). When top coals are partially covered with ash, pour evenly over grill. Set cooking grate in place, cover, and open lid vent completely. Heat grill until hot, about 5 minutes.

1B for a gas grill Turn all burners to high; cover; and heat grill until hot, about 15 minutes. Leave all burners on high. (Adjust burners as needed to maintain grill temperature of 350 degrees.)

2 Clean and oil cooking grate. Lightly brush eggplant with extra oil and sprinkle with ¼ teaspoon salt and pepper. Cook until dark grill marks appear, about 10 minutes, flipping eggplant halfway through cooking. Let cool completely, then cut into bite-size pieces.

3 Meanwhile, bring 4 quarts water to boil in large pot. Whisk oil, garlic, lemon zest and juice, pepper flakes, and remaining ¾ teaspoon salt together in large bowl.

4 Add pasta and 1 tablespoon salt to boiling water and cook, stirring often, until al dente. Drain pasta. Whisk dressing again to blend; add tomatoes, basil, eggplant, and pasta to bowl with dressing; toss to mix thoroughly; and let salad cool completely. Season with salt to taste, and serve. (Salad can be refrigerated in airtight container for up to 24 hours; return to room temperature before serving.)

spinach pesto pasta salad

SERVES 4 TO 6

1½ teaspoons plus 2 tablespoons extra-virgin olive oil, divided

1 pound cherry or grape tomatoes, halved

1½ teaspoons sugar

3 garlic cloves, minced, divided

4 teaspoons plus 2 tablespoons chopped fresh basil, divided

1 large onion, chopped fine

⅛ teaspoon red pepper flakes

10 ounces (10 cups) baby spinach

1 teaspoon table salt, plus salt for cooking pasta

12 ounces spaghetti

1 ounce Parmesan or Pecorino Romano cheese, grated (½ cup)

2 teaspoons lemon juice

2 cups drained jarred whole baby artichoke hearts packed in water or thawed frozen artichoke hearts, quartered

2 ounces (¼ cup) whole-milk or part-skim ricotta cheese (optional)

why this recipe works Pesto is often associated with basil. But pesto just means "paste" in Italian, so you can make it with almost any vegetable, herb, cheese, nuts, or seasonings. Here we used spinach and left out the nuts. We sautéed onion and garlic; added spinach; and then processed it in a food processor with Parmesan, lemon juice, and pasta water. We added earthy, nutty artichoke hearts, and topped the pasta with sautéed cherry tomatoes, which contributed bright color. A sprinkle of basil added pleasant freshness. You can also top the salad with ricotta, if desired. Sautéing highlights the tomatoes' sweetness. If your tomatoes are sweet, you may want to reduce or omit the sugar. For a spicier dish, add more pepper flakes.

1   Heat 1½ teaspoons oil in 12-inch nonstick skillet over medium-high heat until just smoking. Add tomatoes and sugar and cook, tossing often, until tomatoes begin to soften, about 1 minute. Stir in 1 teaspoon garlic and cook until fragrant, about 30 seconds. Transfer tomatoes to bowl, stir in 4 teaspoons basil, and season with salt and pepper to taste. (Tomatoes can be refrigerated for up to 2 days; rewarm before using.)

2   Heat remaining 2 tablespoons oil in now-empty 12-inch skillet over medium heat until shimmering. Add onion and cook until softened and lightly browned, 5 to 7 minutes. Stir in pepper flakes and remaining garlic and cook until fragrant, about 30 seconds. Add spinach, 1 handful at a time, and salt and cook until spinach is wilted, about 2 minutes.

3   Meanwhile, bring 4 quarts water to boil in large pot. Add pasta and 1 tablespoon salt and cook, stirring often, until tender. Reserve 1 cup cooking water, then drain pasta and return it to pot.

4   Transfer spinach mixture to food processor with Parmesan, lemon juice, and ½ cup reserved cooking water. Process until smooth, about 1 minute, scraping down sides of bowl as needed. Add spinach pesto and artichokes to pot with pasta and stir to coat. Adjust consistency of sauce with remaining ½ cup reserved cooking water as needed and season with salt and pepper to taste. Divide among individual plates. Serve, topping individual portions with tomatoes, remaining 2 tablespoons basil, and ricotta, if desired. (Salad can be refrigerated in airtight container for up to 24 hours; to serve, add warm water and additional oil as needed to refresh its texture and toss remaining basil before serving.)

creamy corn farfalle salad

why this recipe works In this ingenious recipe, uncooked corn serves as the sauce for a simple, creamy farfalle salad that comes together in a flash. We started by processing corn to a smooth puree, adding some hot water to get it smooth. We then tossed it with cooked pasta, adding sun-dried tomatoes, lemon juice, and red pepper flakes for tang and a subtle kick. A sprinkle of fresh mint and roasted pepitas finished the dish for a final result that is satisfying and easy to make any day of the week. You can substitute 20 ounces of frozen corn for fresh, if desired.

1   Bring 4 quarts water to boil in large pot. Add pasta and 1 tablespoon salt and cook, stirring often, until tender. Drain pasta and set aside.

2   Meanwhile, stand 1 reserved corn cob on cutting board and firmly scrape downward with back of butter knife to remove any pulp remaining on cob. Repeat with remaining reserved cobs then transfer pulp to blender along with 3½ cups corn kernels.

3   Process corn mixture on low speed until thick puree forms, about 30 seconds. With blender running, add hot water, melted butter, and salt. Increase speed to high and process until smooth, about 3 minutes longer. Pour puree through fine-mesh strainer set over large bowl or 4-cup liquid measuring cup. Using back of ladle or rubber spatula, push puree through strainer, extracting as much liquid as possible; discard solids. Combine reserved pasta and corn puree in large bowl, tossing to combine. Let cool to room temperature, about 30 minutes. (Salad can be refrigerated in airtight container for up to 24 hours; to serve, add warm water and additional oil as needed to refresh its texture.)

4   Stir in tomatoes, scallions, lemon juice, pepper flakes, and remaining 1½ cups corn kernels. Season with salt and pepper to taste and adjust consistency with additional hot water as needed. Sprinkle with feta, pepitas, and mint. Serve.

SERVES 4 TO 6

- 1 pound farfalle
- ¼ teaspoon table salt, plus salt for cooking pasta
- 5-7 ears corn, kernels cut from cobs (5 cups), divided, cobs reserved
- ¼ cup hot water
- 4 tablespoons unsalted butter, melted
- 1 cup oil-packed sun-dried tomatoes, rinsed, patted dry, and chopped coarse
- 2 scallions, sliced thin
- 2 tablespoons lemon juice
- ½ teaspoon red pepper flakes
- 6 ounces feta cheese, crumbled (1½ cups)
- ⅓ cup roasted pepitas
- 3 tablespoons chopped fresh mint

pasta salad with asparagus and smoked mozzarella

SERVES 4 TO 6

4 ounces asparagus, trimmed and cut into 1-inch lengths

¼ teaspoon table salt, plus salt for cooking asparagus and pasta

½ red, orange, or yellow bell pepper, stemmed, seeded, and chopped

3 tablespoons red wine vinegar, divided

2 tablespoons finely chopped red onion

8 ounces (2½ cups) whole-wheat penne

1½ ounces smoked mozzarella or aged or smoked gouda, shredded (⅓ cup)

1 teaspoon minced fresh oregano or basil

2 teaspoons Dijon mustard

1 garlic clove, minced

⅛ teaspoon red pepper flakes

2 tablespoons extra-virgin olive oil

why this recipe works This recipe is a lovely make-ahead summer salad, using fresh asparagus, creamy smoked mozzarella, and penne. The vibrant dressing—red wine vinegar, Dijon mustard, garlic, and red pepper flakes—is bold enough to stand up to the hearty whole-wheat pasta. It can be doubled to serve a crowd and it can be refrigerated and served hours later at a picnic. Be sure to set up the ice bath before cooking the asparagus, as plunging it in the cold water immediately after blanching preserves its bright green color and ensures that it doesn't overcook.

1 Bring 4 quarts water to boil in large pot. Fill large bowl halfway with ice and water. Add asparagus and 1 tablespoon salt to pot and cook until asparagus is crisp-tender, about 3 minutes. Using slotted spoon, transfer asparagus to ice bath (do not discard cooking water) and let cool, about 2 minutes.

2 Drain asparagus from ice bath and pat dry with paper towels. Toss bell pepper, 1 tablespoon vinegar, onion, salt, and asparagus together in large serving bowl; set aside.

3 Return cooking water to boil; add pasta; and cook, stirring often, until tender. Drain pasta, rinse with cold water to cool, and drain thoroughly again. Add mozzarella, oregano, and pasta to bowl with vegetables and toss to combine.

4 Whisk mustard, garlic, red pepper flakes, and remaining 2 table-spoons vinegar together in small bowl. Whisking constantly, slowly drizzle in oil until emulsified, then pour over salad and toss to coat. Season with salt and pepper to taste before serving. (Salad can be refrigerated in airtight container for up to 4 hours.)

spicy roasted red pepper pesto pasta salad

SERVES 8 TO 10

1 pound penne, fusilli, or campanelle

½ teaspoon table salt, plus salt for cooking pasta

2 ounces (¼ cup) whole-milk or part-skim ricotta cheese

1¼ cups jarred roasted red peppers, drained and chopped, divided

½ cup slivered almonds or chopped walnuts, toasted, divided

¼ cup grated Asiago cheese

¼ cup extra-virgin olive oil

1 garlic clove, minced

2 tablespoons chopped fresh parsley or basil

¼ teaspoon red pepper flakes

why this recipe works In the heat of summer, a cool pasta salad tossed with a light, fresh vegetable puree sounds like an appealing supper but many of these recipes end up bland and dry. So for this salad, we made pesto with velvety roasted red peppers, pureeing them with ricotta for creaminess and pasta water to smooth out the pesto. Red pepper flakes added heat and garlic and olive oil were vital along with almonds, Asiago cheese, and parsley.

1 Bring 4 quarts water to boil in large pot. Add pasta and 1 tablespoon salt to boiling water and cook until just al dente. Reserve ¾ cup pasta water. Drain pasta in colander, rinse with cold water until cool, drain once more, and transfer to large bowl.

2 Process ricotta and 2 tablespoons hot pasta water in food processor until smooth, 15 seconds. Add ¾ cup roasted red peppers, ¼ cup almonds, Asiago, oil, garlic, parsley, pepper flakes, and salt and process until smooth, 30–45 seconds, scraping down sides of processor bowl as needed. Stir pesto into pasta until well coated, adding reserved pasta water as needed to adjust consistency. Fold in remaining ¼ cup roasted red peppers and almonds. Season with salt to taste. Serve. (Salad can be refrigerated in airtight container for up to 3 days; to serve, add warm water and additional oil as needed to refresh its texture.)

summer garden pasta salad with olives and feta

why this recipe works For some make-ahead pasta salads, we want to ensure that the pasta tastes good even if served 1 or 2 days later, so we boil the pasta in salted water until fully tender rather than keeping it al dente. Cooking the pasta until it's softer than usual prevents it from developing a tough, chewy texture when chilled and allows it to absorb more flavor from the dressing. Tossing hot pasta with the vinaigrette, rather than letting it cool off first, also increases absorption. To moisten this salad, we landed on the idea of adding pasta cooking water to the vinaigrette, which increased its volume without overpowering its flavors. We like the size of farfalle (bow-tie) pasta here, however you can substitute any small pasta. If using a different pasta shape, note that the yield may change significantly. Cooking the pasta until it is completely tender is crucial here—otherwise pasta can become tough as it sits in the salad overnight.

1 Whisk vinegar, lemon juice, shallot, mustard, oregano, salt, garlic powder, and pepper together in medium bowl. Whisking constantly, slowly drizzle in oil until emulsified; set aside.

2 Bring 4 quarts water to boil in large pot. Add pasta and 1 tablespoon salt and cook until completely tender. Reserve 1 cup cooking water, then drain pasta. Transfer pasta to large bowl.

3 (To make ahead, toss salad with half of vinaigrette; refrigerate pasta mixture and remaining vinaigrette separately for up to 2 days. To serve, bring to room temperature, then stir in remaining vinaigrette and add warm water as needed to refresh its texture.) Stir reserved pasta water into dressing. Pour vinaigrette over pasta and toss to coat. Stir in tomatoes, carrots, bell pepper, feta, olives, and parsley. Serve.

SERVES 8 TO 10

- 3 tablespoons red wine vinegar
- 3 tablespoons fresh lemon juice (2 lemons)
- 1 shallot, minced
- 1 tablespoon Dijon mustard
- 1 tablespoon minced fresh oregano leaves or ½ teaspoon dried
- 1 teaspoon table salt, plus salt for cooking pasta
- ¼ teaspoon garlic powder
- ¼ teaspoon pepper
- 6 tablespoons extra-virgin olive oil
- 1 pound farfalle or other bite-size pasta
- 12 ounces cherry or grape tomatoes, quartered
- 2 carrots, peeled and shredded
- 1 yellow, orange, or red bell pepper, stemmed, seeded, and cut into ¼-inch-thick strips
- 8 ounces (2 cups) crumbled feta or goat cheese
- 1 cup (6 ounces) pitted olives, chopped coarse
- ½ cup minced fresh parsley or basil

summer garden pasta
salad with olives and feta,
page 343

cool and creamy macaroni salad

SERVES 8 TO 10

1 pound elbow macaroni

   Table salt for cooking pasta

½ cup finely chopped red onion

1 celery rib, minced

¼ cup minced fresh parsley or chives

2 tablespoons lemon juice

1 tablespoon Dijon mustard

⅛ teaspoon garlic powder

   Pinch cayenne pepper

1½ cups mayonnaise

why this recipe works Our traditional macaroni side salad features elbow macaroni, chopped red onion, and minced celery tossed with a creamy dressing. We generously seasoned the pasta cooking water with salt to flavor the macaroni and then cooked the pasta until fully tender—not just al dente. We drained the pasta briefly but made sure to leave a little water on it; the pasta absorbed the water rather than the creamy dressing (which would have left the salad dry and bland). Two tablespoons of lemon juice helped balance the richness of the mayonnaise. We prefer garlic powder to fresh garlic here because the flavor isn't as sharp and the powder dissolves easily into the dressing. Cooking the pasta until it is completely tender and leaving it slightly wet after rinsing are important for the texture of the finished salad.

1 Bring 4 quarts water to boil in large pot. Add macaroni and 1 tablespoon salt and cook, stirring often, until tender. Drain macaroni; rinse with cold water; and drain again, leaving macaroni slightly wet.

2 Toss onion, celery, parsley, lemon juice, mustard, garlic powder, cayenne, and macaroni together in large bowl and let sit until flavors meld, about 2 minutes. Stir in mayonnaise and let sit until salad is no longer watery, 5 to 10 minutes. Season with salt and pepper to taste. Serve. (Salad can be refrigerated in airtight container for up to 2 days.)

variations

cool and creamy macaroni salad with roasted red peppers and capers

Add 1 cup jarred roasted red peppers, chopped, and 6 tablespoons capers, rinsed and chopped, with onion in step 2.

cool and creamy macaroni salad with sharp cheddar and chipotle

Add 1½ cups shredded extra-sharp cheddar cheese and 2 tablespoons minced canned chipotle chile in adobo sauce with onion in step 2.

orzo salad with broccoli and radicchio

SERVES 4 TO 6

12 ounces broccoli florets, cut into 1-inch pieces

1 teaspoon table salt, plus salt for cooking broccoli and pasta

1⅓ cups orzo

1 head radicchio (10 ounces), cored and chopped fine

2 ounces Parmesan or Pecorino Romano cheese, grated (1 cup)

½ cup oil-packed sun-dried tomatoes, rinsed, patted dry, and minced, plus 3 tablespoons packing oil

½ cup pine nuts or walnuts, toasted

¼ cup balsamic vinegar, plus extra for seasoning

1 garlic clove, minced

1 teaspoon honey

3 tablespoons extra-virgin olive oil

½ cup chopped fresh basil or parsley

why this recipe works Orzo salad is a great all-purpose side for a picnic, a day at the beach, or a patio dinner. In this simple version, we included vibrant broccoli, bitter radicchio, salty sun-dried tomatoes, and crunchy pine nuts for a lovely, colorful, and tasty salad. Cooking the orzo in the water that we used to blanch the broccoli imparted a delicate vegetal flavor and streamlined the recipe. To ensure the orzo was tender even when served cold, we cooked it past al dente. To bring all the elements of the dish together, we used a bold dressing, with hints of sweetness from balsamic vinegar and honey. Toasting the pine nuts intensified their nuttiness. Parmesan added a salty accent, and chopped basil offered freshness. Leaving the pasta slightly wet after rinsing is important for the texture of the finished salad. Be sure to set up the ice bath before cooking the broccoli, as plunging it in the cold water immediately after blanching preserves its bright green color and ensures that it doesn't overcook.

1 Bring 4 quarts water to boil in large pot. Fill large bowl halfway with ice and water. Add broccoli and 1 tablespoon salt to boiling water and cook until crisp-tender, about 2 minutes. Using slotted spoon, transfer broccoli to ice bath (do not discard cooking water) and let cool, about 2 minutes; drain and pat dry.

2 Return pot of water to boil. Add orzo and cook, stirring often, until tender. Drain orzo; rinse with cold water; and drain again, leaving orzo slightly wet. Toss orzo, broccoli, radicchio, Parmesan, tomatoes, and pine nuts together in large bowl.

3 Whisk vinegar, garlic, honey, and salt together in small bowl. Whisking constantly, slowly drizzle in olive oil and tomato oil until emulsified. Stir vinaigrette into orzo mixture. (Salad can be refrigerated in airtight container for up to 24 hours; refresh with warm water and additional olive oil as needed and toss with basil before serving.) Stir in basil and season with salt, pepper, and extra vinegar to taste before serving.

radicchio

Radicchio, with its compact head of waxy red, white-veined leaves, is neither a cabbage nor a lettuce. It belongs to the red chicory family and has the distinctive bitterness of chicory. That flavor, bright color, and sharp crunch have made radicchio a salad favorite, especially when juxtaposed with milder green lettuces or vegetables such as broccoli. Historically, in Italy, radicchio was served cooked. Making the best of both worlds, we serve it raw in some salads and grilled in others. Radicchio varieties are named after the Italian towns they come from. In the United States, the most common of these late winter vegetables is Rosso da Verona. Also available are field-grown, less bitter varieties—Chioggia, Castelfranco, and Treviso. When buying radicchio, look for tightly bound heads without brown spots, which the vegetable easily gets when separated from its core.

orzo salad with cucumber, red onion, and mint

SERVES 4 TO 6

1¼ cups orzo

½ teaspoon table salt, plus salt for cooking orzo

6 tablespoons extra-virgin olive oil, divided, plus extra for drizzling

¼ cup lemon juice (2 lemons)

2 garlic cloves, minced

½ teaspoon pepper

½ English cucumber, halved lengthwise and sliced thin

2 ounces feta or goat cheese, crumbled (½ cup)

½ cup finely chopped red onion

½ cup chopped fresh mint or parsley

2 scallions, sliced thin

why this recipe works Cucumber really shines when paired with rice-shaped orzo in this pasta salad. An assertive lemony dressing and ingredients that work nicely with cucumber—namely red onion, feta, and mint—ensured an appealingly bright and flavorful light lunch. To start, we cooked the orzo in salted water, stirring frequently to keep all the pieces separate; when it was al dente, we drained it and tossed it with a tablespoon of oil to further ensure that it wouldn't clump. For our dressing, plenty extra-virgin olive oil and ¼ cup of lemon juice ensured that there would be enough dressing to coat the orzo and all the mix-ins and those plus minced garlic also delivered bright flavor.

1   Bring 2 quarts water to boil in large saucepan. Add orzo and 1½ teaspoons salt and cook, stirring often, until al dente. Drain orzo and transfer to rimmed baking sheet. Toss with 1 tablespoon oil and let cool completely, about 15 minutes.

2   Whisk lemon juice, garlic, pepper, salt, and remaining 5 table-spoons oil in large bowl until combined. Add cucumber, feta, onion, mint, scallions, and orzo and toss to coat. Season with salt and pepper to taste.

3   Let salad sit at room temperature for 30 minutes to allow flavors to meld. Serve, drizzling with extra oil.

grilled vegetable and orzo salad with lemon, basil, and feta

why this recipe works With fresh produce abundantly available in the summer, grilled vegetables are perfect for an al fresco supper. Here we pair chunks of grilled vegetables with orzo, fresh herbs, and feta cheese. Zucchini, red onion, and red bell peppers worked well since their cooking times are similar. Cutting zucchini lengthwise and bell peppers into quarters creates pieces that are easy to grill.

1   Whisk basil, lemon zest and juice, mustard, garlic, ½ teaspoon salt, and ¼ teaspoon pepper together in bowl. Whisking constantly, slowly drizzle in oil until emulsified.

2   Thread onion rounds evenly onto two 12-inch metal skewers. Spray onion rounds, bell peppers, and zucchini lightly with oil spray and sprinkle with remaining ⅛ teaspoon salt and remaining ⅛ teaspoon pepper.

3A   for a charcoal grill Open bottom vent completely. Light large chimney starter half filled with charcoal briquettes (3 quarts). When top coals are partially covered with ash, pour evenly over grill. Set cooking grate in place, cover, and open lid vent completely/halfway. Heat grill until hot, about 5 minutes.

3B   for a gas grill Turn all burners to high; cover; and heat grill until hot, about 15 minutes. Turn all burners to medium.

4   Grill vegetables, covered, until spottily charred, 5 to 8 minutes per side. Transfer vegetables to cutting board and remove onion rounds from skewers.

5   Meanwhile, bring 4 quarts water to boil in large pot. Add orzo and 1 tablespoon salt and cook, stirring often, until tender. Drain orzo, rinse under cold running water, and drain again thoroughly. Add orzo to bowl with dressing.

6   Cut vegetables into 1-inch pieces, add to bowl with orzo and dressing, and toss gently to combine. Season with salt and pepper to taste. Divide among individual plates. Serve, topping individual portions with feta.

SERVES 4

- ½ cup chopped fresh basil or parsley
- 2 teaspoons grated lemon zest plus 2 tablespoons juice
- 2 teaspoons Dijon mustard
- 1 garlic clove, minced
- ½ teaspoon plus ⅛ teaspoon table salt, divided, plus salt for cooking pasta
- ¼ teaspoon plus ⅛ teaspoon pepper, divided
- 3 tablespoons extra-virgin olive oil
- 1 red onion, sliced into ½-inch-thick rounds
- 2 red, orange, or yellow bell peppers, stemmed, seeded, and quartered
- 2 zucchini or summer squash, halved lengthwise
-    Vegetable oil spray
- 1 cup orzo
- 2 ounces feta or goat cheese, crumbled (½ cup)

**grilled vegetable and orzo salad with
lemon, basil, and feta,** *page 351*

tortellini salad with asparagus and fresh basil vinaigrette

why this recipe works For a supereasy but attractive pasta salad that would impress any picnic crowd, we paired convenient store-bought cheese tortellini with crisp asparagus and a dressing inspired by the flavors of classic pesto. First, we blanched the asparagus in the same water we later used to cook the cheese tortellini, giving the pasta some of the asparagus's delicate flavor. We tossed the cooked tortellini in a bold dressing of extra-virgin olive oil, lemon juice, shallot, and garlic. Just before serving, we tossed in some bright, juicy cherry tomatoes; fresh basil; grated Parmesan; toasted pine nuts; and the blanched asparagus. Cooking the tortellini until it is completely tender and leaving it slightly wet after rinsing are important for the texture of the finished salad. Be sure to set up the ice bath before cooking the asparagus, as plunging it in the cold water immediately after blanching preserves its bright green color and ensures that it doesn't overcook.

1   Bring 4 quarts water to boil in large pot. Fill large bowl halfway with ice and water. Add asparagus and 1 tablespoon salt to boiling water and cook until crisp-tender, about 2 minutes. Using slotted spoon, transfer asparagus to ice bath (do not discard cooking water) and let cool, about 2 minutes; drain and pat dry.

2   Return pot of water to boil. Add tortellini and cook, stirring often, until tender. Drain tortellini; rinse with cold water; and drain again, leaving tortellini slightly wet.

3   Whisk oil, lemon juice, shallot, garlic, pepper, and salt together in large bowl. Add tortellini and toss to combine.

4   Add tomatoes, Parmesan, basil, pine nuts, and asparagus and toss gently to combine. Season with salt, pepper, and extra lemon juice to taste. Serve. (Cooled tortellini, cooked asparagus, and dressing can be refrigerated separately for up to 2 days. Toss before serving.)

SERVES 4 TO 6

- 1 pound thin asparagus, trimmed and cut into 1-inch lengths
- 1 teaspoon table salt, plus salt for cooking asparagus and pasta
- 1 pound dried cheese tortellini
- ¼ cup extra-virgin olive oil
- 3 tablespoons lemon juice, plus extra for seasoning
- 1 shallot, minced
- 2 garlic cloves, minced
- ¾ teaspoon pepper
- 12 ounces cherry or grape tomatoes, halved
- 1 ounce Parmesan or Pecorino Romano cheese, grated (½ cup)
- ¾ cup chopped fresh basil, mint, or parsley
- ¼ cup pine nuts or walnuts, toasted

smoked trout

We love the rich flavor and flaky, moist texture of smoked trout and think that it's perfectly suited for use in salads. The richness of the fish means that it adds a different unctuousness than tuna and its smokiness elevates it as a salad topper, especially when paired with a lemony dressing. Smoked trout can be found sold whole, in full fillets, in fillet pieces, and canned in water or oil. Vacuum-packed fillets are typically located next to smoked salmon in the deli case.

Use whichever type you prefer. Fillets are often sold with additional flavorings and spices; make sure to purchase an unflavored variety for this recipe. Smoked mackerel is a great substitution too. But be sure with both fish to check for pin bones before adding them to your salad.

couscous salad with smoked trout and pepperoncini

why this recipe works The smoky richness and buttery texture of smoked trout is brought out by the tangy dressing in this couscous salad. Instead of letting the pepperoncini brine go to waste, we use it in our simple dressing, which gives the salad a tangy, salty bite that complements the fish. Tossing the dressing with warm, cooked couscous helps the pasta absorb the dressing as it cools in the refrigerator. Some smoked trout comes with pin bones in it and some does not. Make sure to check your fish for pin bones before flaking it into pieces. Do not substitute pearl couscous here as it requires a different cooking method and will not work in this recipe.

1   Heat 1½ tablespoons oil in medium saucepan over medium-high heat until shimmering. Add couscous and cook, stirring frequently, until grains begin to brown, about 5 minutes. Add water and salt; stir briefly to combine, cover, and remove pan from heat. Let sit until liquid is absorbed and couscous is tender, about 7 minutes. Uncover and fluff couscous with fork.

2   Meanwhile, whisk remaining ⅓ cup oil, pepperoncini brine, and garlic together in large bowl.

3   Transfer couscous to bowl with dressing and toss to combine. Refrigerate couscous mixture until room temperature, about 10 minutes.

4   Using 2 forks, flake trout into bite-size pieces. Add tomatoes, parsley, scallions, and pepperoncini to couscous and toss gently to combine. Season with salt and pepper to taste, and drizzle with extra oil to taste. Divide among individual plates. Serve, topping individual portions with smoked trout and passing lemon wedges separately.

SERVES 4 TO 6

1½ tablespoons plus ⅓ cup extra-virgin olive oil, divided, plus extra for drizzling

1½ cups couscous

2 cups water

¾ teaspoon table salt

1 cup pepperoncini, stemmed and sliced thin into rings, plus 3 tablespoons brine

1 garlic clove, minced

8 ounces smoked trout or mackerel, skin and pin bones removed

8 ounces cherry or grape tomatoes, halved

½ cup parsley or cilantro leaves

3 scallions, sliced thin

Lemon wedges for serving

pearl couscous salad with peas, feta, and pickled shallots

why this recipe works Pearl or Israeli couscous is hearty, so it makes for a filling and satisfying dinner salad when accompanied by pretty shades of green and fresh flavor from peas, spicy arugula, and pistachios. Feta cheese adds creaminess, and the dish is brightened by tangy pickled shallots. Pearl couscous is hefty enough to take on a tangy dressing of red wine vinegar, lemon juice, and Dijon mustard with red pepper flakes adding heat and mint leaves bringing fresh sweetness. Do not substitute regular couscous in this dish, as it requires a different cooking method and will not work in this recipe. For efficiency, let the shallots pickle while you prepare the remaining ingredients.

1   Heat 1 tablespoon oil and couscous in medium saucepan over medium heat, stirring frequently, until about half of grains are golden, about 5 minutes. Stir in water and ½ teaspoon salt. Bring to simmer; cover; and simmer over low heat, stirring occasionally, until water is absorbed, 10 to 15 minutes. Let sit off heat, covered, for 3 minutes. Transfer couscous to rimmed baking sheet and let cool completely, about 15 minutes.

2   Meanwhile, bring vinegar, sugar, and pinch salt to simmer in small saucepan over medium-high heat, stirring occasionally, until sugar dissolves. Add shallots and stir to combine. Remove from heat; cover; and let cool completely, about 30 minutes. Drain and discard liquid.

3   Meanwhile, whisk lemon juice, mustard, pepper flakes, remaining 3 tablespoons oil, and remaining ⅛ teaspoon salt together in large bowl. Add couscous, arugula, mint, peas, 6 tablespoons pistachios, ½ cup feta, and shallots and toss gently to combine. Season with salt and pepper to taste and transfer to serving bowl. Let sit for 5 minutes. Sprinkle with remaining ¼ cup feta and remaining 2 tablespoons pistachios and serve. (Salad can be refrigerated in airtight container for up to 2 days.)

SERVES 4 TO 6

¼ cup extra-virgin olive oil, divided

2 cups pearl couscous

2½ cups water

½ teaspoon plus pinch plus ⅛ teaspoon table salt, divided

⅓ cup red wine vinegar

2 tablespoons sugar

2 shallots, sliced thin

3 tablespoons lemon juice

1 teaspoon Dijon mustard

⅛ teaspoon red pepper flakes

4 ounces (4 cups) baby arugula or baby spinach, coarsely chopped

1 cup fresh mint or basil leaves, torn

½ cup frozen peas, thawed

½ cup shelled pistachios or almonds, toasted and chopped, divided

3 ounces feta or goat cheese, crumbled (¾ cup), divided

pearl couscous salad with chickpeas, chorizo, and warm spices

SERVES 4 TO 6

1 cup pearl couscous

6 ounces Spanish-style chorizo, cut into ½-inch pieces

2 carrots, peeled and chopped

8 teaspoons extra-virgin olive oil, divided

¼ teaspoon table salt

1⅓ cups chicken or vegetable broth

1 teaspoon smoked paprika

½ teaspoon ground cumin

2 cups canned chickpeas, rinsed and patted dry

⅔ cup chopped fresh parsley or cilantro

½ cup raisins, chopped dried apricots, chopped dates, or chopped dried figs

4 teaspoons lemon juice, plus lemon wedges for serving

why this recipe works In this easy, bright, sweet-tart pasta salad, we toasted pearl couscous with chorizo and carrots, then stirred in broth, plus smoked paprika and cumin to add smokiness. We added pantry-friendly chickpeas for heft, and parsley for some freshness. Dried fruit gave additional textural contrast and a hint of sweetness, and a squeeze of lemon juice brightened up this gorgeous-looking dish. Do not substitute regular couscous in this dish, as it requires a different cooking method and will not work in this recipe.

1 Combine couscous, chorizo, carrots, 2 teaspoons oil, and salt in medium saucepan and cook over medium heat, stirring frequently, until half of grains are golden, about 5 minutes. Stir in broth, paprika, and cumin. Bring to simmer; cover; and simmer over low heat, stirring occasionally, until broth is absorbed, 10 to 15 minutes. Let sit off heat, covered, for 3 minutes.

2 Stir in chickpeas, parsley, raisins, lemon juice, and remaining 2 tablespoons oil. Season with salt and pepper to taste. Serve with lemon wedges. (Salad can be refrigerated in airtight container for up to 2 days.)

couscous

Couscous is a starch made from durum semolina, the high-protein wheat flour that is also used to make Italian pasta. Traditional Moroccan couscous is made by rubbing crushed durum semolina and water between the hands to form small granules. The couscous is then dried and traditionally cooked over a simmering stew in a steamer called a couscoussier. The couscous found in most supermarkets is a precooked version that needs only a few minutes of steeping in hot liquid in order to be fully cooked. Pearl couscous (also known as Israeli couscous), is larger (about the size of a caper) and, like Italian pasta, is made from durum semolina flour. However, it is toasted rather than dried, which gives it a unique, nutty flavor. Both kinds of couscous make great salad bases. Regular couscous resembles quinoa or rice in its texture and form while the larger pearl couscous is heartier and filling and can hold up to stronger dressings and larger pieces of vegetables.

pearl couscous salad with radishes and watercress

why this recipe works We love the satisfying fulsome chew of pearl couscous. For this fresh-tasting salad, we paired it with crunchy radishes and walnuts, plus watercress and scallions for spiciness. A sherry vinegar–smoked paprika dressing with a hint of sugar brought a caramelly quality to the salad and complemented the nuts; a sprinkling of goat cheese finished the dish with tangy creaminess. Do not substitute regular couscous in this dish, as it requires a different cooking method and will not work in this recipe.

1   Heat 1 tablespoon oil and couscous in medium saucepan over medium heat, stirring frequently, until about half of grains are golden brown, about 5 minutes. Stir in water and ½ teaspoon salt. Bring to simmer; cover; and simmer over low heat, stirring occasionally, until water is absorbed, 10 to 15 minutes. Let sit off heat, covered, for 3 minutes. Transfer couscous to rimmed baking sheet and let cool completely, about 15 minutes.

2   Whisk vinegar, mustard, paprika, sugar, and remaining ⅛ teaspoon salt together in large bowl. Whisking constantly, slowly drizzle in remaining 3 tablespoons oil until emulsified. Add couscous, watercress, scallions, radishes, parsley, and 6 tablespoons walnuts and toss gently to combine. Season with salt and pepper to taste and transfer to serving bowl. Let sit for 5 minutes. Sprinkle with goat cheese and remaining 2 tablespoons walnuts and serve. (Salad can be refrigerated in airtight container for up to 2 days; sprinkle with goat cheese and remaining walnuts before serving.)

SERVES 4 TO 6

- ¼ cup extra-virgin olive oil, divided
- 2 cups pearl couscous
- 2½ cups water
- ½ teaspoon plus ⅛ teaspoon table salt, divided
- 3 tablespoons sherry vinegar
- 1 teaspoon Dijon mustard
- 1 teaspoon smoked paprika
- ¼ teaspoon sugar
- 2 ounces (2 cups) watercress or baby arugula, torn into bite-size pieces
- 6 scallions, sliced thin
- 6 radishes, trimmed and cut into matchsticks
- 1½ cups coarsely chopped parsley
- ½ cup walnuts or pine nuts, toasted and chopped coarse, divided
- 4 ounces goat or feta cheese, crumbled (1 cup)

cherry and goat cheese couscous salad

SERVES 4 TO 6

2 tablespoons unsalted butter

2 garlic cloves, minced

2 cups couscous

1 cup water

1 cup chicken or vegetable broth

1 teaspoon table salt

1 cup pecans or walnuts, toasted and chopped

1 cup baby arugula, chopped

1 cup dried cherries, chopped

4 ounces goat or feta cheese, crumbled (1 cup)

6 tablespoons extra-virgin olive oil

4 scallions, sliced thin

3 tablespoons lemon juice

why this recipe works Back-of-the-box instructions for couscous yield mushy, clumpy granules. Toasting uncooked couscous in butter and garlic sets the starch in the pasta, which keeps the granules separate and prevents them from blowing out. It also adds nutty flavor. To enhance the cooked couscous further, we added sweet, tart, and spicy flavors—dried cherries, pecans, arugula, and goat cheese. You can eat the salad immediately, but it will improve if you let the flavors meld for 30 minutes or so. Do not substitute pearl couscous in this dish, as it requires a different cooking method and will not work in this recipe.

1   Melt butter in medium saucepan over medium-high heat. Stir in garlic and cook until fragrant, about 30 seconds. Add couscous and cook, stirring frequently, until grains begin to brown, about 5 minutes. Add water, broth, and salt; stir briefly to combine, cover, and remove saucepan from heat. Let sit until liquid is absorbed and couscous is tender, about 7 minutes. Uncover and fluff couscous with fork.

2   Combine pecans, arugula, cherries, goat cheese, oil, scallions, and lemon juice in large bowl. Stir in couscous until well combined. Season with salt and pepper to taste. Serve.

variations
cilantro and pepita couscous salad
Omit dried cherries and goat cheese. Add 2½ teaspoons ground cumin and ½ teaspoon cayenne pepper to couscous with broth. Substitute roasted, salted pepitas for pecans; ½ cup chopped fresh cilantro for arugula; and 3 tablespoons lime juice (2 limes) for lemon juice.

feta and olive couscous salad
Omit arugula and dried cherries. Substitute 1 finely chopped small red onion for scallions. Substitute 6 ounces crumbled feta for goat cheese. Substitute almonds for pecans. Add 1 cucumber, peeled, seeded, and chopped fine and 1 cup pitted kalamata olives, chopped coarse, with olive oil in step 2.

spiced vegetable couscous salad

SERVES 4 TO 6

1 head cauliflower (2 pounds), cored and cut into 1-inch florets

6 tablespoons extra-virgin olive oil, divided, plus extra for drizzling

1¼ teaspoons table salt, divided

½ teaspoon pepper

1½ cups couscous

1 zucchini or summer squash, cut into ½-inch pieces

1 red, orange, or yellow bell pepper, stemmed, seeded, and cut into ½-inch pieces

4 garlic cloves, minced

2 teaspoons ras el hanout

1 teaspoon grated lemon zest, plus lemon wedges for serving

1¾ cups chicken or vegetable broth

1 tablespoon minced fresh marjoram or oregano

why this recipe works This easy vegetable salad was inspired by aromatic North African flavors and ingredients—the spice blend, ras al hanout, and the region's favorite pasta, couscous. For our vegetables, we chose a colorful combination of cauliflower, zucchini, and red bell pepper. To encourage deep caramelization on our cauliflower, we cut it into small, even pieces. We started the cauliflower in a cold pan, which ensured that it cooked through before developing a golden exterior. We then quickly sautéed zucchini and bell pepper with garlic, lemon zest, and ras el hanout. Finally, marjoram gave the salad some minty freshness. We prefer to use our homemade Ras el Hanout (recipe follows), but you can substitute store-bought ras el hanout if you wish, though flavor and spiciness can vary greatly by brand. You will need a 12-inch nonstick skillet with a tight-fitting lid for this recipe. Do not substitute pearl couscous in this dish, as it requires a different cooking method and will not work in this recipe.

1 Toss cauliflower, 2 tablespoons oil, ¾ teaspoon salt, and pepper together in 12-inch nonstick skillet. Cover and cook over medium-high heat until florets start to brown and edges just start to become translucent (do not lift lid), about 5 minutes.

2 Remove lid and continue to cook, stirring every 2 minutes, until florets turn golden brown in several spots, about 10 minutes. Transfer to bowl and wipe skillet clean with paper towels.

3 Heat 2 tablespoons oil in now-empty skillet over medium-high heat until shimmering. Add couscous and cook, stirring frequently, until grains are just beginning to brown, 3 to 5 minutes. Transfer to separate bowl and wipe skillet clean with paper towels.

4 Heat remaining 2 tablespoons oil in again-empty skillet over medium-high heat until just smoking. Add zucchini, bell pepper, and remaining ½ teaspoon salt and cook until tender, 6 to 8 minutes. Stir in garlic, ras el hanout, and lemon zest and cook until fragrant, about 30 seconds. Stir in broth and bring to simmer.

5 Stir in couscous. Off heat, cover and let sit until couscous is tender, about 7 minutes. Add marjoram and cauliflower to couscous and fluff gently with fork to combine. Season with salt and pepper to taste and drizzle with extra oil. Serve with lemon wedges.

ras el hanout

makes about ½ cup

Ras el hanout is a complexly flavorful Moroccan spice blend that traditionally features a host of warm spices. We use it to give robust flavor to couscous dishes, soups, stews, braises, and more. If you can't find Aleppo pepper, you can substitute ½ teaspoon paprika and ½ teaspoon of red pepper flakes.

- 16 cardamom pods
- 4 teaspoons coriander seeds
- 4 teaspoons cumin seeds
- 2 teaspoons anise seeds
- ½ teaspoon allspice berries
- ¼ teaspoon black peppercorns
- 4 teaspoons ground ginger
- 2 teaspoons ground nutmeg
- 2 teaspoons ground dried Aleppo pepper
- 2 teaspoons ground cinnamon

1 Toast cardamom, coriander, cumin, anise, allspice, and peppercorns in small skillet over medium heat until fragrant, shaking skillet occasionally to prevent scorching, about 2 minutes. Let cool completely.

2 Transfer toasted spices, ginger, nutmeg, Aleppo pepper, and cinnamon to spice grinder and process to fine powder. (Ras el hanout can be stored at room temperature in airtight container for up to 1 year.)

chilled soba noodle salad with cucumber, snow peas, and radishes

why this recipe works Soba noodles are made from buckwheat flour or a buckwheat–wheat flour blend. They have a chewy texture and nutty flavor and are delicious in salads. Here we made a cold noodle salad that's refreshing on a hot day. We cooked the noodles in unsalted boiling water until tender but still resilient and rinsed them under cold running water to remove excess starch and prevent sticking. We then tossed the soba with a miso-mirin dressing, which clung to and flavored the noodles without overpowering their distinct taste. We also cut a mix of vegetables into varying sizes so that they'd incorporate nicely into the noodles while adding crunch and color. Adding strips of toasted nori added more texture and a subtle briny taste. Plain pretoasted seaweed snacks can be substituted for the toasted nori, if desired. This dish isn't meant to be very spicy, but if you like heat, use the full ½ teaspoon of red pepper flakes.

1 Bring 4 quarts water to boil in large pot. Stir in noodles and cook, stirring occasionally, until noodles are cooked through but still retain some chew. Drain noodles and rinse under cold water until chilled. Drain well and transfer to large bowl.

2 Grip nori sheet, if using, with tongs and hold about 2 inches above low flame on gas burner. Toast nori, flipping every 3 to 5 seconds, until nori is aromatic and shrinks slightly, about 20 seconds. If you do not have a gas stove, toast nori on rimmed baking sheet in 275-degree oven until it is aromatic and shrinks slightly, 20 to 25 minutes, flipping nori halfway through toasting. Using scissors, cut nori into four 2-inch strips. Stack strips and cut crosswise into thin strips.

3 Combine miso, mirin, oil, 1 tablespoon water, sesame seeds, ginger, and pepper flakes in small bowl and whisk until combined. Add dressing to noodles and toss to combine. Add cucumber; snow peas; radishes; scallions; and nori, if using, and toss well to evenly distribute. Season with salt to taste, and serve.

SERVES 4 TO 6

- 8 ounces dried soba noodles
- 1 (8-inch square) sheet nori (optional)
- 3 tablespoons white, yellow, red, or brown miso
- 3 tablespoons mirin
- 2 tablespoons toasted sesame oil
- 1 tablespoon sesame seeds
- 1 teaspoon grated fresh ginger
- ¼–½ teaspoon red pepper flakes
- ⅓ English cucumber, quartered lengthwise, seeded, and sliced thin on bias
- 4 ounces snow or sugar snap peas, strings removed, cut lengthwise into matchsticks
- 4 radishes, trimmed, halved, and sliced into thin half-moons
- 3 scallions, sliced thin on bias

chicken and cellophane noodle salad

SERVES 4 TO 6

- 8 ounces cellophane noodles or rice vermicelli
- 3 carrots, peeled and cut into 2-inch-long matchsticks
- 2 English cucumbers, peeled and cut into 2-inch-long matchsticks
- 6 tablespoons unseasoned rice vinegar, divided
- ⅓ cup soy sauce
- 2 tablespoons vegetable oil
- 1 tablespoon toasted sesame oil
- 1 tablespoon grated fresh ginger
- 1 garlic clove, minced
- 2 cups cooked chicken, shredded

why this recipe works We wanted to use slippery cellophane noodles in a satisfying summer salad because we love their coolness and ability to absorb the flavor of our quick-pickled vegetables and soy sauce–rice vinegar dressing. We quick-pickled the vegetables while the noodles cooked. We like using Perfect Poached Chicken (page 43) here but any cooked chicken would work. Note that this recipe uses unseasoned rice vinegar; we don't recommend using seasoned rice vinegar in its place.

1 Bring 4 quarts water to boil in large pot. Off heat, add noodles and let sit, stirring occasionally, until soft and pliable but not fully tender. Drain noodles and rinse under cold running water until chilled. Drain noodles again.

2 Meanwhile, toss carrots and cucumbers with 2 tablespoons vinegar in large bowl; set aside to marinate for 10 minutes. Whisk soy sauce, vegetable oil, sesame oil, ginger, garlic, and remaining ¼ cup vinegar together in bowl.

3 Drain and discard vinegar from marinating vegetables. Add noodles, chicken, and dressing to bowl with vegetables and toss to thoroughly combine. Serve.

cellophane noodles

Chinese fensi or "flour thread" noodles are also called cellophane or glass noodles because of their translucence. They are not to be confused with rice vermicelli, which can be a good substitute for them. The distinctive smooth texture of cellophane noodles comes from the starch they are made with. This starch might come from mung beans, sweet potatoes, or tapioca.

Cellophane noodles can be boiled or soaked, going from translucent to glass-like when cooked. Used for spring rolls and stir-fried dishes because they absorb liquid and flavor easily, they work well in noodle salads for the same reason.

bún chả

SERVES 4 TO 6

noodles and salad

- 8 ounces rice vermicelli
- 1 head Boston or Bibb lettuce (8 ounces), leaves separated and torn into bite-size pieces
- 1 English cucumber, peeled, quartered lengthwise, seeded, and sliced thin on bias
- 1 cup fresh cilantro leaves and stems
- 1 cup fresh mint or Thai basil leaves, torn if large

nước chấm

- 1 small Thai chile, stemmed and minced
- 3 tablespoons sugar, divided
- 1 garlic clove, minced
- ⅔ cup hot water
- 5 tablespoons fish sauce
- ¼ cup lime juice (2 limes)

pork patties

- 1 large shallot, minced
- 1 tablespoon fish sauce
- 1½ teaspoons sugar
- ½ teaspoon baking soda
- ½ teaspoon pepper
- 1 pound ground pork

why this recipe works Vietnamese bún chả—a vibrant mix of grilled pork patties, crisp cucumber and lettuce, and delicate yet resilient rice vermicelli, all united by a light yet potent sauce—makes a flavorful composed salad for which you assemble the elements and eat them in lettuce leaves on a hot summer night. We soaked rice vermicelli in hot water, rinsed the noodles well, and spread them on a platter to dry. Then we mixed up the bold and zesty sauce known as nước chấm using lime juice, sugar, and fish sauce. To ensure that every drop of the sauce was flavored with garlic and chile, we used a portion of the sugar to help grind the pungent ingredients into a fine paste. For juicy pork patties, we mixed baking soda into ground pork because it raised the meat's pH, which helped the meat retain moisture and brown during the 8-minute grilling time. Per tradition, we also seasoned the pork with shallot, fish sauce, sugar, and pepper, and also briefly soaked the grilled patties in the sauce, a step that further flavored the patties and imbued the sauce with grilled flavor. We plated the components separately to allow diners to combine them according to their taste. We prefer the more delicate springiness of vermicelli made from 100 percent rice flour to those that include a secondary starch such as cornstarch. If you can find only the latter, just cook them longer—up to 12 minutes. For a less spicy sauce, use only half the Thai chile. For the cilantro, use the leaves and the thin, delicate stems, not the thicker ones close to the root. To serve, place platters of noodles, salad, sauce, and pork patties on the table and allow diners to combine components to their taste. The sauce is potent, so use it sparingly.

1 for the noodles and salad Bring 4 quarts water to boil in large pot. Off heat, add noodles and let sit, stirring occasionally, until tender but not mushy. Drain noodles and rinse under cold running water until chilled. Drain well, spread on large plate, and let sit at room temperature to dry. Arrange lettuce, cucumber, cilantro, and mint separately on serving platter and refrigerate until needed.

2 for the nước chấm Using mortar and pestle (or on cutting board using flat side of chef's knife), mash Thai chile, 1 tablespoon sugar, and garlic to fine paste. Transfer to medium bowl and add hot water and remaining 2 tablespoons sugar. Stir until sugar is dissolved. Stir in fish sauce and lime juice. Set aside.

3 for the pork patties Combine shallot, fish sauce, sugar, baking soda, and pepper in medium bowl. Add pork and mix until well combined. Shape pork mixture into 12 patties, each about 2½ inches wide and ½ inch thick.

4A for a charcoal grill Open bottom vent completely. Light large chimney starter filled with charcoal briquettes (6 quarts). When top coals are partially covered with ash, pour evenly over half of grill. Set cooking grate in place, cover, and open lid vent completely. Heat grill until hot, about 5 minutes.

4B for a gas grill Turn all burners to high; cover; and heat grill until hot, about 15 minutes. Leave all burners on high.

5 Clean and oil cooking grate. Cook patties (directly over coals if using charcoal; covered if using gas) until well charred, 3 to 4 minutes per side. Transfer patties to bowl with sauce and toss gently to coat. Let sit for 5 minutes.

6 Transfer patties to serving plate, reserving sauce. Serve noodles, salad, nước chấm, and pork patties separately.

summer ramen salad

sesame-scallion vinaigrette

 2 tablespoons soy sauce

 1 tablespoon unseasoned rice vinegar

 1 tablespoon mirin

 1 tablespoon water

 ½ teaspoon chili oil (optional)

 ¼ teaspoon toasted sesame oil

 ½ scallion, minced

salad

 2 teaspoons vegetable oil

 ¼ teaspoon grated orange zest
    plus ¼ cup juice

 12 ounces lump crabmeat, picked over
    for shells and pressed dry between
    paper towels

 4 (3-ounce) packages ramen noodles,
    seasoning packets discarded

 1 avocado, sliced thin

 ½ English cucumber, cut into
    2-inch-long matchsticks

 4 radishes, trimmed, halved,
    and sliced thin

 2 scallions, green parts only,
    sliced thin on bias

 2 teaspoons toasted black
    sesame seeds

why this recipe works A hot, steaming bowl of ramen noodles is the perfect fix on a cold, blustery day. But when the temperature rises, ramen noodles need a cooldown just as much as you do. Hiyashi chuka or summer ramen is that fix: brothless ramen noodles tossed in a sweet-sour soy sauce dressing and served chilled with an array of toppings that provide textural contrast and visual appeal. While vegetables, eggs, and meat are most often found on the noodles, summer ramen presents a perfect opportunity for customizing based on what you have in the fridge or what you just brought home from the farmers' market. We tossed chilled ramen noodles with a soy sauce–based dressing perked up with rice vinegar, sesame oil, chili oil, and scallion. We topped the noodles with crisp cucumbers; rich avocado; and crunchy, spicy radishes. To this elegant base, we added seafood and bright citrus, tossing crab with both orange juice and zest. You could use cooked shrimp or salmon instead. If using crab, be sure to purchase high-quality, fresh lump or jumbo lump crabmeat. For a milder vinaigrette, omit the chili oil. Note that this recipe uses unseasoned rice vinegar; we don't recommend using seasoned rice vinegar in its place. Serve with pickled ginger and cilantro leaves.

1 **for the sesame-scallion vinaigrette** Whisk all ingredients together in bowl. (Vinaigrette can be refrigerated for up to 3 days; whisk to recombine before using.)

2 **for the salad** Whisk oil and orange zest and juice together in medium bowl. Add crabmeat, tossing to coat, then season with salt and pepper to taste; refrigerate until ready to serve.

3 Bring 4 quarts water to boil in large pot. Add noodles and cook, stirring frequently, until tender. Drain noodles and rinse under cold water until chilled. Drain well, toss noodles with vinaigrette, and season with salt and pepper to taste. Divide among individual plates. Serve, topping individual portions with crabmeat mixture, avocado, cucumber, and radishes. Sprinkle with scallions and sesame seeds.

chilled somen noodle salad with shrimp

why this recipe works Served in ice water with a bowl of dipping sauce and pickled ginger, somen noodles are perfect to help you cool off on a scorching day. For our version, we tossed cooled somen with a chilled savory broth turned sauce instead. We made a simple dashi from simmered kombu (dried kelp) and dried bonito flakes and seasoned it with soy sauce, mirin, and sugar before chilling the sauce for 3 hours. After cooking the somen, we rinsed them in cold water to remove extra starch that would make them gummy. We tossed the somen with the sauce, then topped individual bowls with sautéed shrimp, sliced cucumber, pickled ginger, and fresh cilantro and scallions for a refreshing dish. Do not substitute other types of noodles for the somen noodles here.

1   Bring water and kombu to boil in large saucepan over medium-low heat. Off heat, stir in bonito flakes and let sit for 3 minutes. Strain broth through fine-mesh strainer into large bowl, pressing on solids to extract as much broth as possible. Whisk in soy sauce, mirin, and sugar until sugar is dissolved. Cover and refrigerate until well chilled, about 3 hours.

2   Bring 4 quarts water to boil in large pot. Add noodles, and cook, stirring often, until tender. Drain noodles and rinse under cold water until chilled and drain again, leaving noodles slightly wet. Toss noodles with sauce in large bowl. Top individual portions with shrimp, cucumber, pickled ginger, cilantro, and scallions. Serve.

SERVES 4 TO 6

- 1½   cups water
- 1   (2-inch) piece kombu
- ¼   cup dried bonito flakes
- ½   cup soy sauce
- ¼   cup mirin
- 1   teaspoon sugar
- 12   ounces somen noodles
- 1½   cups Sautéed Shrimp (page 43), halved lengthwise
- ½   English cucumber, halved lengthwise and sliced thin
- ¼   cup pickled ginger, chopped coarse
- ¼   cup fresh cilantro or mint leaves
- 2   scallions, sliced thin on bias

sesame lo mein salad

SERVES 4 TO 6

5 tablespoons soy sauce

¼ cup Asian sesame paste or tahini

2 tablespoons unseasoned rice vinegar

2 tablespoons packed brown sugar

1 tablespoon boiling water, plus extra as needed

1 tablespoon grated fresh ginger

2 garlic cloves, minced

1 teaspoon Sichuan Chili Oil (page 187), plus extra for serving

1 pound fresh lo mein noodles or 12 ounces dried lo mein noodles or linguine

½ English cucumber, cut into 3-inch-long matchsticks

¼ cup fresh cilantro or Thai basil leaves

2 scallions, green parts only, sliced thin on bias

1 tablespoon sesame seeds, toasted

why this recipe works The nutty taste of toasted sesame seeds is paired with chewy lo mein noodles in this salad, inspired by ma jiang mian, a deceptively simple dish that delivers creamy, complex flavor. This popular street food in both China and Taiwan works as a quick and easy vegetarian noodle salad. Chewy noodles are tossed in a fresh, aromatic sesame sauce. We first rinsed the cooked noodles with cold water to cool them and wash away excess sticky starch. We also drained the noodles thoroughly to get rid of any water that could dilute our sauce. For the sauce, we used Asian sesame paste, made from toasted white sesame seeds blended with aromatic toasted sesame oil. We added soy sauce, vinegar, brown sugar, ginger, garlic, chili oil, and just a little boiling water to the paste and whizzed everything in a blender to create a smooth consistency. Cilantro and scallions added freshness while English cucumber and sesame seeds provided crunch. We like drizzling some chili oil on at the end for a touch of welcome heat. We use our Sichuan Chili Oil, however any store-bought chili oil will work. Note that this recipe uses unseasoned rice vinegar; we don't recommend using seasoned rice vinegar in its place.

1 Process soy sauce, sesame paste, vinegar, sugar, boiling water, ginger, garlic, and chili oil in blender until smooth, about 30 seconds, scraping down sides of blender jar as needed; transfer to large bowl.

2 Meanwhile, bring 4 quarts water to boil in large pot. Add noodles and cook, stirring often, until tender. Drain noodles and rinse under cold running water until chilled. Drain well and transfer to bowl with dressing. Toss to combine. Adjust consistency with extra boiling water as needed. Transfer noodles to serving platter and top with cucumber, cilantro, scallions, and sesame seeds. Serve, passing extra chili oil separately.

peanut noodle salad

SERVES 6 TO 8

12 ounces (⅜-inch-wide) rice noodles

3 tablespoons toasted sesame oil

¾ cup chunky peanut butter

6 tablespoons soy sauce

6 tablespoons boiling water,
plus extra as needed

3 tablespoons distilled white vinegar

1 tablespoon grated fresh ginger

1 tablespoon hot sauce

1 English cucumber, peeled,
quartered lengthwise, seeded,
and sliced thin

1 red, orange, or yellow bell pepper,
seeded and cut into ¼-inch strips

⅓ cup chopped fresh cilantro or
Thai basil

why this recipe works For a noodle salad that marries crunchy and soft elements and sweetness with tang, we combined peanuts, rice noodles, ginger, and soy sauce with English cucumbers, white vinegar, and hot sauce. Coating the noodles with sesame oil before tossing them in the sauce created a barrier that helped prevent pasty pasta and also added a divine sesame aroma. If you prefer natural peanut butter and use it here, add 1 tablespoon brown sugar to the dressing. Use a mild hot sauce, such as Frank's. If you use a hotter hot sauce, such as Tabasco, reduce the amount to 1 teaspoon. You can substitute 1 pound spaghetti or linguine for the rice noodles.

1   Bring 4 quarts water to boil in large pot. Remove from heat; add noodles; and let sit, stirring occasionally, until fully tender. Drain noodles and rinse under cold running water until chilled. Drain noodles well and toss with sesame oil; transfer to large bowl. Set aside.

2   Whisk peanut butter, soy sauce, boiling water, vinegar, ginger, and hot sauce in medium bowl until smooth. Add dressing, cucumber, bell pepper, and cilantro to noodles and toss to combine. Adjust consistency with extra boiling water as needed. Serve.

udon noodle salad with edamame pesto

why this recipe works For a different take on pasta salad, we paired thick, chewy udon noodles with a pesto featuring frozen edamame (immature soy beans) and lots of parsley, cilantro, and basil in an update on classic pesto ingredients. This herby bean pesto is so hearty that all we needed now was a vegetable to make our noodle salad a complete meal. The pesto takes minimal time to prepare since all the ingredients are simply added to the food processor. We cooked the asparagus and noodles together in the same pot to save time. Once they were drained, we simply combined them with the pesto. We reserved some of the noodle cooking water to loosen the thick sauce into a creamy dressing as needed. We recommend using the thinnest asparagus stalks available to ensure that they'll cook in about the same amount of time as the noodles. Do not substitute other types of noodles for the udon noodles here.

1   Bring 4 quarts water to boil in large pot. Process edamame, parsley, cilantro, basil, pine nuts, Parmesan, oil, lemon juice, and garlic in food processor until smooth, about 20 seconds, scraping down sides of bowl as needed. Transfer to small bowl and season with salt and pepper to taste.

2   Add noodles and asparagus to boiling water and cook, stirring occasionally, until noodles and asparagus are tender, about 4 minutes. Reserve 1 cup cooking water, then drain noodles and asparagus and return them to pot.

3   Stir pesto into pot with noodles. Season with salt and pepper to taste and adjust consistency with reserved cooking water as needed. Serve. (Salad can be refrigerated in airtight container for up to 24 hours; to serve, add warm water and additional oil as needed to refresh its texture.)

SERVES 4 TO 6

- 8 ounces frozen shelled edamame, thawed
- 1 cup fresh parsley leaves
- 1 cup fresh cilantro leaves
- 1 cup fresh basil leaves
- ½ cup pine nuts, toasted
- 1 ounce Parmesan or Pecorino Romano cheese, grated (½ cup)
- ¼ cup extra-virgin olive oil
- 2 tablespoons lemon juice
- 1 garlic clove, minced
- 18 ounces fresh udon noodles
- 1 pound thin asparagus, trimmed and cut on bias into 1½-inch lengths

soba noodle salad with roasted eggplant and sesame

why this recipe works The creamy texture and mild flavor of eggplant is the perfect complement to rich, nutty soba noodles in this recipe. Roasting eggplant proved an easy, hands-off way to cook it; before cooking, we tossed it with soy sauce and vegetable oil to season it and draw out its moisture. For our dressing, we used more soy sauce for savory richness. Oyster sauce, sugar, Asian chili-garlic sauce, and toasted sesame oil added a nice balance of sweet and spicy flavors, while a little sake contributed clean, acidic notes that bolstered the complexity of the dressing. A sprinkling of fresh cilantro and sesame seeds brightened up our earthy noodle salad. Vermouth can be substituted for the sake if necessary. Do not substitute other types of noodles for the soba noodles here.

1 Adjust oven racks to upper-middle and lower-middle positions and heat oven to 450 degrees. Line 2 rimmed baking sheets with aluminum foil and spray with vegetable oil spray. Toss eggplant with 1 tablespoon soy sauce and vegetable oil, then spread evenly between prepared baking sheets. Roast until eggplant is well browned and tender, 25 to 30 minutes, stirring and switching sheets halfway through roasting.

2 Combine sugar, oyster sauce, sesame oil, sake, chili-garlic sauce, and remaining soy sauce in small saucepan. Cook over medium heat, whisking often, until sugar has dissolved, about 1 minute; cover and set aside.

3 Meanwhile, bring 4 quarts water to boil in large pot. Add noodles and cook, stirring often, until tender. Reserve ½ cup cooking water, then drain noodles and return them to pot. Add sauce and roasted eggplant and toss to combine. Add reserved cooking water as needed to adjust consistency. Serve warm or at room temperature; topping individual portions with cilantro and sesame seeds.

SERVES 4 TO 6

3 pounds eggplant, cut into 1-inch pieces

⅓ cup soy sauce, divided

¼ cup vegetable oil

⅓ cup sugar

3 tablespoons oyster sauce

3 tablespoons toasted sesame oil

5 teaspoons sake

1½ tablespoons Asian chili-garlic sauce

12 ounces dried soba noodles

¾ cup fresh cilantro or mint leaves

2 teaspoons sesame seeds, toasted

nutritional information for our recipes

To calculate the nutritional values of our recipes per serving, we used The Food Processor SQL by ESHA research. When using this program, we entered all the ingredients, using weights wherever possible. We also used our preferred brands in these analyses. Any ingredient listed as "optional" was excluded from the analyses. If there is a range in the serving size, we used the highest number of servings to calculate nutritional values. We did not include additional salt or pepper for food that's seasoned to taste.

	CALORIES	TOTAL FAT (G)	SAT FAT (G)	CHOL (MG)	SODIUM (MG)	TOTAL CARB (G)	DIETARY FIBER (G)	TOTAL SUGARS (G)	PROTEIN (G)
The Salad Bar									
Foolproof Vinaigrette *(per 2 tablespoons)*	100	11	1.5	0	90	0	0	0	0
Foolproof Lemon Vinaigrette *(per 2 tablespoons)*	100	11	1.5	0	90	0	0	0	0
Foolproof Balsamic-Mustard Vinaigrette *(per 2 tablespoons)*	110	11	1.5	0	135	1	0	1	0
Foolproof Herb Vinaigrette *(per 2 tablespoons)*	100	11	1.5	0	90	0	0	0	0
Make-Ahead Vinaigrette *(per 2 tablespoons)*	100	11	1.5	0	100	1	0	1	0
Make-Ahead Sherry-Shallot Vinaigrette *(per 2 tablespoons)*	110	11	1.5	0	100	1	0	1	0
Make-Ahead Balsamic-Fennel Vinaigrette *(per 2 tablespoons)*	110	11	1.5	0	100	2	0	2	0
Make-Ahead Cider-Caraway Vinaigrette *(per 2 tablespoons)*	110	11	1.5	0	100	1	0	1	0
Tarragon-Caper Vinaigrette *(per 2 tablespoons)*	100	11	1.5	0	110	0	0	0	0
Maple-Mustard Vinaigrette *(per 2 tablespoons)*	60	5	0.5	0	230	4	0	3	0
Raspberry Vinaigrette *(per 2 tablespoons)*	80	7	1	0	70	4	0	4	0
Sriracha-Lime Vinaigrette *(per 2 tablespoons)*	110	9	1.5	0	210	6	0	5	1
Pomegranate-Honey Vinaigrette *(per 2 tablespoons)*	80	3.5	0	0	150	12	0	10	0
Orange-Ginger Vinaigrette *(per 2 tablespoons)*	70	3.5	0.5	0	150	9	0	7	1
Apple Cider-Sage Vinaigrette *(per 2 tablespoons)*	70	3.5	0	0	150	10	0	9	0
Orange-Lime Vinaigrette *(per 2 tablespoons)*	35	2	0	0	75	5	0	4	0
Oregano-Black Olive Vinaigrette *(per 2 tablespoons)*	100	11	1.5	0	105	1	0	0	0
Creamless Creamy Herb Dressing *(per 1 tablespoon)*	50	4	0.5	0	180	3	0	1	2
Creamless Creamy Ginger-Miso Dressing *(per 1 tablespoon)*	60	4.5	0.5	0	180	5	0	1	2
Creamless Creamy Green Goddess Dressing *(per 1 tablespoon)*	40	3	0.5	0	110	2	0	0	1
Creamless Creamy Roasted Red Pepper and Tahini Dressing *(per 1 tablespoon)*	50	4	0.5	0	280	4	0	1	1

	CALORIES	TOTAL FAT (G)	SAT FAT (G)	CHOL (MG)	SODIUM (MG)	TOTAL CARB (G)	DIETARY FIBER (G)	TOTAL SUGARS (G)	PROTEIN (G)
The Salad Bar (cont.)									
Tahini-Lemon Dressing *(per 1 tablespoon)*	90	9	1.5	0	150	1	0	0	1
Creamy Roasted Garlic Dressing *(per 1 tablespoon)*	130	9	1.5	0	95	11	1	2	2
Yogurt-Dill Dressing *(per 1 tablespoon)*	20	1.5	0	0	85	0	0	0	0
Poppy Seed Dressing *(per 1 tablespoon)*	110	10	1	0	200	6	0	5	0
Blue Cheese Dressing *(per 1 tablespoon)*	45	4	1.5	10	100	0	0	0	1
Ranch Dressing *(per 1 tablespoon)*	40	4	1	5	85	1	0	0	0
Vegan Ranch Dressing *(per 1 tablespoon)*	90	10	1	0	120	0	0	0	0
Green Goddess Dressing *(per 1 tablespoon)*	10	0.5	0	0	40	1	0	1	0
Creamy Peppercorn Dressing *(per 1 tablespoon)*	60	7	1	5	40	1	0	0	0
Creamy Avocado Dressing *(per 1 tablespoon)*	35	3.5	0.5	0	110	1	1	0	0
Creamy Italian Dressing *(per 1 tablespoon)*	80	9	1.5	5	45	0	0	0	0
Caesar Dressing *(per 1 tablespoon)*	70	8	1	5	135	1	0	0	0
Rosemary Oil *(per 1 tablespoon)*	250	28	4	0	0	1	0	0	0
Fennel Oil *(per 1 tablespoon)*	260	28	4	0	0	1	0	0	0
Chipotle-Coriander Oil *(per 1 tablespoon)*	260	28	4	0	1	1	0	0	0
Ginger Oil *(per 1 tablespoon)*	250	28	2	0	0	1	0	0	0
Peppercorn Oil *(per 1 tablespoon)*	250	28	2	0	0	0	0	0	0
Wine Vinegar *(per 1 tablespoon)*	20	0	0	0	0	1	0	0	0
Seasoned Rice Vinegar *(per 1 tablespoon)*	25	0	0	0	870	6	0	6	0
Hot Pepper Vinegar *(per 1 tablespoon)*	5	0	0	0	75	1	0	1	0
Easy-Peel Hard-Cooked Eggs *(per 1 egg)*	70	5	1.5	185	70	0	0	0	6
Perfect Poached Chicken	200	4.5	1	125	220	0	0	0	38
Crispy Tofu	200	7	0	0	190	20	0	0	11
Sautéed Shrimp	90	4.5	0.5	105	270	1	0	0	12
Classic Croutons *(per ¼ cup)*	60	4	0.5	0	60	5	0	1	1
Garlic Croutons *(per ¼ cup)*	60	4	0.5	0	60	5	0	1	1
Herbed Croutons *(per ¼ cup)*	70	2	1	5	75	11	0	2	2
Umami Croutons *(per ¼ cup)*	50	3	0	80	5	0	0	0	1
Buttery Rye Croutons *(per ¼ cup)*	100	8	4	15	65	5	0	0	1
Parmesan Croutons *(per ¼ cup)*	70	4.5	1	0	105	6	0	1	1
Black Pepper Candied Bacon	270	23	8	35	380	10	0	9	7
Crispy Chickpeas *(per ¼ cup)*	70	4	0.5	0	140	6	2	0	2
Cumin-Spiced Crispy Lentils	140	8	0.5	0	290	14	4	1	5
Frico Crumble	100	8	5	25	340	0	0	0	7
Microwave-Fried Shallots	30	2.5	0	0	0	3	0	1	0
Microwave-Fried Garlic	40	2.5	0	0	0	4	0	0	1
Microwave-Fried Leeks	40	2.5	0	0	0	4	0	1	0
Hazelnut-Nigella Dukkah *(per 1 tablespoon)*	40	3.5	0	0	120	2	1	0	1
Za'atar *(per 1 tablespoon)*	20	1.5	0	0	5	2	1	0	1
Spiced Pepitas or Sunflower Seeds *(per 1 tablespoon)*	60	5	1	0	75	1	1	0	2
Quick Candied Nuts *(per ¼ cup)*	60	4.5	0.5	0	35	4	1	2	2
Spiced Nuts *(per ¼ cup)*	110	10	1	0	150	4	2	1	4
Savory Seed Brittle *(per ¼ cup)*	80	5	1	0	135	6	1	2	3

	CALORIES	TOTAL FAT (G)	SAT FAT (G)	CHOL (MG)	SODIUM (MG)	TOTAL CARB (G)	DIETARY FIBER (G)	TOTAL SUGARS (G)	PROTEIN (G)
The Salad Bar (cont.)									
Quick Pickled Red Onion *(per ¼ cup)*	20	0	0	0	35	5	0	4	0
Quick Giardiniera *(per ¼ cup)*	70	0	0	0	1070	17	1	13	1
Pickled Asparagus *(per ¼ cup)*	80	2	0	0	1680	13	2	10	3
Quick Pickled Daikon Radish and Carrot *(per ¼ cup)*	30	0	0	0	260	7	1	4	1
Quick Pickled Fennel *(per ¼ cup)*	45	0	0	0	650	11	1	9	0
Quick Pickled Cabbage with Lemongrass *(per ¼ cup)*	10	0	0	0	600	2	0	1	0
Quick Pickled Grapes *(per ¼ cup)*	20	0	0	0	110	5	0	5	0
Leafy Salads									
Purslane and Watermelon Salad	170	12	4.5	20	220	11	1	8	6
Pea Green Salad with Warm Apricot-Pistachio Vinaigrette	180	10	1	0	150	18	6	10	5
Spring Pea Salad	180	13	2.5	0	370	11	3	5	4
Bitter Greens and Chickpea Salad with Warm Vinaigrette	410	21	4	10	630	46	9	26	10
Salad with Herbed Baked Goat Cheese and Vinaigrette	400	29	11	120	680	14	1	2	17
Roasted Cipollini and Escarole Salad	290	19	4.5	20	880	21	3	5	10
Chopped Winter Salad with Butternut Squash	430	28	5	15	460	42	8	14	8
Creamy Chicken Salad with Fresh Herbs	470	32	5	130	640	1	0	0	44
Curried Chicken Salad with Dried Apricots	630	37	6	130	650	27	5	20	47
Creamy Chicken Salad with Grapes and Walnuts	550	39	6	130	730	10	2	7	46
Crab and Mizuna Salad	400	35	5	90	790	4	2	1	17
Tuna Salad with Hard-Cooked Eggs, Radishes, and Capers	410	31	4.5	130	880	2	1	1	24
Tuna Salad with Apple, Walnuts, and Tarragon	490	39	5	40	650	10	3	6	24
Curried Tuna Salad with Grapes	400	29	4	40	650	9	1	6	21
Chicken and Arugula Salad with Figs and Warm Spices	450	24	3.5	80	380	26	6	14	35
Chicken Salad with Thai Basil and Mango	320	6	1.5	120	460	19	2	5	46
Bibb Lettuce and Chicken Salad with Peanut Dressing	480	25	3.5	120	920	14	3	8	49
Steak Salad with Carrot-Ginger Vinaigrette	600	42	10	110	1170	19	3	12	37
Steak Salad with Pear and Quick Pickled Fennel	400	21	7	85	780	21	3	15	32
Arugula Salad with Steak Tips and Blue Cheese	570	46	16	115	1130	8	2	4	35
Southwest Beef Salad with Cornbread Croutons	670	45	6	160	1400	32	2	9	34
Chef's Salad with Fennel, Asiago, and Salami	480	35	13	75	1350	17	4	6	22
Romaine and Watercress Salad with Asparagus and Prosciutto	160	12	2	10	390	7	4	3	6
Larb	180	2.5	1	75	530	11	1	4	27
Salade Lyonnaise	290	22	6	210	1030	3	1	1	14
Perfect Poached Eggs *(per 1 egg)*	70	5	1.5	185	70	0	0	0	6
Salmon, Avocado, and Watercress Salad	780	55	10	125	620	23	11	11	50
Lemony Salmon and Roasted Beet Salad	550	41	8	170	640	11	3	6	35

	CALORIES	TOTAL FAT (G)	SAT FAT (G)	CHOL (MG)	SODIUM (MG)	TOTAL CARB (G)	DIETARY FIBER (G)	TOTAL SUGARS (G)	PROTEIN (G)
Leafy Salads (cont.)									
Seared Tuna Poke Salad	350	15	2.5	45	810	19	4	5	30
Summer Dinner Salad with Scallops	420	26	4	40	750	19	4	7	23
Shrimp Salad with Avocado and Grapefruit	250	9	1.5	145	800	27	5	13	19
Wilted Spinach and Shrimp Salad with Bacon-Pecan Vinaigrette	450	31	7	170	1420	17	6	8	24
Grilled Caesar Salad	360	32	5	10	600	13	2	2	5
Grilled Chicken Cobb Salad	890	66	16	350	1220	17	8	6	57
Crispy Bacon (per slice)	180	17	6	30	280	1	0	0	5
Grilled Radicchio Salad with Corn, Cherry Tomatoes, and Pecorino Romano	510	41	7	5	580	30	5	13	12
Arugula Salad with Fennel and Shaved Parmesan	130	11	2	5	180	5	2	2	3
Arugula Salad with Grapes, Fennel, Blue Cheese, and Pecans	220	18	4.5	10	310	12	2	8	5
Bibb and Frisée Salad with Apple and Celery	140	12	1.5	0	85	8	4	4	2
Green Salad with Artichokes and Olives	110	9	2	5	270	5	1	2	3
Green Salad with Marcona Almonds and Manchego Cheese	190	17	4	5	200	2	1	1	4
Mâche Salad with Cucumber and Mint	120	11	1.5	0	100	5	2	1	2
Spinach Salad with Egg and Red Onion	210	12	2	95	560	16	1	3	6
Spinach Salad with Raspberry Vinaigrette	190	14	4	15	220	11	3	6	6
Wilted Spinach Salad with Strawberries, Goat Cheese, and Almonds	150	13	2.5	5	70	7	2	3	4
Radicchio, Endive, and Arugula Salad	80	7	1	0	60	3	1	1	1
Pan-Roasted Pear Salad with Watercress, Parmesan, and Pecans	180	9	2	5	240	21	4	14	4
Pan-Roasted Pear Salad with Frisée, Goat Cheese, and Almonds	160	8	2	5	150	21	4	13	3
Pan-Roasted Pear Salad with Radicchio, Blue Cheese, and Walnuts	180	10	3	10	240	22	4	13	4
Fruit & Vegetable Salads									
Apple and Fennel Salad with Bitter Greens and Warm Pancetta Dressing	280	22	5	15	570	12	5	5	9
Apple-Fennel Rémoulade	80	5	1	0	220	7	2	4	1
Crispy Artichoke Salad with Lemon Vinaigrette	190	12	1.5	0	330	16	3	2	4
Asparagus Salad with Radishes, Pecorino Romano, and Croutons	320	28	7	20	490	13	4	4	8
Beet Salad with Spiced Yogurt and Watercress	240	15	6	10	580	19	5	12	8
Grilled Panzanella	670	60	9	10	750	24	3	5	9
Duck Salad with Blackberries and Quick Pickled Fennel	290	8	2	85	980	31	6	22	25
Broccoli Salad with Creamy Avocado Dressing	210	14	1.5	0	320	22	6	12	4
Brussels Sprout, Red Cabbage, and Pomegranate Slaw	140	9	1	0	240	15	5	8	4
Butternut Squash Raita	120	5	2	10	240	15	2	7	4
Roasted Butternut Squash Salad with Za'atar and Parsley	250	13	2	0	600	32	5	12	5
Charred Cabbage Salad with Torn Tofu and Plantain Chips	450	31	5	0	1040	37	6	20	14

	CALORIES	TOTAL FAT (G)	SAT FAT (G)	CHOL (MG)	SODIUM (MG)	TOTAL CARB (G)	DIETARY FIBER (G)	TOTAL SUGARS (G)	PROTEIN (G)
Fruit & Vegetable Salads (cont.)									
Tangy Cabbage-Apple Slaw	110	0	0	0	650	26	4	21	2
Carrot Noodle Salad with Harissa and Honey	390	20	6	15	620	45	10	29	11
Harissa (per 1 tablespoon)	110	11	1.5	0	150	2	1	0	1
Gajarachi Koshimbir	150	8	2	0	340	17	3	11	3
Carrot and Smoked Salmon Salad	210	11	1.5	10	710	19	6	9	9
Chopped Carrot Salad with Mint, Pistachios, and Pomegranate Seeds	240	17	2.5	0	440	20	5	11	5
Chopped Carrot Salad with Radishes and Sesame Seeds	170	12	1	0	550	15	3	9	2
Roasted Grape and Cauliflower Salad with Chermoula	230	18	2.5	0	340	15	4	7	4
Celery Root, Celery, and Apple Slaw	270	19	2.5	0	640	22	4	12	2
Kohlrabi, Radicchio, and Apple Slaw	240	19	2.5	0	520	16	2	12	2
California Chicken Salad	430	19	3	125	1010	21	7	11	43
Mexican Street Corn Salad with Shrimp	410	24	7	115	1000	34	4	10	22
Citrus Salad with Watercress, Dried Cranberries, and Pecans	260	14	2	0	420	36	8	27	3
Nam Tok	350	14	6	115	450	15	3	5	40
Horiatiki Salata	260	21	7	35	980	10	3	6	7
Pai Huang Gua	50	2.5	0	0	650	5	2	3	3
Sichuan Chili Oil (per 1 teaspoon)	100	10	1	0	125	1	1	0	1
Crispy Eggplant Salad	370	28	2	0	850	31	8	18	5
Grilled Vegetable and Halloumi Salad	340	24	9	30	840	22	4	12	11
Fiddlehead Panzanella	290	21	4	5	360	17	0	1	8
Caesar Green Bean Salad	230	15	3	10	580	17	3	4	8
Green Bean Salad with Shallot, Mustard, and Tarragon	110	7	1	0	200	9	3	4	2
Cape Gooseberry Salad with Ginger-Lime Dressing	140	12	2.5	5	140	6	1	1	3
Honeydew Salad with Peanuts and Lime	120	4	0.5	0	340	20	2	15	3
Crispy and Creamy Kale Salad	400	35	3	0	350	17	5	4	8
Shaved Mushroom and Celery Salad	140	12	2.5	5	290	4	1	2	5
Grilled Octopus Salad with Orange and Smoked Paprika	660	31	4.5	220	1270	22	3	7	69
Orange-Jicama Salad with Sweet and Spicy Peppers	230	14	1	0	300	25	9	13	2
Som Tam	100	2.5	0	0	240	19	3	13	3
Roasted Pattypan Squash and Corn Salad	270	20	2.5	0	310	24	4	12	6
Peach Caprese Salad	260	19	9	40	500	10	1	8	13
Grilled Peach and Tomato Salad with Burrata and Basil	290	25	9	35	1370	13	2	11	8
Salade Niçoise	560	39	7	205	460	27	5	7	26
Classic Potato Salad	280	15	2.5	70	410	31	2	4	6
German Potato Salad	210	11	4	20	400	20	2	3	6
Gado Gado	340	18	6	125	1040	36	6	13	13
Rhubarb, Celery, and Radish Salad	200	18	4.5	15	330	5	2	2	3

	CALORIES	TOTAL FAT (G)	SAT FAT (G)	CHOL (MG)	SODIUM (MG)	TOTAL CARB (G)	DIETARY FIBER (G)	TOTAL SUGARS (G)	PROTEIN (G)
Fruit & Vegetable Salads (cont.)									
Seaweed Salad	200	17	1.5	0	650	10	3	7	2
Shrimp Salad with Corn and Chipotle	230	11	2	150	840	11	0	5	16
Smoked Salmon Niçoise Salad	450	19	6	295	480	25	4	5	45
Steak Fajita Salad	420	22	6	85	700	28	5	10	31
Crispy Tortilla Strips (per ¼ cup)	80	3	0	0	10	14	0	2	2
Grilled Sweet Potato Salad	290	15	2.5	10	560	37	6	15	4
Simplest Tomato Salad	100	9	1	0	200	5	2	3	1
Simplest Tomato Salad with Capers and Parsley	90	7	1	0	260	5	2	3	1
Simplest Tomato Salad with Pecorino Romano and Oregano	100	9	2	5	260	5	1	3	2
Cherry Tomato Salad with Mango and Lime-Curry Vinaigrette	140	10	1	0	105	14	3	5	3
Tomato Salad with Steak Tips	430	30	7	85	540	7	2	4	28
Marinated Tofu and Vegetable Salad	360	22	2.5	0	330	18	3	9	22
Shaved Salad with Pan-Seared Scallops	480	25	4	40	1260	38	8	20	25
Appetizer-Sized Shaved Salad with Pan-Seared Scallops	430	25	3.5	25	1040	36	8	20	18
Zucchini Noodle–Chicken Salad with Ginger and Garam Masala	350	15	3	90	390	23	3	18	31
Herb-Yogurt Sauce (per 2 tablespoons)	20	1	0.5	5	15	2	0	2	1
Chipotle-Yogurt Sauce (per 2 tablespoons)	20	1	0.5	5	15	2	0	2	1
Zucchini Noodle Salad with Tahini-Ginger Dressing	380	26	3.5	0	1610	31	8	15	15
Shaved Zucchini Salad with Pepitas	110	8	1.5	5	310	5	1	3	4
Bean & Grain Salads									
Lentil Salad with Spinach, Walnuts, and Parmesan	270	17	2.5	5	310	22	6	1	11
Crispy Lentil and Herb Salad	360	25	7	10	330	24	4	7	11
Spiced Lentil Salad with Butternut Squash	260	13	2	0	220	29	7	3	8
Southwestern Black Bean Salad	130	8	1	0	190	13	4	2	3
Layered Tex-Mex Salad	360	23	7	30	470	30	4	3	11
Marinated Cauliflower and Chickpea Salad	280	22	3	0	790	18	4	7	4
Chickpea Salad with Carrots, Arugula, and Olives	180	11	1.5	0	560	17	4	3	4
Chickpea Salad with Carrots, Raisins, and Almonds	180	11	1.5	0	560	17	4	3	4
Chickpea Salad with Oranges, Red Onion, and Chipotle	200	11	1.5	0	500	22	5	8	5
Chickpea Salad with Roasted Red Peppers and Feta	200	13	3	10	670	15	3	3	6
Fattoush with Chickpeas	290	20	2.5	0	290	24	4	4	6
Edamame and Shrimp Salad	400	21	2.5	145	770	20	2	10	33
Fava Bean and Radish Salad	250	11	1.5	0	320	28	10	14	13
Fava Bean Salad with Artichokes, Asparagus, and Peas	160	3	0	0	790	25	10	10	11
Pinto Bean, Ancho, and Beef Salad with Pickled Poblanos	420	18	6	55	890	40	9	14	25

	CALORIES	TOTAL FAT (G)	SAT FAT (G)	CHOL (MG)	SODIUM (MG)	TOTAL CARB (G)	DIETARY FIBER (G)	TOTAL SUGARS (G)	PROTEIN (G)
Bean & Grain Salads (cont.)									
Black-Eyed Pea Salad with Peaches and Pecans	180	9	1	0	590	21	5	6	6
Shrimp and White Bean Salad	390	19	3	145	1460	30	8	5	25
Squid and White Bean Salad	500	23	3.5	265	1460	43	11	5	32
Classic Three-Bean Salad	180	11	1	0	210	20	3	13	3
Three-Bean Salad with Cumin, Cilantro, and Oranges	190	11	1	0	200	23	4	16	3
Arugula, Roasted Red Pepper, and White Bean Salad	150	10	1.5	0	620	11	3	3	4
Roasted Bell Peppers (per 1 pepper)	20	0	0	0	0	4	1	2	1
White Bean Salad with Valencia Oranges and Celery	220	13	2	0	650	22	6	6	7
Barley Salad with Pomegranate, Pistachios, and Feta	280	10	2.5	10	320	41	7	9	7
Pomegranate Molasses (per 1 tablespoon)	60	0	0	0	0	15	0	13	0
Farro Salad with Asparagus, Snap Peas, and Tomatoes	290	11	2.5	10	210	42	6	5	9
Millet Salad with Corn and Queso Fresco	230	9	1.5	0	230	31	3	4	5
Oat Berry, Chickpea, and Arugula Salad	260	12	3	10	550	30	5	4	9
Quinoa, Black Bean, and Mango Salad with Lime Dressing	450	27	3.5	0	540	45	8	3	9
Quinoa Lettuce Wraps with Feta and Olives	420	27	6	20	410	35	5	6	11
Quinoa Taco Salad	280	14	2.5	5	470	30	9	3	9
Wheat Berry and Endive Salad with Blueberries and Goat Cheese	450	28	5	10	300	43	9	4	11
Black Rice Salad with Snap Peas and Ginger-Sesame Vinaigrette	280	13	1.5	0	250	39	4	4	5
Black Rice and Sea Bean Salad	320	16	2	0	210	43	5	5	5
Brown Rice Salad with Fennel, Mushrooms, and Walnuts	330	15	2	0	1100	43	4	4	7
Harvest Salad	310	16	4.5	15	520	36	5	13	7
Cooked Wild Rice (per 1 cup)	200	2	1	5	290	40	3	1	7
Turmeric Rice and Chicken Salad with Herbs	420	14	3	80	740	45	2	4	31
Nam Khao	290	9	1	5	530	45	1	5	9
Rice Salad with Dates and Pistachios	490	26	3.5	0	0	58	3	7	9
Rice Salad with Oranges, Olives, and Almonds	260	9	1	0	590	41	2	5	5
Red Rice and Quinoa Salad	350	11	1.5	0	100	59	5	24	6
Pasta & Noodle Salads									
One-Pot Pasta Salad with Chicken	410	20	5	75	570	27	3	4	30
Fusilli Salad with Salami and Sun-Dried Tomato Vinaigrette	600	35	10	50	1450	48	4	1	22
Zesty Shrimp Pesto Pasta Salad	560	27	3.5	95	200	60	4	3	22
Pea and Pistachio Pesto Pasta Salad	470	18	3.5	5	270	62	5	3	16

	CALORIES	TOTAL FAT (G)	SAT FAT (G)	CHOL (MG)	SODIUM (MG)	TOTAL CARB (G)	DIETARY FIBER (G)	TOTAL SUGARS (G)	PROTEIN (G)
Pasta & Noodle Salads (cont.)									
Pasta Salad with Eggplant, Tomatoes, and Basil	350	15	2	0	440	46	4	4	8
Spinach Pesto Pasta Salad	490	13	2.5	5	910	78	8	8	18
Creamy Corn Farfalle Salad	510	15	5	25	510	79	4	9	21
Pasta Salad with Asparagus and Smoked Mozzarella	200	7	2	5	190	25	1	2	7
Spicy Roasted Red Pepper Pesto Pasta Salad	270	11	2	5	240	35	2	2	8
Summer Garden Pasta Salad with Olives and Feta	290	12	2.5	10	520	38	3	3	8
Cool and Creamy Macaroni Salad	380	25	4	10	320	34	0	2	6
Cool and Creamy Macaroni Salad with Roasted Red Peppers and Capers	390	25	4	10	510	35	0	3	6
Cool and Creamy Macaroni Salad with Sharp Cheddar and Chipotle	450	30	7	30	430	35	0	2	10
Orzo Salad with Broccoli and Radicchio	430	26	4	5	700	39	2	7	13
Orzo Salad with Cucumber, Red Onion, and Mint	290	17	3.5	10	280	30	1	3	7
Grilled Vegetable and Orzo Salad with Lemon, Basil, and Feta	390	15	4	15	710	52	2	8	12
Tortellini Salad with Asparagus and Fresh Basil Vinaigrette	570	35	7	50	1150	51	3	6	16
Couscous Salad with Smoked Trout and Pepperoncini	360	16	2.5	30	950	37	3	1	17
Pearl Couscous Salad with Peas, Feta, and Pickled Shallots	450	17	4	15	430	61	3	9	14
Pearl Couscous Salad with Chickpeas, Chorizo, and Warm Spices	650	28	8	35	1230	74	7	18	24
Pearl Couscous Salad with Radishes and Watercress	440	20	5	15	460	53	2	3	13
Cherry and Goat Cheese Couscous Salad	640	35	8	20	580	66	5	13	14
Cilantro and Pepita Couscous Salad	510	29	6	10	490	49	5	1	14
Feta and Olive Couscous Salad	620	37	10	35	830	55	6	4	17
Spiced Vegetable Couscous Salad	350	15	2	0	700	45	6	5	10
Ras el Hanout (per 1 tablespoon)	20	0.5	0	0	220	4	2	2	1
Chilled Soba Noodle Salad with Cucumber, Snow Peas, and Radishes	230	7	0.5	0	320	34	1	7	7
Chicken and Cellophane Noodle Salad	460	14	1.5	60	1340	54	3	4	29
Bún Chà	400	17	6	55	850	45	2	9	18
Summer Ramen Salad	530	13	1.5	95	1160	72	4	6	32
Chilled Somen Noodle Salad with Shrimp	490	2.5	0.5	215	3840	73	5	6	38
Sesame Lo Mein Salad	310	7	1	10	1160	50	1	6	12
Peanut Noodle Salad	360	18	3	0	770	42	2	3	10
Udon Noodle Salad with Edamame Pesto	540	23	3	5	1110	64	2	11	23
Soba Noodle Salad with Roasted Eggplant and Sesame	470	18	2.5	0	1280	70	6	20	11

conversions & equivalents

The recipes in this book were developed using standard U.S. measures following U.S. government guidelines. The charts below offer equivalents for U.S. and metric measures. All conversions are approximate and have been rounded up or down to the nearest whole number.

example

1 teaspoon = 4.9292 milliliters, rounded up to 5 milliliters

1 ounce = 28.3495 grams, rounded down to 28 grams

volume conversions

U.S.	METRIC
1 teaspoon	5 milliliters
2 teaspoons	10 milliliters
1 tablespoon	15 milliliters
2 tablespoons	30 milliliters
¼ cup	59 milliliters
⅓ cup	79 milliliters
½ cup	118 milliliters
¾ cup	177 milliliters
1 cup	237 milliliters
1¼ cups	296 milliliters
1½ cups	355 milliliters
2 cups (1 pint)	473 milliliters
2½ cups	591 milliliters
3 cups	710 milliliters
4 cups (1 quart)	0.946 liter
1.06 quarts	1 liter
4 quarts (1 gallon)	3.8 liters

weight conversions

OUNCES	GRAMS
½	14
¾	21
1	28
1½	43
2	57
2½	71
3	85
3½	99
4	113
4½	128
5	142
6	170
7	198
8	227
9	255
10	283
12	340
16 (1 pound)	454

oven temperature

FAHRENHEIT	CELSIUS	GAS MARK
225	105	¼
250	120	½
275	135	1
300	150	2
325	165	3
350	180	4
375	190	5
400	200	6
425	220	7
450	230	8
475	245	9

converting temperatures from an instant-read thermometer

We include doneness temperatures in many of the recipes in this book. We recommend an instant-read thermometer for the job. Refer to the table above to convert Fahrenheit degrees to Celsius. Or, for temperatures not represented in the chart, use this simple formula:

Subtract 32 degrees from the Fahrenheit reading, then divide the result by 1.8 to find the Celsius reading.

example
To convert 160°F to Celsius:
   160°F - 32 = 128°
   128° ÷ 1.8 = 71.11°C, rounded down to 71°C

orange-jicama salad with sweet
and spicy peppers, *page 207*

index

Note: Page references in *italics* indicate photographs.

r